Wood, Water & Grass: Meek Cutoff of 1845

James H. and Theona J. Hambleton

Books may be purchased at your local bookseller or
directly through Caxton Press
www.caxtonpress.com
1-800-657-6465

James H. Hambleton or Theona J. Hambleton
18483 W. Campbell Loop Rd.
Baker City, Oregon 97814
Telephone #541-524-1256
go4gold@q.com

Library of Congress Cataloging-in-Publication Data

Hambleton, James H.
Wood, water & grass : Meek Cutoff of 1845 / James H. and Theona J. Hambleton ; foreword by Stafford Hazelett.
pages cm
Includes bibliographical references and index.
ISBN 978-0-9903860-2-5
1. Meek's Cutoff (Or.)--History--19th century. 2. Pioneers--Oregon--Meek's Cutoff--History--19th century. 3. Pioneers--Oregon--Meek's Cutoff--Diaries. 4. Meek, Stephen Hall, 1805-1889. 5. Wagon trains--Oregon--Meek's Cutoff--History--19th century. 6. Overland journeys to the Pacific. 7. Frontier and pioneer life--Oregon. 8. Oregon Territory--History. I. Hambleton, Theona J. II. Title. III. Title: Wood, water and grass.
F880.H193 2014
979.503--dc23
2014028455

Foreword by Stafford Hazelett

Copyright Acknowledgments
The Autobiography of a Mountain Man by Stephen Hall Meek. 1805-1889,
Oregon Historical Society 92M4946a
Stephen Meek's signed Photo California Biography Project
Stephen Meek's last home site Photo in Scotts Valley, California, from Richard Silva
Stephen Meek Photos, Oregon Historical Society Image #19905 and 25856
Eli Casey Cooley's Photo, Michael F. Cooley and Mary Lou Cooley
Eli Casey Cooley's original Handwritten Diary, from Mrs. Grace Berry Armstrong
Excerpts from John Herron's Diary, Oregon Historical Society MSS #224
Samuel Parker Diary, Oregon Historical Society MSS #1508
Jesse Harritt Overland Handwritten Diary, Oregon Historical Society MSS #947
James Field, Oregon Historical Society MSS #520
Andrew McClure's Handwritten Diary, Oregon Historical Society MSS #732
Oregon Pioneer Association Letter from Mrs. Grace Armstrong
Hudson Bay Co. Trappers Campsite photos from Joe Molter
1845 Lost Meeks Limb Photo, Families of Keith Clark and Lowell Tiller

Cover design by James H. Hambleton.

Printed in the United States of America
by The Caxton Printers, Ltd., Caldwell, Idaho

TABLE OF CONTENTS

USGS QUADRANGLE MAPS

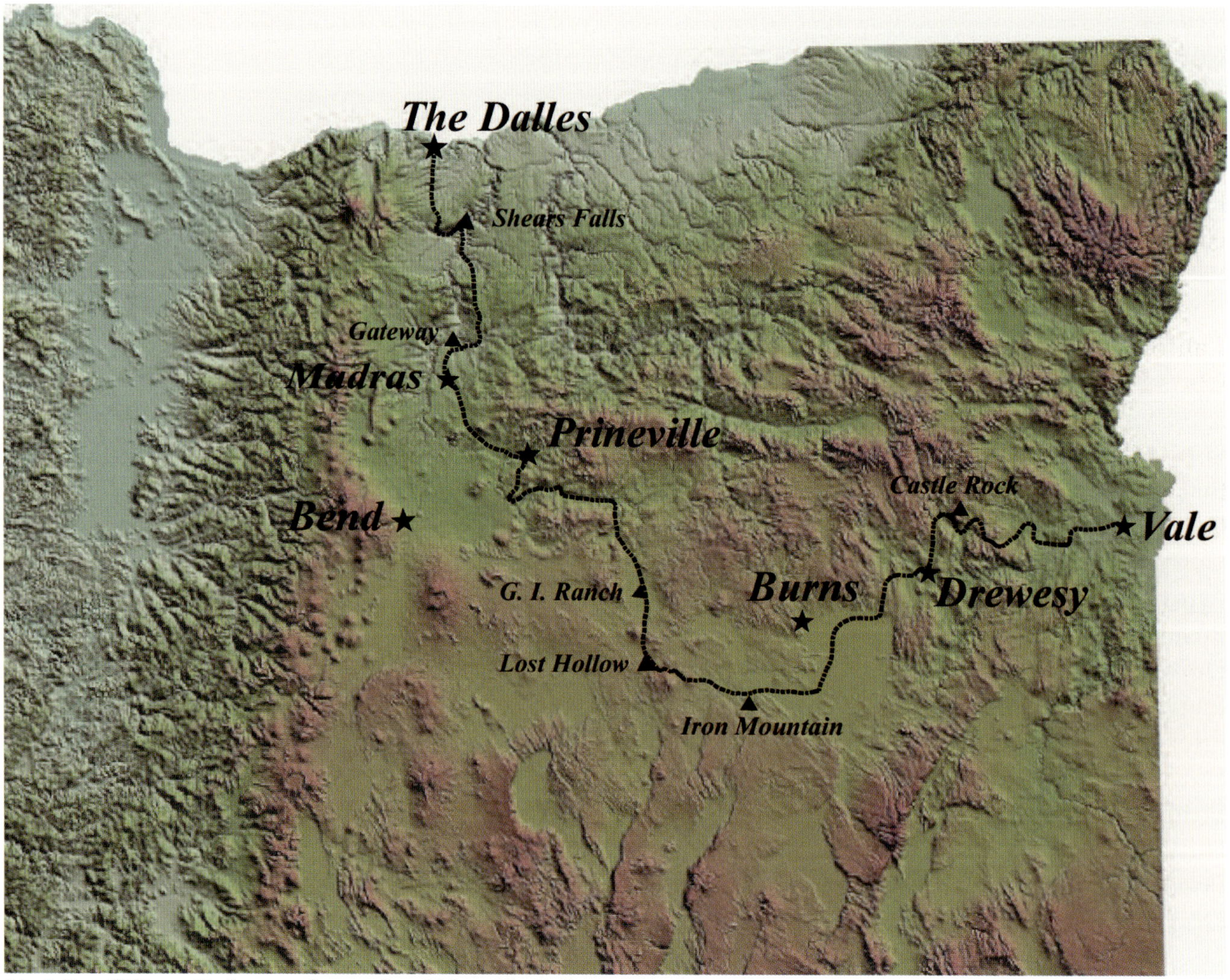

Meek Cutoff Wagon Trail across Oregon from Vale to The Dalles.
Map courtesy of 2009 topocreator.com with modifications by author.

ACKNOWLEDGMENTS

So many people have been helpful in our research. All were so friendly and interested. We wish to thank everyone for whatever part they played in our project:

The late Lowell Tiller, one of the co-authors of *Terrible Trail: Meek Cutoff 1845,* for placing a challenge to continue our research on the trail and also for being able to review our ongoing work in February of 2010. He gave us his sincere blessing on our project. We will cherish his thoughts forever. We will be forever grateful to Lowell who passed away July 1, 2010.

Grace Berry Armstrong, a great-granddaughter of Eli Casey Cooley, thank you so very much for giving us permission to use a copy of Eli Casey Cooley's handwritten diary and also for the letter that was given to the family from the Oregon Pioneer Association.

Donna Sanders, also a direct descendant of Eli Casey Cooley, for taking the time to visit with us and the input you provided was very much appreciated.

Margaret Heater, a descendant of Christopher Columbus Cooley, for your interest and enthusiasm in our effort to tell the true story.

Michael F. Cooley and his wife Mary Lou Cooley, for making us aware that Eli Casey Cooley's diary even existed and for the photograph of Eli Cooley and his family.

Stafford Hazelett for your interest, excitement, enthusiasm, support, and the great amount of assistance you so freely provided and for writing our Foreword. Thank you.

Lee Kreutzer for your interest, enthusiasm, and much needed encouragement in the completion of this work.

To our daughter Catherine Marie Martin and our son-in-law Scott Martin for their listening ear, helpful comments, and especially a great big thank you Cathy, for the many, many hours you spent in editing out all of Dad's grammar problems.

To our granddaughter Anne Marie Martin for her assistance in preparing the index.

To our son Daniel Hambleton and daughter-in-law Sherrie Hambleton for driving us to Etna, California, so that we could vistit the grave site of Stephen Hall Meek and visit the museum at Etna. Also to Sherrie for finding documents on the internet and emailing them to us and for their continued support of our project.

To my brother Albert Hambleton and his wife Marlene Hambleton of Redding, California, for their continued interest and encouragement and sending data they found in the museum in Yreka, California.

Julianne Williams and her late husband Del Williams for their interest and courage to go on a long, rough, and grueling road trip, being the first people we led on a field tour on one of the important mountainous legs of the Meek Cutoff Wagon Trail. Thank you Julianne, for your continuing support, interest, and exhaustive efforts in helping to edit our final work. You are greatly appreciated.

Bryan Metke for his knowledge and experience as a history teacher and his interest, enthusiasm, and guidance in our book.

Jack Kleinhoff, the holder of the keys to the old townsite of Auburn, Oregon, for his interest and enthusiasm helped spur us on in our pursuit of the Meek Cutoff Wagon Trail.

Jack Peila and his son, Bill Peila, owners of property on Wagontire Mountain and vicinity, for granting us permission to research the trail and allowing us to camp along the trail as we worked, specifically in Lost Hollow, which was a very memorable camp site on the Meek Cutoff.

The owner of Castle Rock Ranch, Thomas Hammond and his manager, Steven Jay, for granting us permission to research the trail through their property.

Jeff Hussey and Sheri Hussey, Pat Wilber, and Rod Robertson, all ranchers in the Otis Valley area, for their interest and permission to research the trail through that locality.

Patrick O'Toole for his insight of the trail and granting us permission to research on his property.

Loren Irving for his interest and enthusiasm in our project.

Richard Silva for his important knowledge, assistance, and interest in our work.

Joe Molter for his interest in Stephen Meek and the photos of the Hudson Bay Co. Trappers Campsite of 1836.

Oregon Historical Society and in particular, Scott Daniels, the Research Librarian, for his help copying and sending us data.

Perry Stokes of the Baker County Library for his assistance in acquiring materials.

To Les Schwab Ranch Manager Jodi LaRey, and Ranch Foreman, Brad Wigle, for so graciously providing access to the Les Schwab ranch lands. Especially a great big thank to you both for coming to our rescue when the battery in our vehicle died, leaving us stranded many miles from help. Cell phone technology is a real blessing.

Herbert Bryce Vibbert for his valuable insight and his permission to research the trail through his property.

William Butler and his son, William, for their help and permission to research the trail on their property and surrounding area in Agency Valley.

Robert Marheine, Portland General Electric manager of the Trout Creek Ranch property, for his interest in our project and allowing us access onto their property.

Ed Hagen for his interest and helping us gain access to private lands in the Bakeoven area.

Jennie Ward, who grew up on the Trout Creek Ranch, for the information she gave us about her Grandfather using the Meek Cutoff Wagon Trail for several years to haul the wool from his sheep to Shaniko until he was able to build an improved road.

The families of Keith Clark and Lowell Tiller and especially Tim Clark-McKitrick for searching through numerous family photos to come up with a photo for us.

Any people that we have inadvertently failed to mention, we thank them deeply for their interest and assistance.

FOREWORD

James and Theona Hambleton honored me by taking me out in the field to show me the remnants of the 1845 Meek Cutoff. When it turned out that documents I had found in the Oregon Historical Society Research Library assisted them to illuminate the story of the 1845 emigrants and the places they traveled on the Meek Cutoff of the Oregon Trail, I was thrilled to share my research. They did the hard work before we met by coincidence as they were putting finishing touches on the documentation of their research.

If you think you know the story, you are in for some surprises. If you think you know where the wagons of 1845 crossed central Oregon, you are in for some surprises. They have built on the fine work of Keith Clark and Lowell Tiller, published in the *Terrible Trail*; and Leah and Donald Collins with Lowell Tiller, published as "Cutoff Fever" in five consecutive issues of the *Oregon Historical Quarterly,* December 1977 to December 1978.

James and Theona have taken a painstaking approach to the best possible evidence. Their attention to details is the hallmark of their work. Relying only on first person accounts and personal observation in the field, they have assembled a remarkable reconstruction of the route and the places where the wagons traveled and camped.

Where the diaries may seem to be inconsistent or contradictory, they have supplied the sort of analysis that produces a sensible result. Their conclusions are based on their observations in the field, comparing the diaries, and considering preceding and following diary entries. By working closely with the landowners, they have located places that match the descriptions given by the emigrant diarists and documented their observations with clear photography. If they are mistaken in their conclusions about places, it will require some very convincing evidence better than the descriptions of the first viewers recording their impressions at the time.

The Hambletons persisted to get the original handwritten diaries. You will see how a mistaken transcription produced some uncertainty. With the original handwriting deciphered correctly and other contemporaneous evidence, they have resolved the uncertainty about the existence of a split-off company. As we have received it, the story of the split-off company suggested that some families left the main group in the neighborhood of what is now the G I Ranch and traveled west along the route of US Highway 26 to the Deschutes River before turning north and rejoining the main party north of Prineville.

Many of the old wagon company emigrants told their stories to Fred Lockley, a columnist for the Oregon Journal, a Portland daily newspaper. In my own research, I saw that no one who traveled with Meek and talked to Fred Lockley in the late nineteenth and early twentieth century mentioned a split-off company. I had my doubts that such a split would have gone unmentioned.

The Hambletons tracked down the various threads of that story and looked at the evidence in the field. They have come to a logical conclusion that makes sense of the evidence we have. You may not agree with their conclusion, but then you should explain how the split-off group traveled farther and faster than the main group over unexplored country to get to an unexpected rendezvous and how no one expressed surprise at the alleged reunion.

Stafford Hazelett

AKA Levi Pringle

INTRODUCTION

People traveling across an unfamiliar country with a destination in mind would need a reliable guide to lead them, be it a reliable map, an experienced guide, or a Global Positioning System unit. Otherwise, they could be like Moses traveling in the desert for forty years. The emigrants of 1845 who were traveling across the Oregon Territory didn't have that many guide tools to choose from. There were no GPS units to attach to their covered wagons. The maps of the Oregon Territory were very sketchy at best. They certainly weren't reliable. So that left them one thing to do and that was to hire a reliable guide. The guide available was Stephen Meek. Was he reliable? According to previously published articles written about him and the Meek Cutoff, he wasn't. These authors' goal in writing this book is to clear up misconceptions and misinformation about Stephen Meek and the Meek Cutoff and to define the trail as accurately as possible through the use of text, maps, and photos.

These authors have been researching the Meek Cutoff Wagon Trail for the past nine years, locating and walking as much of the trail as possible over its total length of 435 miles across the state of Oregon. We have used a combination of valuable tools in our intense research. These tools include United States Geological Survey Quadrangle Maps, Google Earth Satellite Imagery, Bureau of Land Management cadastral survey, field notes, and maps, the autobiography of Stephen Hall Meek, as well as the complete original 1845 handwritten diaries of Eli Cooley, Jesse Harritt, and Samuel Parker. In addition, we have used the incomplete transcribed diaries of James Field and John Herron. These last two diaries only cover a portion of the journey. We have also used the original handwritten diary of Andrew McClure who was with the Elliott Wagon Train of 1853 and who followed a large portion of the Meek Cutoff Wagon Trail.

In order to attempt to learn the real truths of the Meek Cutoff Wagon Trail and be as factual as possible, these authors have refrained from using any documented memories, hearsay reports, or reminiscences and cancerous embellishments. We feel the Meek Cutoff story has been infected with a mixture of extra details, some taken from stories written about the Elliott Wagon Train of 1853 and the Macy Wagon Train of 1854. Both of these trains followed a large portion of the Meek Cutoff before leaving the trail. Many writers have researched the subject from libraries and the internet with very little effort, if any, of following the trail out in the field. It would be pointless for us to repeat their written opinions and findings.

The most important diarist of the Meek Cutoff of 1845 was Eli Cooley. Cooley realized the extreme importance of the main essentials of each night's camping location. A common thread throughout the entire journey can be found in his comments of almost every day's camp when he makes note of those camping essentials: wood, water and grass. Thus, these authors felt it fitting to make them part of the title of this book, *"Wood, Water and Grass: Meek Cutoff of 1845."*

The diarists mention water at nearly every night's encampment, although their opinions vary to some degree as to the actual quantity of water being available. Usually the type of wood being available was willow wood. This is an important fact as willows require a large amount of water just to survive. Today these springs continue to flow, but in nearly all cases there is not a sufficient volume of water to sustain the growth of willows as there are very few willows present. This shows that even though 1845 was known to be an extremely dry year, there was definitely more water at the springs and creeks than what is there now.

There are many stories written pertaining to travels along the Oregon Trail. Therefore, these authors took the liberty of just briefly mentioning the beginning of the wagon train of 1845. This is done in an attempt to have a better understanding of the journey and what companies made up the 200+ wagons that eventually took what was later named the Meek Cutoff of 1845.

The year 1845 was a memorable year of the early onset of the Great Western Emigration although there were small, but growing emigration movements starting in about 1840. Small companies began making their way west into the Oregon Territory, and word made its way back East of the successful journeys into the Oregon Territory, telling of the milk and honey of this new land, as well as the freedom and prosperity it had to offer. Excitement began to build with the success of each small company completing the journey west.

The first really large movement west took place in 1845. It has been reported with varying degrees of accuracy that between 450 and 500 wagons, about 2000 to 2500 people, and about 6000 to 6500 head of livestock, including oxen, horses, mules, and loose cattle made up the large emigration movement of the year 1845. Stephen Hall Meek stated in his autobiography, that he had secured *"the position as guide to the immense emigrant train of 480 wagons then preparing to go to Oregon"* and leaving on May 11, 1845. Common sense dictates that an immense emigration of this size could not, in one's wildest dream, be able to travel in unison day-by-day. It was quickly deemed necessary for the large train to be broken into several smaller companies traveling several miles apart, or even days apart. Some of the companies traveled much more aggressively and faster, while other companies were taking their time traveling much slower. These later groups possibly did not understand the magnitude of the task they were undertaking. Soon they found themselves using up their precious supplies. Thus, rationing became a must if they were to complete the long journey. Even then, they found themselves running out of food. Days were beginning to separate the guide and the companies in the lead from the slower straggling companies. Some of these later companies were beginning to think they were on their own, and that their guide had abandoned them.

Personalities played a big role in what formation the companies traveled along the trail. This huge wagon train contained the same diverse range of personalities as any large gathering of people today. Tempers were sharp and quick; patience was very thin. Selfishness and greed were in command of many of the pioneer souls. A number of writers have envisioned life along the wagon trail as one great big happy family with the emigrants having a big party with dancing, singing, and having a good time at nearly every night's encampment. This might have been the case at the beginning of the trip on a very small scale when several family members or very close neighbors were traveling together. However, there was none of this type of action on a large-scale basis. Long before the pioneers reached their destination, a far different picture actually emerged.

It is extremely difficult for one to understand their story with all the conveniences that are enjoyed today. Put yourself in their shoes and walk in their footsteps. This would help you understand their long, hard journey. Picture fathers and sons walking alongside the oxen teams that were pulling the heavily loaded wagons; dust and grime of the trail mixed with sweat running from their foreheads, turning to mud and running down their cheeks, day after day along the toilsome journey. If they were with the lead wagons, they had to run ahead to help clear the trail of large rocks and debris so the wagons could pass over them. Picture the women and daughters trudging along ankle-deep in the dust, walking mile after mile, believing it to be easier to walk than ride in the wagon that was rocking, swaying and bouncing along over the rough, rocky ground. Women's workdays began at daylight preparing something to eat, and ended after dark cleaning up the dinner dishes. Their days were extremely long and tiring, but endure they must. These are only small examples of what the emigrants faced day after day for over 1700 miles along the trail to The Dalles, Oregon.

Each day's travel would repeat the challenges of the day before. In many cases, with a new day, new challenges would present themselves. For the most part, these people met each of these challenges with grace, courage, and perseverance, and above all, a great deal of intestinal fortitude.

Stephen Hall Meek
(Courtesy of California Biography Project.)

STEPHEN HALL MEEK'S AUTOBIOGRAPHY

I was born in Washington County, Virginia, on the 4th of July 1805, and am a relative of Pres. Polk. I attended the common schools of the day. Scarcely 20 years of age, I became imbued with that restless spirit of a venture that has since been a marked characteristic of my life, and left my home for the then comparatively unknown West. St. Louis was at the time, the center of the fur trade of the United States, and when I reached that city, I engaged with the Rocky Mountain Fur Company, to work in their warehouses. I was placed in the cellar by the celebrated William Sublette with several other green hands to "rum the beaver," which operation consisted of spreading the skins out upon the cellar floor and sprinkling them with rum for preservation. Sublette left us with the remark "don't you boys get tight now," at which idea we all laugh. Soon, the fumes of the rum began to affect us, and it was not long before we were reeling around the room apparently helplessly drunk. Sublette then put in an appearance, and pretended to be angry with us "can't I leave you here alone for a few minutes, without you getting drunk? Here!" Said he "drink this," and he drew a cup from the barrel. This had the effect of making us over again, and Sublette again left us with the remark "the next time you rum the beaver, just rum yourselves first."

In 1829, I went to Lexington, Missouri, and worked in a steam sawmill erected by my brother, Hiram C. Meek, then a merchant of that place. In the spring of 1830, I joined the party being taken to the Mountain by William Sublette and Robert Campbell, and then commenced that wild life of adventure, which I led so many years. The great annual meeting of the trappers that season was held at the favorite rendezvous on Green River, and four rival companies were then competing for the patronage of the Indians and free trappers, the Rocky Mountain Co., the American Co., the Hudson Bay Co. and an independent company. It was the custom to send trapping parties or brigades, in different directions to trap, all of them assembling the next summer at some rendezvous previously agreed upon.

I joined the brigade of Milton Sublette, and went to the Lewis Fork of the Columbia River and wintered at Blackfoot Lake. In the fall of 1831 I was again with Milton Sublette and trapped the Black Hills, near where Fort Laramie was afterwards built, on the headwaters of the Platte. The winter was spent on the Powder River, and in the spring we went to Wind River and trapped on that stream, the Yellowstone, Muscle Shell River, and back through Jackson's Hole to Wind River, the rendezvous being at the mouth of Tar, or Popyoisa, River, a tributary of that stream. In the fall of 1832 I went to the Blackfoot country with Bridger's brigade; crossed to Powder and Yellowstone, and then to the Missouri; went up that stream to Three Forks, and at the left-hand fork to the head of Big Gray Bull River, a tributary of the Yellowstone; then to Green River, and finally wintered on the Snake River, where Fort Hall was afterwards built. In the spring we trapped Salmon, Snake and Point Neuf, and then went to Green River rendezvous. There I hired to Capt. B. L. E. Bonneville to accompany an expedition of 34 men, under Joseph Walker, to explore the Great Salt Lake. We got too far West, and finally started down the Mary's, or Humboldt River for California, over a country entirely unknown to trappers.

We discovered Truckee, Carson and Walker rivers, Donner Lake and Walker's pass, through which we went and pitched our camp for the winter on the shore of Tulare Lake, in December, 1833. Walker, with a party of ten men, went to Monterey and returned in March, when they broke camp and retraced their steps to Humboldt River, thence south to the Colorado, thence up that stream, thence north again, passing West of Great Salt Lake to Bear River, where we met Bonneville. In the fall of 1834 I went with Bonneville and 22 men and trapped Snake River and all its tributaries to Walla Walla; then up John Day River, over to Lake Harney; then to Malheur, Owyhee and Powder rivers, and wintered on Snake River. In the spring of 1835 I started for the Willamette Valley, and when I reached Walla Walla, engaged to the Hudson Bay Co., staying until the spring of 1836 at Vancouver. That spring I went with a party of men under the celebrated, Tom McKay to California, trapping Scott River and the Sacramento. We went to Yerba Buena (San Francisco) and left our furs with the agent of the company, Mr. Ray, and then returned, trapping on the American, Yuba, Feather, Pit, McLeod and Shasta rivers, and then to Vancouver. In the spring of 1837, I went to the Rocky Mountains with a few companions, trapping on the way, selling pelts to Bridger at Green River. I then trapped in the Black Hills, on the Sweetwater and Platte, and wintered at Fort Laramie, which was built by William Sublette. In the spring of 1838 I went south to Pike's Peak; then to Taos, New Mexico; then to the Arkansas and to the north fork of the Platte, and wintered at the mouth of Cherry Creek, where Andrew Sublette built Fort Robert (Campbell), opposite the city of Denver. That winter I went to Independence on horseback, carrying the annual express. Having ten days to spare, I went to Lexington to see my brother and sister. While there I called on some young ladies, to whom I related many incidents of my mountain life, which so startled there worthy mother that she exclaimed: "Law sakes! Mr. Meek, didn't you never get killed by none of them Indians and bears?" "Oh, yes, madam," said I gravely, "I was frequently killed."

Going back to Laramie with the express, I made the spring hunt with Trapp's brigade, and in July went as wagon-master of the train of ox-teams, taking the furs to Independence. I spent the winter in St. Louis, and in the spring of 1840 engaged with McGoffin Bros. to take a train of wagons to Santa Fe and Chihuahua. I wintered in the latter place, and in the winter of 1841 joined a party of American mountaineers under James Kirke, engaged by the Governor of Chihuahua to fight the Apaches. Several battles were fought, but in the fall a new governor was appointed, who thought Mexican troops should fight Mexican battles, and the Americans were recalled. We came in with fifteen thousand head of captured stock, for which we received two and one-half dollars each, according to agreement. I again spent the winter there, and in March, 1842, returned to Independence, where I found 17 families waiting to go to Oregon, who engaged me as a guide. I took them as far as Green River, where they were overtaken by Fitzpatrick's brigade on the way to Fort Hall, and several of the families cut up their wagons and made packsaddles, and packing their effects on their animals went along with Fitzpatrick. The balance of the wagons I conducted safely to Fort Hall, and by going through a new route, known as "Meeks and Sublette's cut-off," I arrived there the same day the others did, much to their surprise.

The wagons were left there, and the goods were then packed upon the animals. They went down the Snake, and by Boise River to its mouth, crossed Snake again, down to Brule or Burnt River, up to Powder and Grand Ronde, crossed the Blue Mountains at Jason Lee's encampment to the Umatilla, down the Columbia and to the Dalles, then by the Mt. Hood trail to Oregon City, which was laid out that fall by L. W. Hastings, of this train, as agent of Dr. McLaughlin, I carrying the chain.

In the spring of 1843, I piloted a few of those who had become dissatisfied with Oregon, to California, over the Old Hudson Bay Trail, meeting Capt. Joe Walker and others in Rogue River Valley, with two thousand head of cattle, coming from California. I went to Sutter's Fort on Monterey, where I spent the winter. Here I met Capt. Smith, with the trading vessel, George and Henry, of Baltimore, who persuaded me to start on a voyage with him around the world.

When we reached Valparaiso, Smith received advice that called him at once to Baltimore, and he and I started in a packet for the Isthmus. We reached Guaquil, Columbia, where I nearly died with yellow fever, then to Panama, where we took the vessel for New York. Arriving there in July, 1844, I went to Pittsburgh with some Santa Fe traders, then to my old home in Virginia, where I found an absence of 17 years had made me almost a stranger.

In March, 1845, I went to New Orleans, and then up the river to St. Louis, where I got letters of recommendation from Fitzpatrick, William Sublette and Robert Campbell, which secured me the position as guide to the immense emigrant train of 480 wagons then preparing to go to Oregon. We started on May 11, 1845, on which day I first saw Elizabeth Schoonover, whom I married a week later.

Arriving at Fort Hall, one third of the train under William D. Ide, of bear flag notoriety, went to California, guided by the old trapper, Greenwood. The remainder, I conducted safely to Oregon, the first large train of wagons ever taken there.

I lived in Linn City and Oregon City, till the spring of 1848, when I went with my wife and child to San Francisco. In October of that year I went to the mines at Coloma, and in January, 1849, opened a butcher shop there. That summer my wife went to Oregon and in December, 1850, I followed.

In the spring of 1851, I started for Scott River, but stopped at Yreka and mined till October, when I returned with $6000. In the spring I went by sea to San Francisco with my family and took a stock of goods to Coloma, which I sold and went to mining. The mine caved in, and I sold out and went to Santa Cruz and opened a butcher shop. While here, I paid $3,400 for a Mexican grant near Watsonville, which the former owner's heirs got away from me again in the courts. Being now poor again, I went to Fraser River in the excitement of 1858, but returned poorer than before. In 1859 I went to Jackson, Amador County, and mined until the death of my wife in 1865. Taking my youngest child, George, then four years of age, I went in search of my wife's father, and found him at Humboldt Bay. In the spring of 1867 I took a train of 22 wagons, loaded with quartz machinery from Sacramento to South Boise, Idaho, and then went to the ranch of my brother, the well-known Joe Meek, near Portland, where I spent the winter. In 1868 I piloted a party of 30 men to Malheur River, where rumor had located the famous Blue Bucket diggings. This wild-goose chase being over, I engaged as wagon master for the government during the Bannock war, and soon became scout for General Cook, finding in a few days the hiding place of the Indians, Sugarloaf and Crater Hole, which the troops had sought in vain all summer. The war being ended by the battle that took place there, I went to Silver City, Idaho, thence by stage to Winnemucca, and by rail to Sacramento. I spent the winter in Amador County, and the summer at Humboldt Bay, the next winter in Amador, and then lived in Truckee till the fall of 1871. Being now advanced in years and having lost all the money my good fortune and hard labor had brought me, I was compelled to take to the mountains to secure a livelihood. I went to Red Bluff, bought animals and traps, and have ever since been trapping the waters of Sacramento, Pit, McLeod, Scott, Trinty and other rivers of Northern California. I make my house of Josiah Doll, in Scotts Valley, my headquarters, and from there range through the mountains with my son George or as guide to hunting parties.

Stephen Hall Meek made his last home at Josiah Doll's in Scotts Valley, Siskiyou County, California. Josiah Doll homesteaded 160 acres about 1½ miles east of the town of Etna, which is located in northern California in Scotts Valley along Scotts River. Scotts Valley's local historians place Stephen's residence as that of Josiah Doll's milk house. (See photos page 178.) The historic structure remained standing until sometime in 2008 when it was torn down and pushed into a pile of rubble. He died at the old milk house and is buried in the Etna Cemetery on the south edge of the town. Buried beside him is his beloved son George and George's wife, Matilda. The birth year on Stephen Meek's headstone does not agree with his autobiography. It appears that all these headstones were erected at the same time at a later date which could explain the difference.

Meek said *"We started on the trail May 11, 1845, on which day I first saw Elizabeth Schoonover, whom I married a week later."* It is quite apparent Stephen saw Elizabeth as a young lady that was very attractive to him. Likewise Elizabeth, being 18 years old and basically on her own, traveling with relatives or family friends, was very attracted to Stephen Meek. She was a very courageous young lady to be traveling without her parents and willing to travel by horse back with Stephen. She apparently had a very strong will and constitution, as well as having an adventurous pioneer spirit. With a very short courtship of a week, a wedding was performed uniting these two lovers in holy matrimony. It has been purported by other writers that Stephen Meek married a young orphan child with the insinuation that he might have taken advantage of her. It must be emphasized that Elizabeth Schoonover was not an orphan child. Elizabeth was the oldest daughter of 13 children born to Peter Schoonover through two marriages, although five of her siblings died during early infancy. In 1857, Elizabeth's father followed her westward to the Humboldt County area of northern California. There he lived out his final years until his death in 1888. Stephen also mentions going to Elizabeth's father's place at Humboldt Bay shortly after Elizabeth's death in 1865. Elizabeth was the love of Stephen Meek's life. Stephen and Elizabeth were married for 20 years and had a family of at least five children. The 1860 U.S. Federal Census of Amador County, California, shows a daughter S.S. Meek age 13, a son S.A. Meek age 9, a daughter Mary E. Meek age 5, a daughter Estella Meek age 2, and a son George E. Meek age 13 months. Later Stephen and George went to Scotts Valley where Stephen passed away in 1889.

It is interesting to note that Stephen Meek did not mention much about the early years of his life. Being a member of a large family of 13 siblings, he only mentions one sister who he does not name, his older brother Hiram Meek, and his younger brother Joseph Meek. He does mention returning home after 17 years and finding himself nearly a total stranger. He continued to have ties to his brothers Hiram and Joseph.

Stephen Meek mentions that in 1825 when he was barely 20 years old, he left home and headed west, arriving at St. Louis, Missouri. At that time, William Ashley and Jedediah Smith were the owners of a fur trading company. William Sublette was in charge of the warehouses for the company where Stephen was hired to work. In 1826, Jedediah Smith, William Sublette and David Jackson purchased William Ashley's interest in the company. It was then named the Rocky Mountain Fur Company. In 1829, Stephen went to Lexington, Missouri, where he worked in a sawmill for his brother Hiram Meek.

In the spring of 1830, Stephen joined the party led by William Sublette and Robert Campbell carrying supplies to the favorite rendezvous site in the Green River area. This is a very significant fact placing Stephen with what is said to have been the first wagons along the Oregon Trail to the Rocky Mountains led by William Sublette. This group consisted of 81 men on mules, 10 wagons drawn by five mules each, 12 head of cattle, and a milk cow.

Over the next two years, Stephen Meek traveled with the Milton Sublette brigade and the Jim Bridger brigade, trapping on many of the streams and rivers of the Rocky Mountains. At the 1833 rendezvous on Horse Creek, Stephen and his brother Joe were hired by Captain Bonneville to go on an expedition into the California country under the command of Joseph Walker. Joseph Walker was one of the best all-around mountain men and explorers of the time. However, he was not well known as he did not have a boastful or bragging spirit.

Stephen Meek says they spent the winter camped on the shores of Tulare Lake. Tulare Lake covered approximately 750 square miles in the southern San Joaquin Valley of California. It is interesting to know that today, Tulare Lake does not exist.[1] Upon leaving their winter camp, Joseph Walker's Company was obliged to follow along the shoreline of this great body of water in order to make their journey around the Sierra Nevada mountain range through Walker's Pass.

Stephen appeared to be a quiet, matter-of-fact individual, similar in nature to Joseph Walker. He was a man of few words, unlike his brother Joseph Meek, who enjoyed telling tall tales, be they true or not, but pleasing to his audience at hand. In Stephen's autobiography, he told of his many journeys as a mountain man, trapping and traveling across the great West. He did not complain of hardships along the trail; they were all just part of a day's journey. His writing does not reflect a bragging boastful attitude; he simply told it like it was.

By 1840, the fur trade began to die out and the heyday of the mountain man died with it. Mountain men in general began seeking other methods of making a living. Becoming guides for wagon trains

[1] Tulare Lake's demise began in the late 1800s when its water sources were diverted into agriculture and municipalities.

of emigrants heading west to Oregon and California was one of the jobs that they were best suited for. Some of the men that became guides were Caleb Greenwood, Moses Black Harris, Joseph Meek, Robert Newell, and Stephen Hall Meek to name a few. So in the spring of 1840, Stephen Hall Meek led the McGoffin Brothers' Wagon Train to Santa Fe and on to Chihuahua, Mexico.

In 1842, Stephen led a group of wagons from Independence, Missouri, to Fort Hall in the Oregon Territory, and then by pack animal on into the Willamette Valley. There he helped Lansford Hastings and Dr. McLoughlin layout Oregon City. Records show that Stephen Meek acquired ownership of the first lot of this new town site from Dr. McLoughlin. This was probably payment for the work he did, carrying the survey chain and helping Hastings survey the town site. In 1843, he guided dissatisfied Oregon settlers into California by way of the Old Hudson Bay Trail.

By 1845, Stephen's lifestyle and travels qualified him to be worthy as a guide. This was his field of expertise. Twenty years of exploring the countryside provided him the experience and knowledge. Thomas Fitzpatrick, William Sublette and Robert Campbell all knew Stephen Meek very well. They knew he was trustworthy, strong-willed, soft-spoken and a hard worker. They knew him as a real mountain man familiar with much of the west and especially the Oregon Territory. With these qualities, he had the ability to guide large wagon trains west. For that reason, they were more than willing to give him their support by writing letters of recommendation. This would allow him to attain a guiding position for the large wagon trains preparing to head west.

These authors became acquainted with Richard Silva, a prominent historian who resides in Yreka, California. Richard grew up and spent his 80 years in the area of Scotts Valley, Siskiyou County, California. Richard related a very interesting story to us, which was a hand-me-down bit of history pertaining to Stephen Hall Meek. This story came by way of Oral Lewis, another very prominent historian of the Scotts Valley area. Oral Lewis lived out his life of 94 years in and around Scotts Valley and Yreka, California. As the story went, not long before Stephen Meek's death in the year of 1889, he showed his friend, Jacob Lewis and some other settlers, one of the campsites he stayed at when he was with the 1836 Hudson Bay trapping expedition led by Thomas McKay. Jacob Lewis was Oral Lewis' grandfather, who was living very close to the camp site in Scotts Valley. Stephen Meek stood on a large rock with the settlers, showing them the campsite where he had camped in 1836, nearly 50 years before. He then went to a specific spot and proceeded to dig up charcoal and a fire pit. He described the fire pit saying that they dug pits deep for their fires in order to restrict the light the fire would give off at night time. They were attempting to protect themselves as much as possible and not attract attention from Indians that might be on the warpath. (See photos of this campsite on page 179).

This story shows a very important fact; Stephen Hall Meek was a true mountain man and guide with an uncanny ability to return to a specific spot nearly 50 years later. It was apparent that Stephen Meek's memory was very clear even up to his death. This fact enforces our belief that Stephen Hall Meek was not lost as he guided the wagon train of 1845 across the Central Oregon desert, even though it has been proported by many writers that he was lost.

It can be further noted that in the history of Scotts Valley, the name Meek is attached to a number of landmarks such as a cabin site, field, stream, meadow, mountain pass, etc. It is clear to us the name Meek is a very renowned and well-respected name throughout parts of California. Scotts Valley has a rich history, from the Indians, to the mountain men, and the trappers, with Stephen Hall Meek being one of the earliest, as well as the last real mountain man that explored that great region. He enjoyed that adventuresome lifestyle until his dying day.

Eli Casey Cooley and his family in later years
Courtesy of Michael F. Cooley and Mary Lou Cooley.

Away and away to the setting sun
Our troops are bound for the Oregon.
On the Rocky Mountains snow capt highth
Our flag shall stream in the Morning light
And over the plains of Oregon.

Away and away for a thousand miles.
To the climes where summer ever smiles.
For a few stout hearts can lead the mass
Through the hostile Tribes, and the Mountains pass
Away and away for the Oregon.

This poem appears in Eli Casey Cooley's diary. It appears that the first verse is signed by Christopher Columbus Cooley and the second verse is signed by Eli Casey Cooley. This was their tribute to the excitement of the long planned journey West.

1845 OREGON TRAIL EMIGRATION

In the spring of 1845, 450 to 500 wagons assembled in St. Joseph, and Independence, Missouri. They were readying themselves for the long and grueling journey to the Oregon Territory. Some came as far away as Pennsylvania, Ohio, Iowa, Indiana, and many of the other eastern states as well as Missouri. They came with the expectation of starting a new life in the far West. They would be going to a new land with new opportunities. They were a part of a growing list of people that wanted to better their lot in life.

The Oregon Trail Emigration started with a person expressing a desire to go "out West." Family members, relatives, neighbors, and friends joined in. It was important to go as a group for safety. Rules and requirements for the members were drawn up. A particular date and place to start this trip was decided on. When all were assembled, a wagon master was chosen and other officers as they felt necessary. Depending on the size of the group, smaller companies would be formed, each with their own captain.

The main companies setting out on this journey to Oregon in 1845 were:

The Savannah Oregon Emigrating Society Wagon Train, under the command of Solomon Tetherow as Wagon Master, was made up of emigrants from Elizabethtown, Indiana, as well as Platte County, Missouri, and other locations throughout Missouri and Indiana. Their place of rendezvous was on Wolf River, 15 or 20 miles west of St. Joseph, Missouri. They began their journey on Tuesday, May 6, 1845. This company consisted of 66 wagons, 292 people, 624 loose cattle, 398 oxen, 74 mules and horses, and 170 weapons. This company was well-organized and well-provisioned, as they had planned for this trip well in advance, preparing for hardships and the unexpected. There were 39 young men designated as cattle drovers. Eli Cooley was one of those drovers. It was the responsibility of the drovers to handle about 33 head of stock each, or their proportioned number of the whole herd. The Savannah Oregon Emigrating Society was broken up into several companies. Not only was Solomon Tetherow Wagon Master, he was the captain in charge of one company of wagons. Nicholas Ownbey was in charge of another company. Lewis Thompson was in command of a small company of ten wagons, including the families of James Officer, Christopher Cooley, Zachariah Moreland, and Abraham Patterson. This company followed closely behind Nicholas Ownbey's Company. There may have been some other small companies.

The St. Joseph Wagon Train was also referred to as the Military Emigrant Wagon Train and consisted of 66 wagons, 293 people, 453 oxen, 649 loose cattle, and 185 shooting irons. No mention is made of the number of horses and mules with this company. One key man that traveled with the St. Joseph Company was William Green T'Vault, the original captain until May 16, 1845, when he resigned the post. At that time James McNary became the captain. Some other men were John Waymire, James Miller Allen, John I. Packwood, James Barry Riggs, James Field who traveled with the Riggs family and kept a diary of the journey, and Jesse Harritt who traveled with the McNary family and also kept a diary of the journey. As the journey progressed, the St. Joseph Company divided into smaller groups. Other wagons joined in and some left. This made it very difficult to have an accurate account of what the company actually consisted of by the time they reached their destination at The Dalles on the Columbia River. It is quite clear from studying the diaries that this company remained behind the Savannah Oregon Emigrating Society Wagon Train, and part of the time, was also following the Samuel Parker Company.

Samuel Parker's Company, also known as the Van Buren Company, was under the command of Samuel Parker, and consisted of 48 wagons, 160 people, 340 loose cattle, 260 cattle, 61 mules and horses, and 90 weapons. Samuel Parker and his family, along with John Butts and his family, were neighbors and very close friends. They, along with several other families, began making the long hard journey to the Oregon Territory from Winchester Union township in Van Buren County, Iowa Territory. This is where Samuel Parker's diary picks up the journey beginning April 14, 1845. Though Samuel Parker was a man of very few words, his diary does include some important information when it is correlated with the other diaries.

The Independence Group was under the command of Presley Welch. Records and recollections seems to be very sketchy, therefore it is hard to arrive at an accurate count of this large wagon train. These authors have settled with the numbers as follows: 233 wagons, 1007 people, 3361 loose and working cattle, 182 mules and horses. At first, Joel Palmer was traveling alone with his friend, Spencer Buckley. Joel Palmer was a young writer and politician that had just served as a State Representative in Indiana for two terms, 1843 to 1845. The two young men were from Rushville, Indiana, and were making their way to Oregon to see if it was worth the effort to make it their future home. Joel Palmer and Spencer Buckley then joined the Independence Group. This large wagon train experienced personality clashes, disagreements, and unrest to a point that by May 19, 1845, it had split into several groups that would set their own pace of progress along the trail. Some of the captains named in the Independence Group were Dr. Presley Welch, Thomas Stevens, Lawrence Hall, Samuel Barlow, Horace M. Brown, and Joel Palmer. Joel Palmer and Spencer Buckley were with a group of 30 wagons and Joel became the captain of this company. He maintained that position throughout the remainder of the journey. Joel Palmer and Spencer Buckley's method of travel was using two horses and an ordinary wagon. A horse-drawn wagon could travel much faster than an ox-drawn wagon as long as there was a good road, but when the road was rough and steep, it was a different story. That's when the oxen outshined the horses. So during the course of the journey over rough roads, Joel Palmer's Company was forced to fall back several days before reaching the Snake River at Fort Boise. This left them well behind the main wagon train which had taken what is known as the Meek Cutoff. Therefore, Palmer's group did not take the cutoff but stayed on the main Oregon Trail. In fact, none of the companies named from the Independence Group followed the Meek Cutoff Wagon Trail. These companies followed the Oregon Trail over the Blue Mountains and down the Columbia River to The Dalles. They were continually jockeying for lead position as they made their journey. It was clear that Samuel Barlow's Company arrived in The Dalles one to two days in advance of Joel Palmer's Company. It is not clear when the other companies arrived. It can only be assumed it was in the following days.

The New London Emigrating Company was under the command of Abner 'Abe' Hackleman and was the last group making up the 1845 emigration. This company consisted of 50 wagons, 214 people, 666 loose cattle, 184 oxen, 19 mules and horses, 100 firearms, and 66 dogs.

One might take note of the similarities in the size of the Savannah Oregon Emigrating Society wagon train and the St. Joseph Wagon Train. The number of wagons and the number of people are nearly the same. However, there is a variation in the number of adults and the number of children listed in both wagon trains. Apparently, it is just a coincidence as the numbers appeared on rosters and diaries that give the accounting of the census of both wagon trains.

As near as can be determined, since records, documented memories, and recollections do not agree with one another, there is an accounting of at least 463 wagons advancing along the Oregon Trail in 1845. This count is only 17 wagons (3 ½ %) short of the claim made by Stephen Hall Meek in his autobiography, when he states he guided an immense wagon train of 480 wagons going to the Oregon Territory.

DIARIES

With all of the misinformation that has been printed about the Meek Cutoff, these authors decided to rely only on the words in the diaries. The following are the diary accounts we have used:

Eli Casey Cooley's Diary of 1845. Eli Cooley was a cattle drover with the Savannah Oregon Emigrating Society. In 1925, a descendant of Eli Cooley, Mrs. D.C. Remington, whose husband was Eli Cooley's grandson, was in possession of Eli Cooley's diary. Mrs. Remington offered to make Eli Cooley's diary available to the public through the Oregon Pioneer Association which was later renamed the Oregon Historical Society. Mrs. Remington realized the value of Eli Cooley's diary and offered the diary to the Oregon Pioneer Association for some undetermined monetary consideration. In response to her offer, George H. Himes, secretary of the Oregon Pioneer Association, refused the diary and minimized its importance in hopes that the diary would be gifted to the society. No doubt, Mrs. Remington was insulted by the response, and the diary was placed away as just that, a keepsake. It remained tucked away in safekeeping until sometime in 2006 or 2007 when the diary was brought out of moth balls and displayed at a Cooley family reunion. A Cooley descendant, Michael F. Cooley and his wife Mary Lou Cooley, realizing the importance of this diary, requested permission from the present owner of the diary to transcribe the diary and place it on the Internet for the world to read. This was done and was the first time the diary became available to the public. These authors were very blessed when we contacted the present diary owner, Grace Armstrong, the great-granddaughter of Eli Cooley, and requested a copy of Eli Cooley's original handwritten diary and the letter from the Oregon Pioneer Association. Grace Armstrong was very gracious in granting our request.[1] We must emphasize the importance of Eli Cooley's diary as it gives insight into a better understanding of the other diaries. Eli Cooley's diary was very helpful in properly locating and following many portions of the wagon traces of 1845 that we have verified on the ground. It is unfortunate that it was not appreciated in 1925 when it surfaced for the first time.

Samuel Parker's Diary of 1845. Samuel Parker was the captain of his own company. We have used a copy of his original handwritten diary.

John Herron's Diary of 1845. We have used a transcribed copy of his diary.[2] We do not know which company Herron was attached to, but he was following very closely to the Ownbey Company.

Jesse Harritt's Diary of 1845. Jesse Harritt was a cattle drover with the James McNary Company with the St. Joseph Wagon Train. We have used a copy of his original handwritten diary.

James Field's Diary of 1845. James Field, a teamster, was with the James Barry Riggs Company with the St. Joseph Wagon Train. We have used a transcribed copy of his diary.[3]

Andrew McClure's Diary of 1853. Andrew McClure was a member of the Elliott Wagon Train of 1853. They followed the Meek Cutoff into the Harney Valley. This diary added more information to the 1845 diaries. We have used a copy of his original handwritten diary.

We found that it is very important to use the original handwritten diaries when available rather than repeating the transcribed diaries if at all possible. Interpretations in transcriptions can confuse or alter the location of the trail. In copying the diaries into this book, we felt it was important to maintain the writing in its original form as much as possible. Grammar, punctuation, and spelling errors remain unchanged. We correlated the dates and mileage of the diaries with the locations such as landmarks and campsites.

---

[1]See a copy of the Oregon Pioneer Association's letter on page 180.

[2]Excerpts from John Herron's diary from August 23 to September 8, 1845 had been printed in an Albany, Oregon, newspaper. But before all of the diary could be printed, it burned up in a fire at Heppner, Oregon, on July 4, 1918, leaving only the excerpts as a record.

[3]See a copy of the letter that James Field wrote on page 181.

The various companies began their journey westward in April and early May. These authors began researching and correlating the diaries at the beginning of the emigrants journey in Missouri. Thereby becoming acquainted with their thoughts and the terminology they used in describing the landmarks they passed, as well as comparing their day-by-day mileage.[1] Joel Palmer mentions on June 1, 1845, when his company was traveling between Republican Fork and the Platte River, that they actually used a survey chain measuring the distance of the day's travel along a good road. They found this distance to be 18½ miles. This is the basis that Palmer used to determine average miles traveled per day. However, this actually proves very little as there are too many variables such as: What was the road condition? What was the amount of time actually spent on the trail in the day's travel? What was the mode of travel, horse or oxen? Joel Palmer and Spencer Buckley were using horses to pull their wagon. When road conditions were good, horses traveled faster and made better time than the ox-drawn wagons. This fact alone would greatly affect the average number of miles traveled per hour in any given day. After compiling the diaries and tracking their travel on a day-by-day basis over the 1700 miles, a mathematical assumption was made that Joel Palmer spent seven hours on the trail from Republican Fork to the Platte River. By putting that assumption in place, simple mathematics would determine the travel rate of 2.64 miles per hour on that given day. Further study revealed that over the 1500 miles distance the companies traveled before reaching The Dalles, a consistent daily average rate of between 2 to 2½ miles per hour seems to be most prevalent, depending solely upon the condition of the weather and the trail. This rate of travel proved to be very consistent with the actual mileage between prominent landmarks that the diarists mention along their journey. Joel Palmer's rate of travel of 2.64 mph for the day he actually measured with the survey chain appears consistent with this line of thought. It is also these authors belief that the emigrants determined their daily mileage traveled by the fact that they knew the consistent speed their oxen traveled under normal conditions.

It might be interesting to note that after correlating the three complete diaries of Eli Cooley, Jesse Harritt, and Samuel Parker, the overall average distance these emigrants estimated they traveled along the Meek Cutoff Wagon Trail was 423 miles. The actual distance of the trail is 435 miles mathematically determined based on latitude and longitude coordinates taken by a Global Positioning System.[2] We found the emigrants overall average mileage to be short of the actual mileage by only 2.68% or 12 miles. Eli Cooley's mileage appears to be quite conservative, while Samuel Parker makes a rather liberal estimate on much of his mileage. James Field, Jesse Harritt, and John Herron were much closer in their daily mileage estimate to the actual mileages between prominent landmarks, as well as the overall total distance along the Meek Cutoff.

The organization and gathering of the companies preparing to make the journey into the Oregon Territory and a brief mention of the beginning days along the Oregon Trail has been emphasized primarily as a reference for the reader. These facts have been posted on the internet and repeated by the writers of many previous books. The main emphasis and purpose of this book is to cover the facts as accurately as possible pertaining to the journey from Fort Boise along the Snake River, following an Indian trail, that was later named the old Hudson Bay Trappers Trail, crossing central Oregon, and continuing on to The Dalles. This trail was later named the Meek Cutoff after the guide Stephen Hall Meek.

A large portion of the trail is on government land, but where the trail crosses private ground, permission from the land owner must be obtained to access the trail location.

---

[1]Some writers believe that crude odometers were used to determine the daily mileage. Those writers explain that the discrepancies in the mileage between the diaries could be the result of broken teeth in the wooden wheel odometers, thus rendering them unreliable, or the odometer was not calibrated. They appear to have given little thought of what the actual mileage might be.

[2]Global Positioning System (GPS) is defined as a satellite navigation system that provides location by coordinates anywhere on Earth where there is an unobstructed line of sight to four or more GPS satellites. This is accessible to anyone with a GPS receiver. Also, these coordinates can be used in conjunction with Google Earth.

ARRIVING AT FORT BOISE AND ON TO VALE

Aug Wen 20: The road to day has been Verry good Weather fine though a sprinkle of rain at nite Come about 1 mile and Crossed Boise River then Traveled down it on the north side about 15 miles and Camped on Snake River near Fort Bosie The fort is on the north side of Snake River on the Bank and Just Below the Mouth of Bosie. Saw severel Indians to day 16 miles to day **Eli Cooley Diary**

21: Got to fort Boisy. 13 mi. **Samuel Parker Diary**

Aug Thu 21: The Weather fine to day Crossed Snake River today Wee crossed Just Below Fort Bosie and camped on the South Side plenty of grass here They is but Verry little timber here on the River Siveril Indians here the River is between ¼ and ½ mile Wide Wee crossed over nearly Square to a point of an Island then bore up the River to the other side the water ran over the top of some of the Waggon Beds but got all over safe. **Eli Cooley Diary**

Aug Fri 22: Laid by to day Weather fine Mr. Meak, for the sum of 50 Dollars proffers to take the company a new rout which he says is about 150 miles nearer than the old one and a Better one it Will leave Fort Walla Walla to the rite some Distance and Will strike the Columbia near the place of Taking Water[1] **Eli Cooley Diary.**

22: Crosed the Snake River Verry deep. **Samuel Parker Diary**

23rd: 4 ms braught us down to Fort Bois this Fort is situated on the north bank of the Louis R or Snake R and is oned by the Hudson bay company Crassed over to the south side were we encamped found grass and a fiew small willows the river here is about 3/4 of a mile wide the water is about 4 feet deep and runs with a geentel current **Jesse Harritt Diary**

Nicholas Ownbey's Company, the advanced portion of the Savannah Oregon Emigrating Society Wagon Train, reached the Snake River crossing at Fort Boise on August 20th. Along the trail, the Savannah Oregon Emigrating Society had grouped themselves into smaller companies even though they were still recognizing the banner under which they had been traveling. Samuel Parker's Company arrived on August 21st. Several other companies arrived later. The St. Joseph Wagon Train had also

ORIGINAL OREGON TRAIL AT CAPTAIN KEENEY PASS INTERPRETIVE SITE LOCATED SOUTHEAST OF VALE, OREGON
Location 1 viewed northerly on Vale (Modified) map, p. 15.

[1]Stephen Meek said he would guide the emigrants to the location he called "Taking Water." This is where The Dalles is located on the Columbia River and, at that time, was where the wagons had to be abandoned. Traveling next to the river by oxen and wagon was impossible. Therefore, at this location they had to take to the water and float the river by boats or rafts, and thus the term "Taking Water."

broken up into several smaller companies. James Riggs' Company and James McNary's Company arrived at Fort Boise on August 23rd. Solomon Tetherow's Company was about four days behind Nicholas Ownbey's Company thereby arriving on August 24th.

During the heat of the early August sun of 1845, the tempers of the Indians in the Blue Mountains and Umatilla region came to a boiling point. The renegades among these Indians felt that the emigrating movement was robbing them of their freedom and of their hunting grounds. Thus, these Indians went on the warpath in an attempt to stop such destruction of their homeland. Word of the renegade Indians traveled easterly along the Oregon Trail reaching the emigrants. A sense of fear quickly possessed the companies as they reached the banks of the Snake River at Fort Boise. Most of them did not want to confront the Indians in battle, and had great concerns and were very worried. Other emigrants assumed that all Indians were alike; they had not encountered any real hostilities from the Indians along the trail, so why should there be any problems ahead? Stephen Meek understood the concerns and fears of the emigrants. He could answer these question, as he was very familiar with Indians and their tactics. He had engaged in many Indian battles. He knew that when Indians were on the warpath, they were not to be taken lightly. Meek told the emigrants that he knew of a new route through central Oregon and on into The Dalles. This route had never been traveled by wagons, but it would bypass the possible threat of the Indian uprisings to the north. This new route appealed to the emigrants. They voted and the majority agreed to take the new route and pay Stephen Meek fifty dollars for his services. Everyone was well aware this was a pack trail and not a wagon road, and that they would be making it a new road.

Stephen was familiar with the trail and the landmarks along the way. This new route was an old Indian trail that had been used for hundreds of years. It had been used as a pack trail by the trappers from the Hudson Bay Company. In addition, this pack trail had been used by the Bonneville Expedition in 1834, of which Stephen Meek had been a member. He also knew that the wagons would have to deviate from the trail in some locations as the terrain would not always be conducive to wagon travel.

It must be emphasized that up to this time, these emigrants had been following the Oregon Trail, which was an already established wagon road. Now, as they turned westward leaving the Oregon Trail, they were entering into a country totally unfamiliar to them. They began following a trail where they had to develop their own wagon road. Even though they had read about the splendors and grandeur of the wonderful West, they only had dim visions with a few names of locations sprinkled around in their thoughts like a light dose of pepper. In other words, they were totally lost from the very beginning. They couldn't even begin to imagine what the next turn in the trail might bring. By the time they had traveled 25 miles from Fort Boise, they were already grumbling and complaining about the rough, rocky, mountainous country through which they were traveling, even though Stephen Meek was leading them on the best possible route wagons could travel through the country. Unbeknownst to them, any other route through central Oregon by wagon would have been virtually impossible.

Aug Sat 23: Traveled to day the road has been Verry good Weather fine Come up a small valley and down an other to Mallaer River and Camped plenty of grass and Willow here The corse has been to day a little north of West They was an other Company got to the Crossing of the River to day. 10 miles. **Eli Cooley Diary**

August 23rd: This morning our company was called together, for the purpose of hiring a pilot to conduct us across the bend in Boise River and over the Blue Mountains, down to the Dalles, on the Columbia River. This route will cut off the bend of the road that leads down Burnt River, and is said to be one hundred and fifty miles nearer than the old route. Price agreed on with Mr. Meek to take us through the new route was fifty dollars, so we got up our oxen and started about 9 o'clock and traveled a northwest course to a beautiful stream of water called Malheur, about twelve miles from where we crossed the river, found plenty of grass and small willows to build a fire to get super with, so there was no grumbling. **John Herron Diary**

23: Went to Malhure Creek. 16 mi. **Samuel Parker Diary**

24th: leaveing the river we travleed a south west coarse over a good road made an advance of 12 ms and encamped on a stream affording grass and willows. **Jesse Harritt Diary**

Sun Aug 24th: The story of the murder of the two Frenchmen by the Walla Wallas is pronounced a humbug by the people of the fort. They say that the Walla Wallas entertain a hostile feeling toward us, and will probably try to injure us as we pass through their territory, but their numbers or their equipment would not render them dangerous to such sized companies as we are in at present. Still, the nature of the country is such that if they took advantage of it they could damage us considerably. We had traveled thus far as three companies without any general commander, and previous to our starting this morning it was agree to choose one. Accordingly, James B. Riggs, our own old captain, was elected captain of the whole company by a unanimous vote. A man named Meek has engaged to pilot the leading company Capt. Owensby's, which is the only one now ahead of us.[1] He was to guide the outfit through to the Dalles of the Columbia River by a new and nearer route, following the pack trail from Fort Boise and missing The Walla Wallas altogether, leaving Fort Walla Walla on his right and cutting off between 100 and 200 miles travel. A vote was taken wheather we should follow them or keep the old way, and a majority decided on the new one. We traveled about 16 miles, camping upon Malheur Creek near the forks of two roads. **James Field Diary**

As the Oregon Trail leaves Fort Boise on the Snake River, it runs in a northwesterly direction over gently sloping sandy hills. The trail was a good road. It enters Cow Hollow and gradually ascends the northerly fork of Cow Hollow Creek to Captain Keeney Pass. A paved county highway called Lytle Boulevard runs parallel to the Oregon Trail, where wagon swales are clearly visible and well marked, up Cow Hollow, over Captain Keeney Pass, and all the way into Vale, Oregon.

Deep swales through this vicinity reveal the traces of the Oregon Trail. Many pioneer settlers traveled this way. These authors' own ancestors left their footsteps along these wagon swales in 1862. Though the trail is no longer used, erosion over the years has continued to work on the trail, cutting the swales even deeper from heavy run off in the spring or an occasional cloudburst during the summer.

The emigrants' campsite was at present-day Vale, Oregon. The two roads that James Field mentions are the Oregon Trail going to the north and the other road that turned to the west which is the route they took. Field was a day behind the lead companies, so he could see where the road went.

Standing at Captain Keeney Pass on the Oregon Trail. Looking northwesterly with Vale Butte in the distance. Swales of the wagon trail are visible throughout the center of the photo. Present highway is to the left. Location 2 viewed northwesterly on Vale (Modified) map, p. 15.

[1]Throughout James Field's diary, he calls Nicholas Ownbey "Owensby".

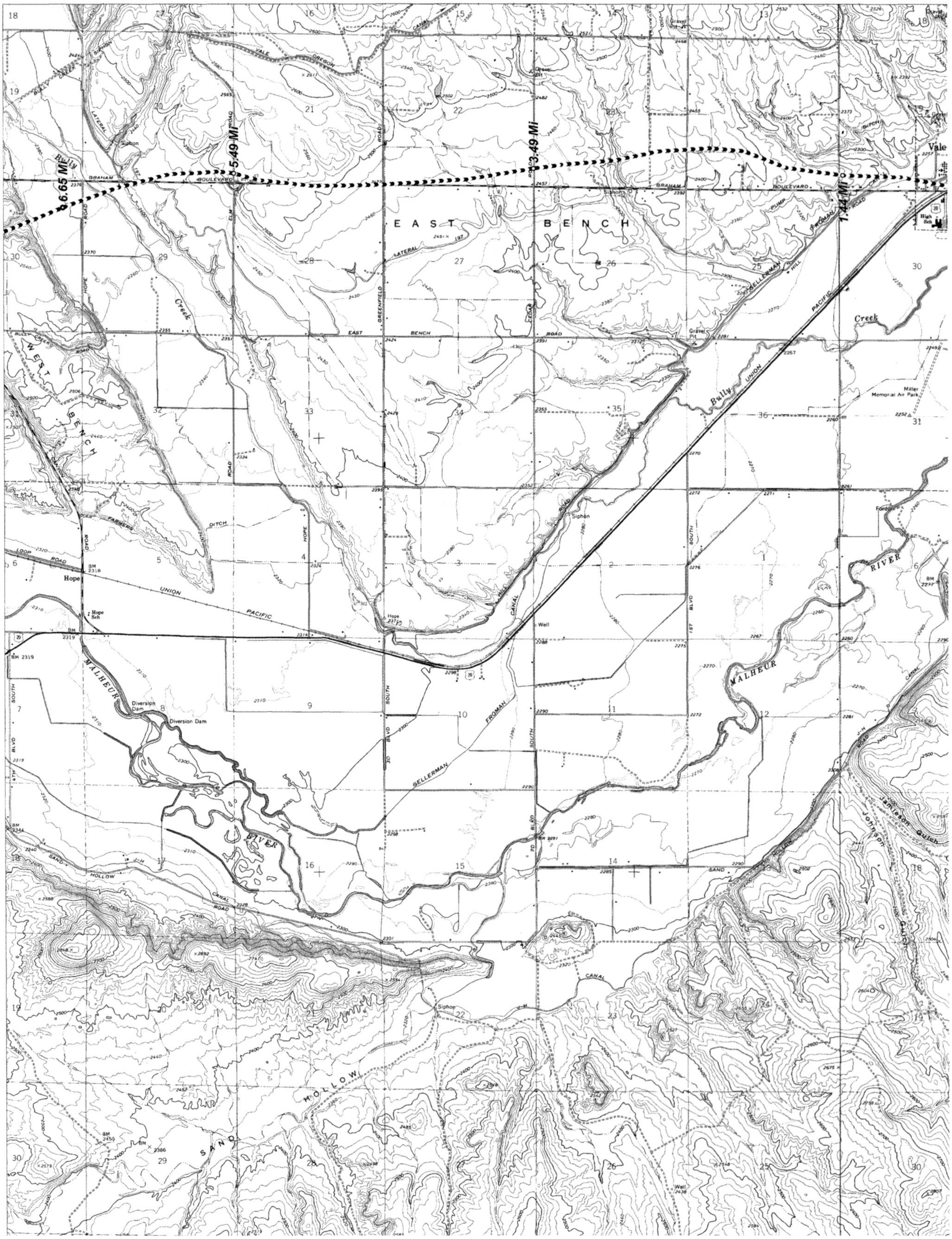

Vale West

Dashed Line: Projected Trail Location. Verified on the ground by these authors.

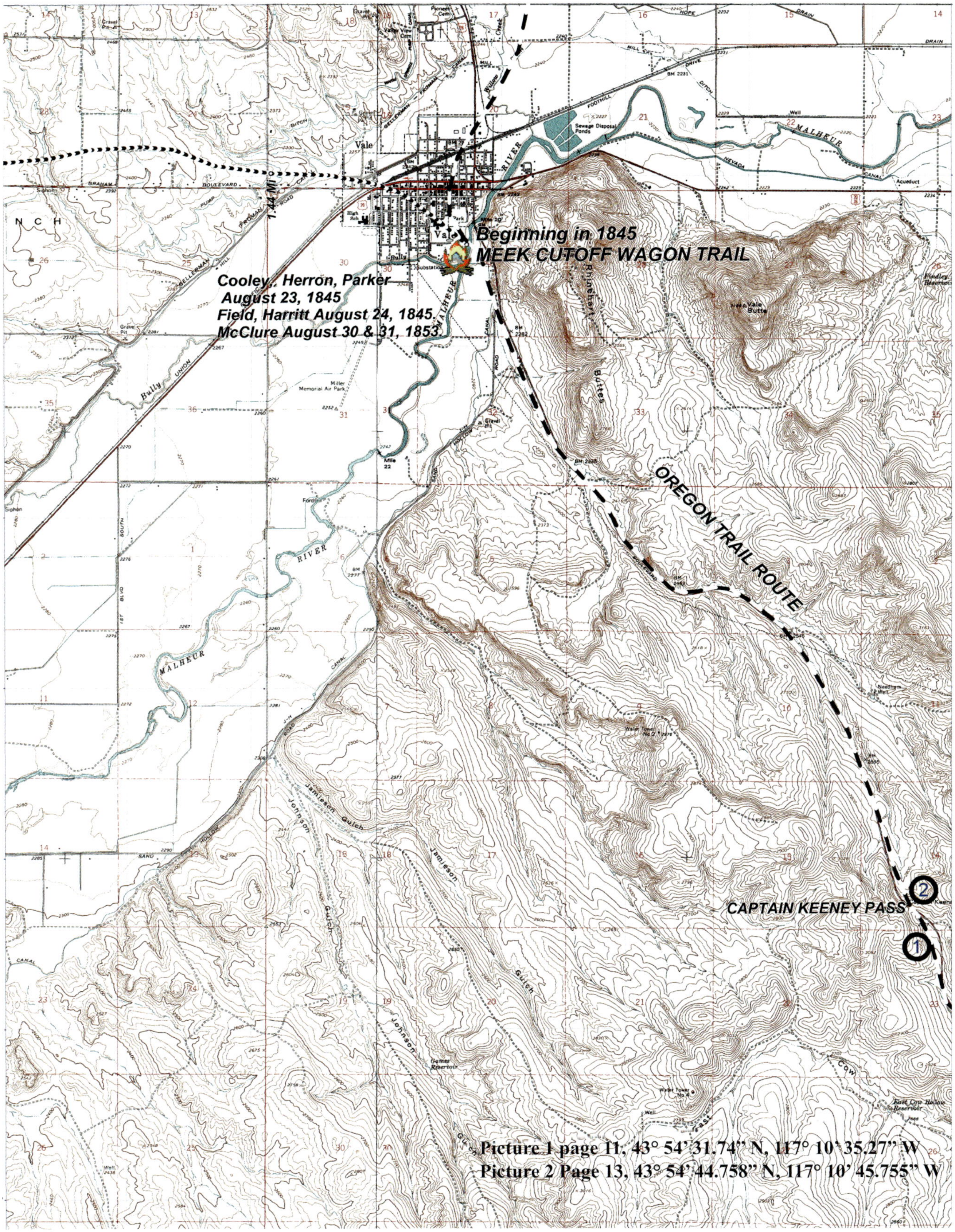

Vale (Modified)

Circles: Picture Number and Its Location.
Dashed Line: Projected Trail Location. Verified on the ground by these authors.
Large Dashed Line: Oregon Trail

1853 Andrew McClure Diary.

Tuesday, August 30. From the Fort the road strikes the bottom and in one mile ascends the bluffs which give a fine view of the Snake and a range of mountains far in the north. Travelling four miles over a sage plain and enter a valley and travelling up the valley five miles and pass over the ridge. A little bunch grass on the hills. From the ridge the road descends into another valley and follows it winding for three miles when it enters the valley of Malheur. Here the cut-off into the Willamette known as Elliotts trail. From here the old trail turns to the right around the bluff passes down two miles and crosses the river. Good grass.

The Malheur is about sixty feet wide and is a dull sluggish and shallow stream on the ripples, but the still water is deep and looks more sickly than the generality of streams in this part of the country.

Traveled about fifteen miles today no grass on the road no water. The day has been very warm. One cow belonging to William Bond fell in the yoke and died. Several others were nearly exhausted when they got here. These long drives without water and grass are very hard on teams. The trading post of Mr. Turner is stationed here.

The clouds gathered this evening and had another refreshing shower of rain nearly sufficient to lay the dust. This seems like cool weather for August, sufficiently so to wear overcoats morning and evenings

Wednesday, August 31. After some deliberation our men came to the conclusion to follow Elliott on the old Meeks trail. The next thing in order was to look out for company. They formed a union with two small trains one of five and the other of four wagons making a company of thirteen wagons. The day was spent in making arrangements and many other men making alike arrangements and with the quantity of cattle and the confusion of men and teams mixed produced more confusion than I have met on the road. All seems to be in readiness and tomorrow we start upon an unknown road and to stand the difficulties of savage cruelty at the doors of their own wigwams. *[Remained at Malheur River Camp.]*

VALE TO MALHEUR RIVER

Aug Sun 24: this morning started to pilott us the new rout wee left the old rout and Turned to the left Crossed the Mallaer River whare wee Camped and have Traveled up it to day though only in site of it until wee Camped struck it and Camped on it the road has been verry good Weather fine The corse has been nearly west. 8 miles. **Eli Cooley Diary**

24th: More oxen missing this morning. 11 o'clock before all the wagons were out of camp, traveled about 12 miles, 6 first miles northwest, then changed our course to southwest until we came to same stream of water that we encamped on last night, and found plenty of water and grass and dry willows to make fire with. The route today has been dry and uncommonly dusty, and entirely destitute of timber or vegetation of any kind, except wild sage, and it is dying very fast for want of rain; country tolerably level but not fit for cultivation. The Indians stole one horse last night within thirty yards of our encampment. **John Herron Diary**

24: Tuck what is also the meeks Cut Off. Misses But tuck Sick this day A Bad Cut of fore all that tuck it.[1] 14 mi. **Samuel Parker Diary**

Mon Aug 25th: Went about 11 miles across the hills, camping on Malheur River again. Since crossing to this side of the Snake River again the road has been fearfully dusty. In fact, a person who has never traveled these wormwood barrens can form no idea as to what depth dust may be cut up in them by passing of a few wagons. To a person walking in the road it is frequently more than shoe deep, and if the wind happens to blow lengthwise of the road, it raises such a fog that you cannot see the next wagon in front. **James Field Diary**

August 25: here we left the former rout baring a litle south of west we steared our corse over a tolerable good road 13 ms and encamped on the same stream found grass and a fiew willows **Jesse Harritt Diary**

The Meek Wagon Train turned westward leaving the Oregon Trail, beginning their journey across central Oregon on August 24, 1845. The trail crossed Bully Creek, and then turned in a southwesterly direction toward the narrows on the Malheur River at the western extremities of Malheur Valley.

It has been speculated and rumored by some researchers that an undetermined portion of the Meek Wagon Train turned up Bully Creek making its way to Westfall, Oregon. This theory can be easily discounted because the emigrants were total strangers to any part of this vast desert region. They were relying entirely upon the knowledge and experience of their guide, Stephen Meek. Therefore it does not seem logical that any of them would be striking off on their own. However, there was a freight wagon road later developed in about 1915 that made a shortcut from Vale, Oregon, to intersect the Winnemucca

[1] It appears that Parker added this last sentence after the journey was over.

to Baker City Wagon Road. It left Vale and followed Bully Creek to Westfall, Oregon, continued up Bully Creek and across the Indian Creek area. There it crossed the northerly end of Bendire Ridge, over the Bendire Mountains to the north end of Hunter Mountain, where it joined the Winnemucca to Baker City Wagon Road.

1853 Andrew McClure Diary:
Thursday, September 1. After much confusion respecting the stock, we succeeded in getting started about half past eight o'clock. After traveling about two miles from camp or three from the proper point for the junction of the roads where the Boise road first enters the valley, we ascended the bluff. Tolerably steep. After ascending, traveled five miles over a sage plain and came to a dry creek with water in pools the descent is steep good coarse grass in the valley. Malheur about three miles on the left. Traveled five miles, crossing two deep ravines over sage barrens and came to the valley of the river again. The descent is steep the surface of the hill composed of coarse gravel.

Travelled two and a half miles and came to the river good grass-coarse grass. One and a half miles further brought us to camp between two high hills which are near the river. Plenty of grass.

There are forty seven wagons that started from the Trading Post this morning for this cut off and are encamped within two miles. Mr. Elliott is said to be leading twenty which will make about sixty seven or nearer seventy wagons that are within three days drive of each other. Energy alone ought to bring about success.

Some sickness of light character in formally our train. One child with some of our fellow travellers is said to be very bad. *[Camped in the narrows on Malheur River.]*

MALHEUR RIVER TO LITTLE VALLEY AND HARPER VALLEY

Aug Mon 25: Traveled up Mallear to day Come about 1 mile and ½ and crossed the River and in a few hundred yards crossed it again and in about 1 mile crossed again and in a short Distance crossed again and thare turned to the rite up the Bluff and in about 2 mile struck it again went ½ mile up it and Camped plenty of grass and willow here the road to whare wee crossed the first time is verry good it then is quite Broken and rough to whare wee struck it the last time it then is verry good Weather fine to day. 6 miles. **Eli Cooley Diary** *[Camped in Little Valley.]*

25th: Started about 8 o'clock and encamped about 4. Traveled over some very rough road today, the fords of the creek very rough and rocky. The country very poor and broken, no timber only along the water courses. There are some willows and grass is very good on the low bottoms near the creek. Course today generally southwest, distance about 10 miles. **John Herron Diary** *[Camped in Harper Valley.]*

25: Went over hills all day and come to the Malhure at nite. 14 mi. **Samuel Parker Diary** *[Camped in Harper Valley.]*

Tues Aug 26th: Went about ten miles still keeping up Malheur, crossing and recrossing it twice, and camping upon it. We were obliged to take to the bluffs to get across several narrow bends of the river, and we there found some as hard road as any we had yet traveled. Indeed, I begin to think wagons can go anywhere. **James Field Diary** *[Camped in Harper Valley.]*

26th: proceded 10 ms farther up the creek and encamped found grass and a fiew willows. had about 4 ms of verry bad road balance good. **Jesse Harritt Diary** *[Camped in Harper Valley.]*

As they made their way up the Malheur River following the old pack trail, they came to some locations where the terrain forced the wagons to deviate from the trail. In these locations, the emigrants had to improve their own road. They were becoming convinced wagons could go anywhere.

1853 Andrew McClure Diary
Friday, September 2. The sick child died last night and was buried this morning near a rocky mound in a bend of the river on the left of the road. It is strange how little sympathy is shown to persons on this road. There should be more feeling.

Travelled four miles up the river and crossed it four times. The road is very rocky and the river bottom composed of large stones which make it bad fording. Water shallow not exceeding two feet. Willows along the stream.

Here we ascended the bluff by turning to the right up a ravine, proceeding one hundred and fifty yards turned to the left. The ascent is rocky and tolerably steep. The bluff is four hundred feet high. After ascending, the bluff strikes southwest across a sage plain the river coming from the left among the hills out of a canyon. Travelling three miles we descended by a long hill into the bottom which is broad and fertile for these parts producing good grass. Travelled one mile and grazed in the valley. A good place to camp [sic]. Willows in the margin of the stream. From the river the

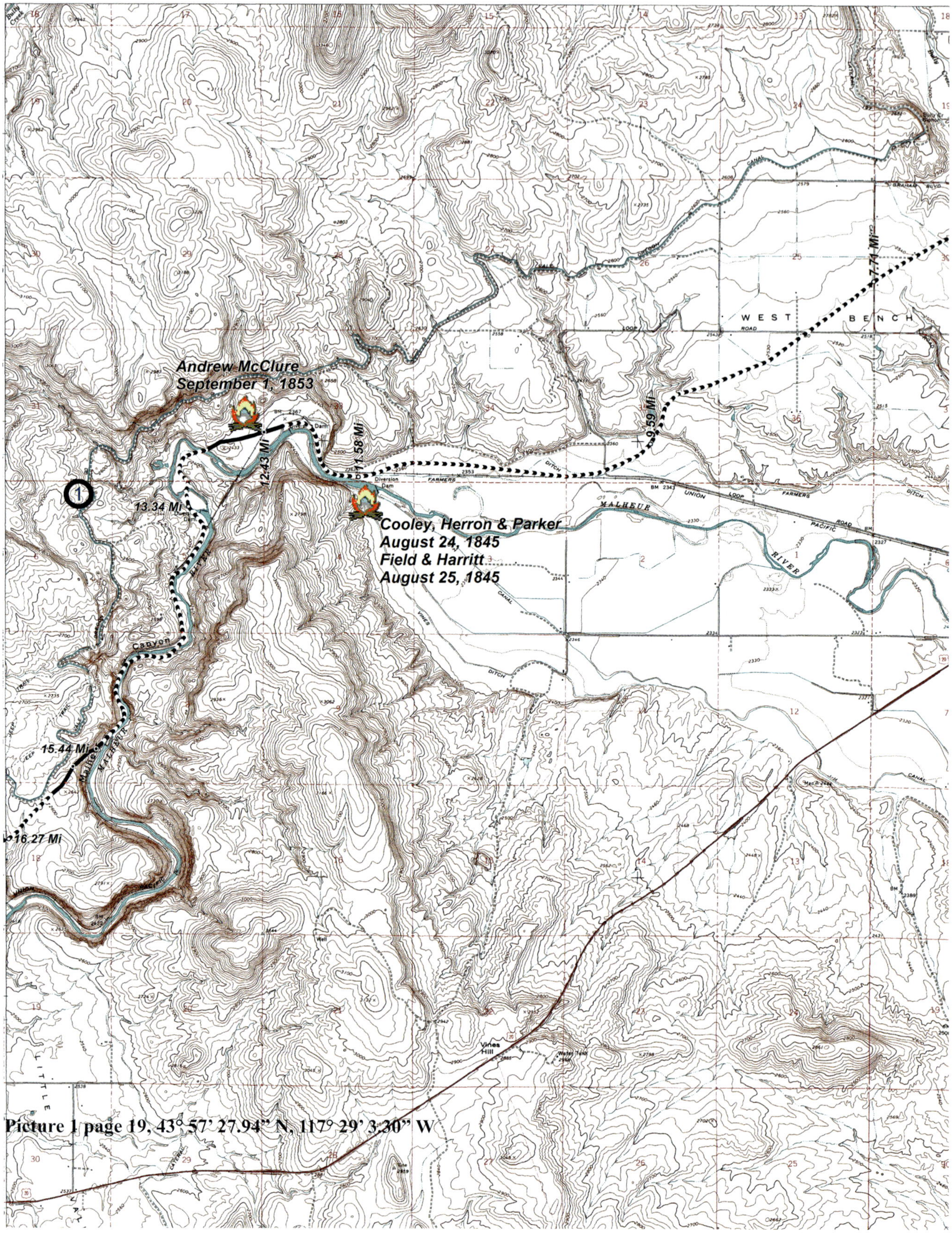

Circles: Picture Number and Its Location.
Solid Line: Traces of the Trail. Verified on the ground by these authors.
Dashed Line: Projected Trail Location. Verified on the ground by these authors.

Vines Hill

road turns to the right and ascends the bluff over a sage plain travelled about three miles mostly uphill and descending a long hill, came to the river and crossing it twice in a half a mile. The fords are deep and crooked and will be impassable except in the lowest stages of the water.

Travelled one and a half miles up the river and camped. The valley here is spread before us to the width of two or three miles and would produce good grass were it not for the washing of the mountains which covers the surface of the valley. Some good grass.

One of our wagons upset in the river today covering the inmates with wagon box beds and bed clothing clothes sacks overcoats, etc. Fortunately, no person was hurt. The team came out with naked wagon leaving the remainder in the stream. Luckily nothing was damaged. Those who have been unwell seem better. All in good cheer. Not so much rock here as we met this forenoon. The rock found in this stream is basalt.

The clouds thickened and presented some indications of rain. The ground shows there has been a shower lately. *[Camped in Harper Valley area.]*

The Meek Cutoff was used by the Meek Wagon Train in 1845, the Elliott Wagon Train of 1853, the Macy Wagon Train of 1854, and then settlers began moving into this area. Cadastral Surveyors were sent out to divide the state into sections. They were instructed to make note of land features, types of soil, and any improvements that may have been made to the area. Some surveyors were very good at making notations while others were negligent. By the year 1874, eastern Oregon was being surveyed in preparation for these homesteaders. John W. Meldrum, Deputy Cadastral Surveyor, under Contract No. 210 dated July 3, 1874, was surveying in this area.[1] His field notes indicate each time his line crossed the trail which he calls "wagon road" as well as any other physical improvements. Using these field notes enabled us to accurately locate the actual traces of the trail on the ground as it appears today.

At the end of the valley, the river narrows and the trail goes around the point of a ridge. The trail parallels the river a short distance, then cuts across a large bend in the river, passing through a low saddle leaving a rocky knob between the trail and the river. It was on this rocky knob that Andrew McClure of the Elliott Wagon Train of 1853 writes in his diary that a sick child died and was buried near a rocky mound in a bend in the river and to the left of the road. (See the photo below). From here the trail follows in and out of the river for a couple of miles. Then it leaves the river, ascends a draw, and crosses over the summit of a ridge and continues out across gently rolling hills.

Malheur River. The mound, shown by the arrow, is where the child's grave was placed. Location 1 viewed northeasterly on Vines Hill map, p. 18.

[1]Cadastral Surveyor is defined as a surveyor locating and determining land boundaries and areas.

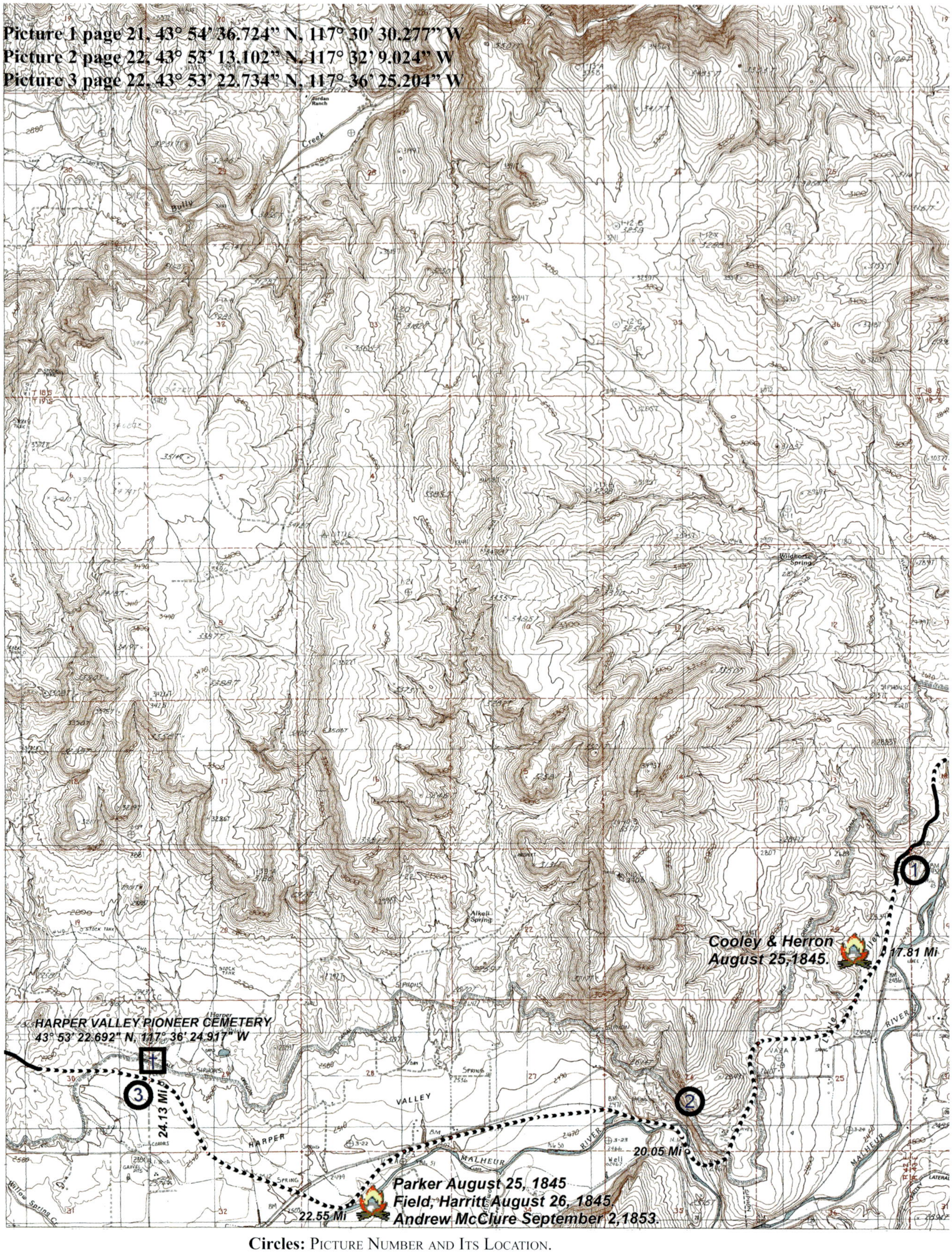

Circles: Picture Number and Its Location.
Solid Line: Traces of the Trail. Verified on the ground by these authors.
Dashed Line: Projected Trail Location. Verified on the ground by these authors.

Little Valley

TRACES OF THE WAGON ROAD. These authors' vehicle is sitting near the Section Corner common to Sections 13, 24, 18, and 19, T 42 & 43 E, W.M. Arrows point to the "Wagon road". Field notes below. Location 1 viewed northerly on Little Valley map, p. 20.

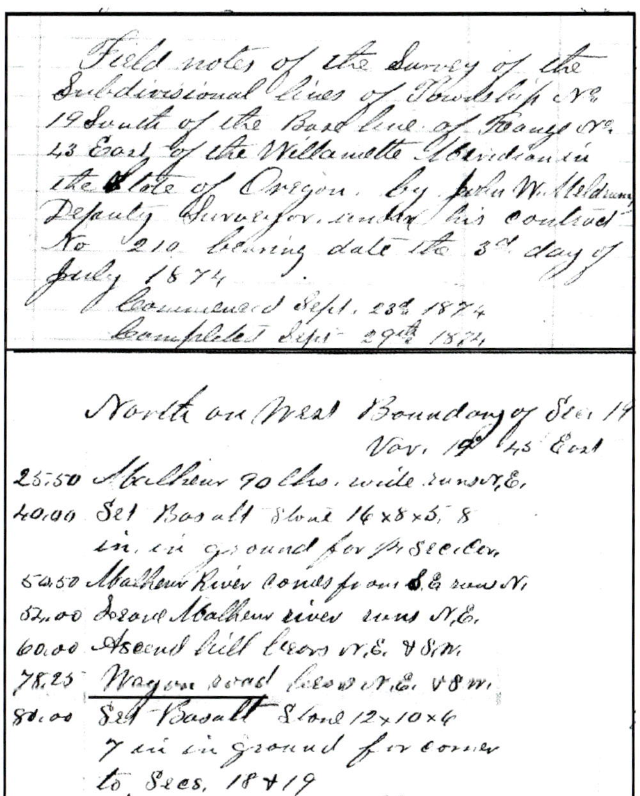

Field notes of the Survey of the Subdivisional lines of Township No. 19 South of the Base line of Range No. 43 East of the Willamette Meridian in the State of Oregon, by John W. Meldrum Deputy Surveyor, under his contract No. 210 bearing date the 3rd day of July 1874.

Commenced Sept. 23rd 1874
Completed Sept. 29th 1874

North on West Boundary of Sec. 19
Var. 19° 45' East

25.50 Malheur 90 lks. wide runs N.E.
40.00 Set Basalt Stone 16×8×5, 8 in. in ground for 1/4 sec. cor.
54.50 Malheur River bends from S.E. runs N.
52.00 Leave Malheur river runs N.E.
60.00 Ascend hill bears N.E. & S.W.
78.25 Wagon road bears N.E. & S.W.
80.00 Set Basalt Stone 12×10×6 7 in in ground for corner to Secs. 18 & 19

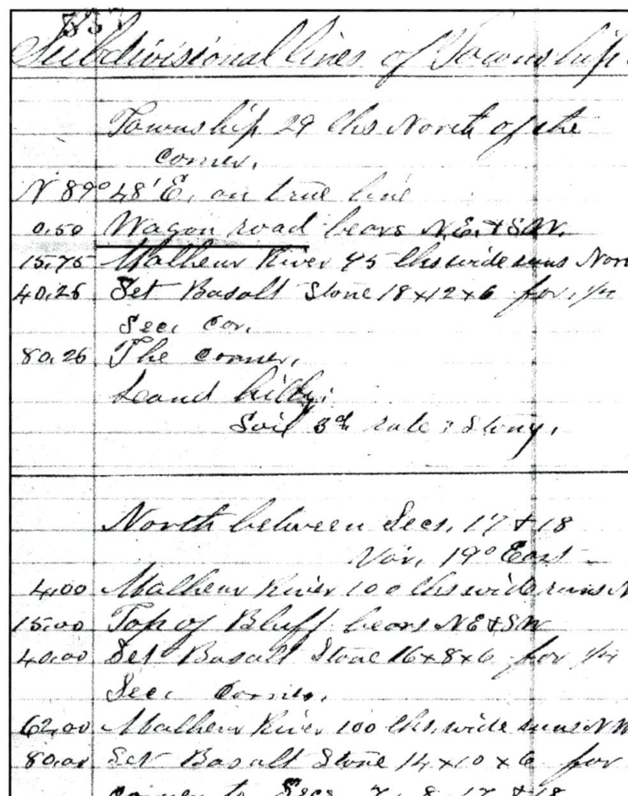

Subdivisional lines of Township

Township 24 lks North of the corner.
N 89°48' E. on true line
0.50 Wagon road bears N.E. & S.W.
15.75 Malheur River 45 lks wide runs North
40.26 Set Basalt Stone 18×12×6 for 1/4 Sec. Cor.
80.26 The corner.
Land hilly.
Soil 3rd rate & stony.

North between Secs. 17 & 18
Var. 19° East
4.00 Malheur river 100 lks wide runs N.
15.00 Top of Bluff bears NE & SW.
40.00 Set Basalt Stone 16×8×6 for 1/4 Sec. corner.
62.00 Malheur River 100 lks wide runs N.W.
80.00 Set Basalt Stone 14×10×6 for corner to Secs. 7, 8, 17 & 18

FIELD NOTES OF DEPUTY CADASTRAL SURVEYOR JOHN W. MELDRUM. Contract No. 210, dated July 3, 1874. T 19 S, R 43 E,W.M. (Township 19 South, Range 43 East, Willamette Meridian). The field notes show where his line crossed the "Wagon road."

Harper Valley. Looking across the easterly end of Harper Valley to Castle Rock. Castle Rock is the jutting point on the horizon just to the right of the center of the photo. Location 2 viewed northwesterly on Little Valley map, p. 20.

Between Little Valley and Harper Valley there is a ridge that the river makes a bend to go around. As the trail short cuts across this ridge, a prominent landmark, Castle Rock, formerly known as Fremont's Peak, is visible on the horizon. It is looming on the skyline about 35 miles in the distance. This was an important landmark to Stephen Meek as he led the wagons westward.

Descending back into the river canyon, the emigrants were forced to cross the river twice in a very short distance. The trail crosses Harper Valley in a westerly direction passing near the Harper Pioneer Cemetery.

The Harper Pioneer Cemetery
Located close to the Meek Cutoff Wagon Trail.
Location 3 on Little Valley map, p. 20

Naked Rocks. Andrew McClure writes, *"...passes over a ridge and passing near some large naked rocks comes into a valley a little grass."* Photo taken from Oregon Highway 20. Location 1 viewed northerly on Westfall map, p. 26.

LITTLE VALLEY TO COTTONWOOD CREEK

Aug Tue 26: Left the River this Morning and in about 1 mile struck it again and crossed 2 and come up about 2 mile and left it and come about 9 mile and camped on a drean plenty of grass Wood and Water Road quite Rough Weather fine. 12 miles. **Eli Cooley Diary**

26th: Started about half past seven. Still keeping up Malheur creek and crossed it the second time, then we left it and turned into a gap into the Blue Mountains, over some tolerably rough road near our encampment and on the east of it was a boiling spring that afforded water enough where we found first rate water and grass and willows, and a kind of soft wood called Balm. Distance 18 mi. **John Herron Diary**

26: Very rocky and hilly Camped on a small stream. 14 mi. **Samuel Parker Diary**

27th: commenced winding our way through the blue mountains at noon we left this pleasant stream to the left turning gradually to the north west travleed over a tolerable bad road reached the head of a small sinking rivulet affording exelent water and timber cottonwood willow and aulder the latter being the principal part of which there is some of the largest I ever saw, measuring from 12 to 14 inches in diameter 12 ms. **Jesse Harritt Diary**

Wed Aug 27th: Went about 18 miles today. The road although leadng across the bluffs which in a country in which mountains are a rarity would pass for pretty goodsized ones, was tolerably fair, but there is an abundance of small, sharp stones in it, black and hard as iron, and very wearing on the feet of the cattle. We camped upon Carter's fork, from its appearance a branch of Burnt River. **James Field Diary**

1853 Andrew McClure Diary

Saturday, September 3. This morning one ox was left dead at camp. From the river the road strikes obliquely about the bottom and passes over a ridge and passing near some large naked rocks comes into a valley a little grass. Passing over another ridge came into another valley wider than the first. Passing on in a westerly direction and six miles from the river came to a ravine and spring on the right of the road. Travelling two miles from the spring up a ravine we stopped to graze. Here a horse died having been bitten by a snake or stung by a scorpion. The road rough most of the way. From here the road passes up a ravine about N 70° W and we took the high and rough hills. The road is crooked here and the general bearing is about N 20° W over rocks and a more fertile country than the barren hills. Bunch grass grows well here but is very dry. Travelling ten miles and descending a long rocky hill came into a green valley and came to a dry branch. Water in pools. The grass is good, but the valley is narrow and would not afford grass sufficient for large quantity of stock.

This quite a gloomy looking place for the emigrant three or four thousand miles from home. The blue hills on the east. The thick willows on the banks of the creek. The narrow defile on the west and the high black rocky hills on the north and south all add to the gloom of the scene. The stone here is basalt. *[Camped on Cottonwood Creek.]*

In 1875, John W. Meldrum surveyed the line between Sections 17 and 18, T 19 S, R 41 E, W.M. (See Westfall map, Location 2, p. 26). His line crossed what he calls the "Old Emigrant road" showing that he recognized the road the early emigrants and settlers used in coming into this part of Oregon. Throughout this area, John Meldrum crossed a wagon road several times. As there weren't many settlers in the area yet, he recognized that the road he was crossing had to be from the emigrants that crossed the central part of Oregon. Therefore he referred to it as the "Old Emigrant road."

Just as Andrew McClure describes in his diary of September 3, 1853, the trail "*...passes over a ridge and passing near some large naked rocks [crossing Oregon Highway 20] comes into a valley...*" which is a small portion of Harper Valley. Then *"Passing over another ridge came into another valley wider than the first."* This larger valley is just more of Harper Valley. Many people have misinterpreted Andrew McClure's diary by thinking that he was referring to the cliffs at Danger Point which are located along the highway several miles north toward the town of Westfall, Oregon. However, Danger Point cannot be seen from the trail, as the trail lies toward the northwest, completely bypassing the cliffs at Danger Point. Andrew McClure writes, "*Passing on in a westerly direction and six miles from the river came to a ravine and spring on the right of the road.*" Upon leaving Harper Valley and the last of the agricultural lands, the trail enters undeveloped sagebrush covered desert. Andrew McClure writes, "*...the road passes up a ravine about N 70° W and we took the high and rough hills.*" The trail crosses the valley and up a drainage called Burnt Willow Creek, passing by a spring that is called Hart

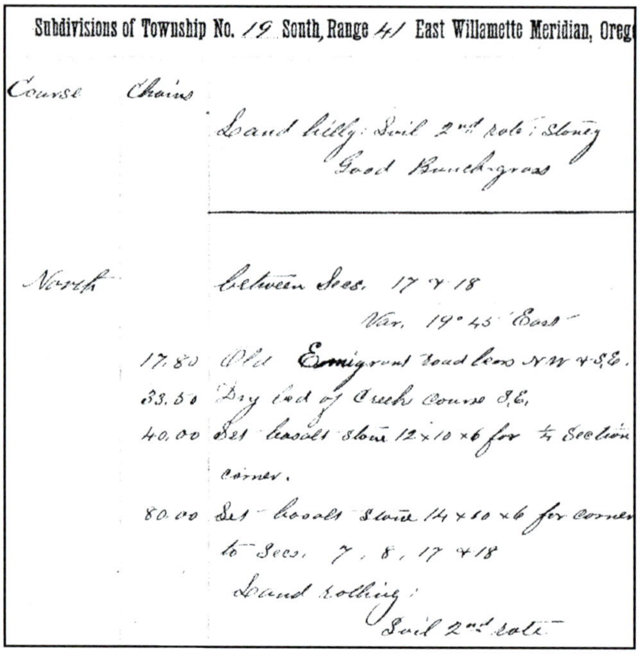

Subdivisions of Township No. 19 South, Range 41 East Willamette Meridian, Oreg

Course | Chains

Sand hilly: Soil 2nd rate: Stony
Good Bunch-grass

North | Between Secs. 17 & 18
Var. 19° 45' East

17.80 Old Emigrant road bears N.W. & S.E.
33.50 Dry bed of Creek course S.E.
40.00 Set basalt stone 12×10×6 for ¼ Section corner.
80.00 Set basalt stone 14×10×6 for corner to Secs. 7, 8, 17 & 18
Land rolling:
Soil 2nd rate

John W. Meldrum's survey notes of 1875. These notes show what he referred to as the "Old Emigrant road."

Spring. These authors were able to identify traces of wagon swales on the ground for several miles running in a northwesterly direction.

Andrew McClure mentions compass bearings along the trail in his diary. Here it must be noted that it appears the compass he was using was a magnetic compass without any declination.[1] Therefore, all of his bearings appear to be magnetic bearings. With respect to the bearings that he mentions throughout his diary, this author has found about 5 degrees variance in the magnetic bearings of today. Thus, making the necessary declination adjustments, the bearings fit the land reasonably well due to the changes in the magnetic declination over the past 169 years.

Andrew McClure again writes, *"...about N 20° W..."*. From Picture 2 location on Westfall map, p. 26 the trail turns more northwesterly as McClure writes, and passes near the corner described by John Meldrum (as shown above) where his line passes the "Old Emigrant Road." This is located near Hart Creek and about four tenths of a mile northeasterly of Hart Reservoir. From Hart Creek, the trail continues in a northwesterly direction for about two miles passing a quarter of a mile to the east of a small reservoir called Allotment Reservoir No. 3. Then the trail turns northeasterly, descending into Cottonwood Creek where all the companies camped, each in their turn as they came to it.

During these authors' research, we camped along the trail near the location that Cadastral Surveyor John W. Meldrum had identified in his field notes. On a few occasions, we took along metal detectors. However, they were seldom used as they consumed a lot of time, but did on this particular trip. A short distance from this campsite, we uncovered an old rusty ox shoe which reassured us that the trail we were following had been used by oxen such as the emigrants used. Using the diaries of the Meek Cutoff and the field notes led to this discovery and helped to confirm that we were indeed following the same trail Stephen Meek had used as he guided the wagon train.

Camping on the Trail. These authors' camp at the location John W. Meldrum described in 1875 as the "Old Emigrant road" on the line between Section 17 and 18, T 19 S, R 41 E, WM. Field notes above. Location 2 viewed westerly on Westfall map, p. 26.

[1]Declination is defined as the angle between the true north pole which is on the axis of the earth and the magnetic north pole which is east of the true north pole.

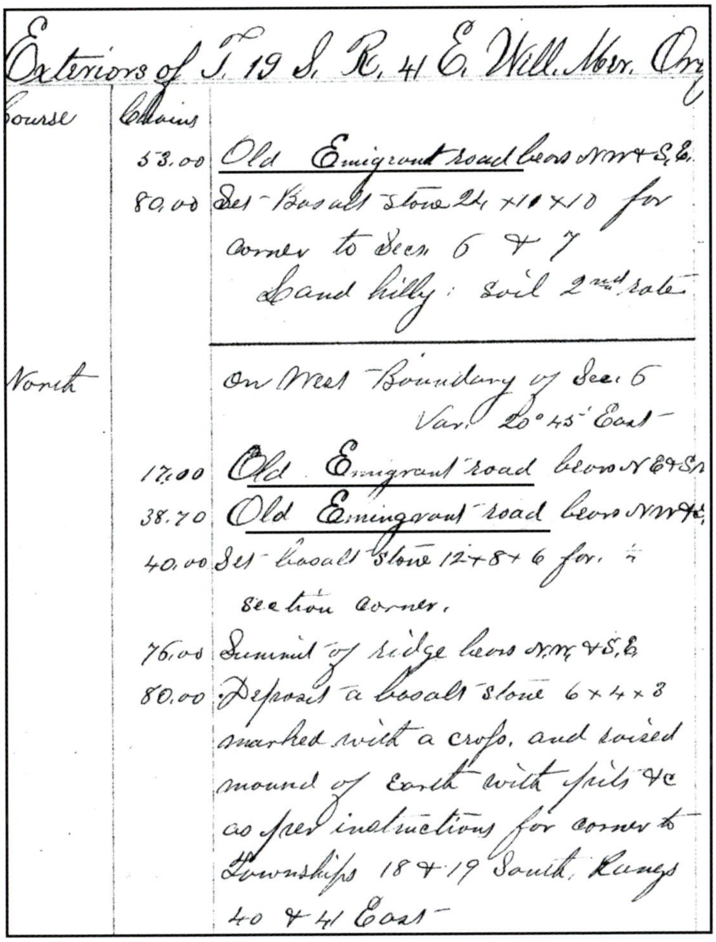

Exteriors of T. 19 S. R. 41 E. Will. Mer. Or.

Course	Chains	
	53.00	Old Emigrant road bears NW & SE.
	80.00	Set Basalt stone 24 x 10 x 10 for corner to Secs 6 & 7 Land hilly: soil 2nd rate
North		On West Boundary of Sec. 6 Var. 20°45' East
	17.00	Old Emigrant road bears NE & SW
	38.70	Old Emigrant road bears NW & SE
	40.00	Set basalt stone 12 x 8 x 6 for ¼ section corner.
	76.00	Summit of ridge bears NW & SE
	80.00	Deposit a basalt stone 6 x 4 x 3 marked with a cross, and raised mound of earth with pits &c as per instructions for corner to Townships 18 & 19 South, Range 40 & 41 East

Transcription of John W. Meldrum's field notes:
Exteriors of T 19 S, R 41 E, Willamette Meridian Oregon

At 53 chains he crosses an Old Emigrant road that bears NW & SE.
At 80 chains he sets a basalt stone 24" x 10" x 10" for corner to sections 6 & 7. Land hilly, Soil 2nd rate.

North on West Boundary of Section 5 with a variation 20 degrees 45 minutes east.
At 17 chains he crossed the Old Emigrant road that bears NE & SW.
At 38.70 chains he again crosses the Old Emigrant road that bears NW & SE.
At 40 chains he set a basalt stone 12" x 8" x 6" for 1/4 section corner.
At 76 chains he crossed a summit of a ridge that bears NW & SE.
At 80 chains he deposited a basalt stone 6" x 4" x 3" marked with a cross, and raised mound of earth with pits as per instructions for corner to Townships 18 & 19 South Range 40 & 41 East.

John Meldrum's Field Notes

Old Emigrant Road. Arrow facing to the right, near the center of the picture, is at a fence post depicting the location of the monument Meldrum set for the quarter corner. The "Old Emigrant road" Meldrum mentioned in his field notes above, runs from the bottom center of the photo up to the horizon, including a section of the road that is traveled on today. Location 1 viewed north on Little Black Canyon map, p. 28.

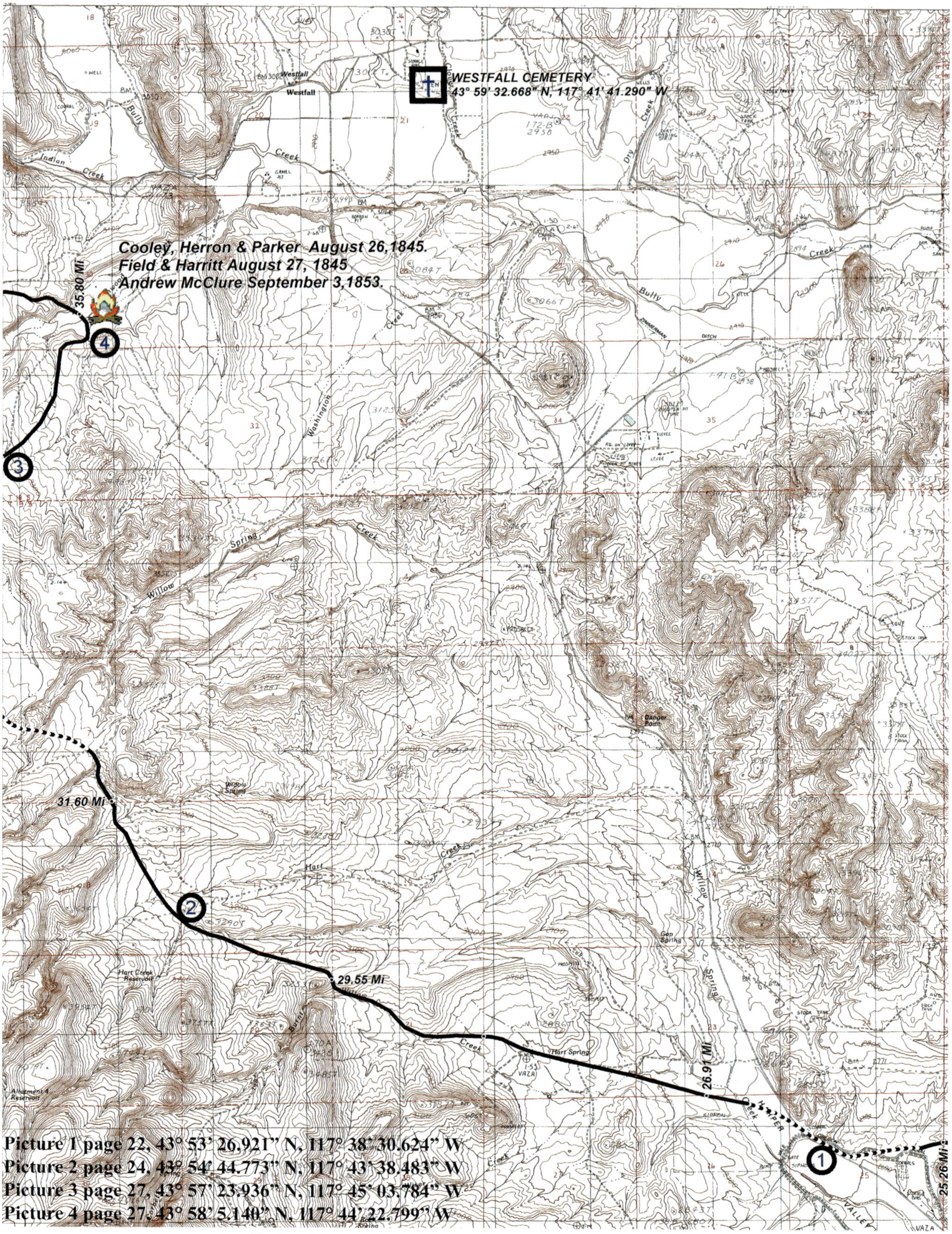

Circles: Picture Number and Its Location.
Solid Line: Traces of the Trail. Verified on the ground by these authors.
Dashed Line: Projected Trail Location. Verified on the ground by these authors.

Westfall

TRACES OF THE TRAIL AS IT DESCENDS INTO COTTONWOOD CREEK
Cottonwood Creek is where the emigrants made their camp the nights of August 26th and 27th. Location 3 viewed northeasterly on Westfall map, p. 26.

COTTONWOOD CREEK CAMPSITE
When leaving the campsite, the trail ascends the narrow ravine just off-center to the left in the photo. Location 4 viewed northwesterly on Westfall map, p. 26.

COTTONWOOD CREEK TO SOUTH FORK OF COTTONWOOD CREEK

Aug Wen 27: The road quite Broken and Rough to day weather fine left the hollow and in about 2 mile struck it again and Traveled up it about 3 mile and Camped some Wood, grass and Water here.[1] 5 miles. **Eli Cooley Diary**

27th: Late start this morning; nine oxen missing. 11 o'clock before all of the wagons were out of camp, then we moved off a southwest coarse about ten miles to the head of the same branch that we camped on last night; had some very rough road today. Passed down one very rocky ravine the valley of the little stream where we are tonight, and had it very dusty down the bench, found plenty of water and some willows, grass not good, very much dried up, mountains entirely barren, no soil here. **John Herron Diary**

27: Bad road went. 12 mi. **Samuel Parker Diary** *[Camped at mouth of Jones Canyon.]*

28th: turned to the south west passed over a range of mountains had bad road travleed 5 ms and encamped on a small stream found but little grass wood plenty. **Jesse Harritt Diary**

Thurs Aug 28th: Went about 6 miles, camping upon the same branch as before. The sharp stones spoken of yesterday were more plentiful today, and a few more such days travel as this will entirely use up our cattles feet. **James Field Diary**

1853 Andrew McClure Diary

Sunday, September 4. Ascended the bluff this morning and following a crooked trail over rough road for four miles descended the bluff down a rocky ravine for one half mile. The bluff being about five hundred feet high came to the same creek grass but no water. Four miles up the creek brought us to water in pools. Tolerably good water. Grass plentiful. Grazed here.

Having grazed about two hours started and turning to the right followed a ravine four miles and found water. Willows, Balm of Gilead and Elder here. The Balm of Gilead is the largest I have seen. Watered the cattle filled the water vessels and made a start from here and ascended a ravine by turning to the left, passed up a short distance and commenced the ascent of the bluff. Passing on four and a half miles and came to the ravine and encamped without water. Some grass it is not good. The water is supposed to flow into Burnt river from here. The road has been rocky the principal part of the day. The road is bad. The rock is black and the narrow valley present a gloomy appearance. *[Camped near Jones Reservoir on Jones Canyon.]*

Andrew McClure describes the Cottonwood Creek encampment on Saturday September 3, 1853, as, "*... The grass is good, but the valley is narrow... This quite a gloomy looking place... The narrow defile on the west and the high black rocky hills on the north and south all add to the gloom of the scene.*" Today, the area where they camped has been developed into a pleasant, green and inviting place. Westfall, Oregon, is about two miles northeasterly of the Cottonwood Creek campsite.

When they were camped at Cottonwood Creek on August 26th, John Herron mentions balm trees. Jesse Harritt actually called them Cottonwood. As these authors were researching the trail, we also found a small group of Cottonwood trees located there.

[1]The word hollow is a colloquial expression used by the diarists meaning either valley or canyon.

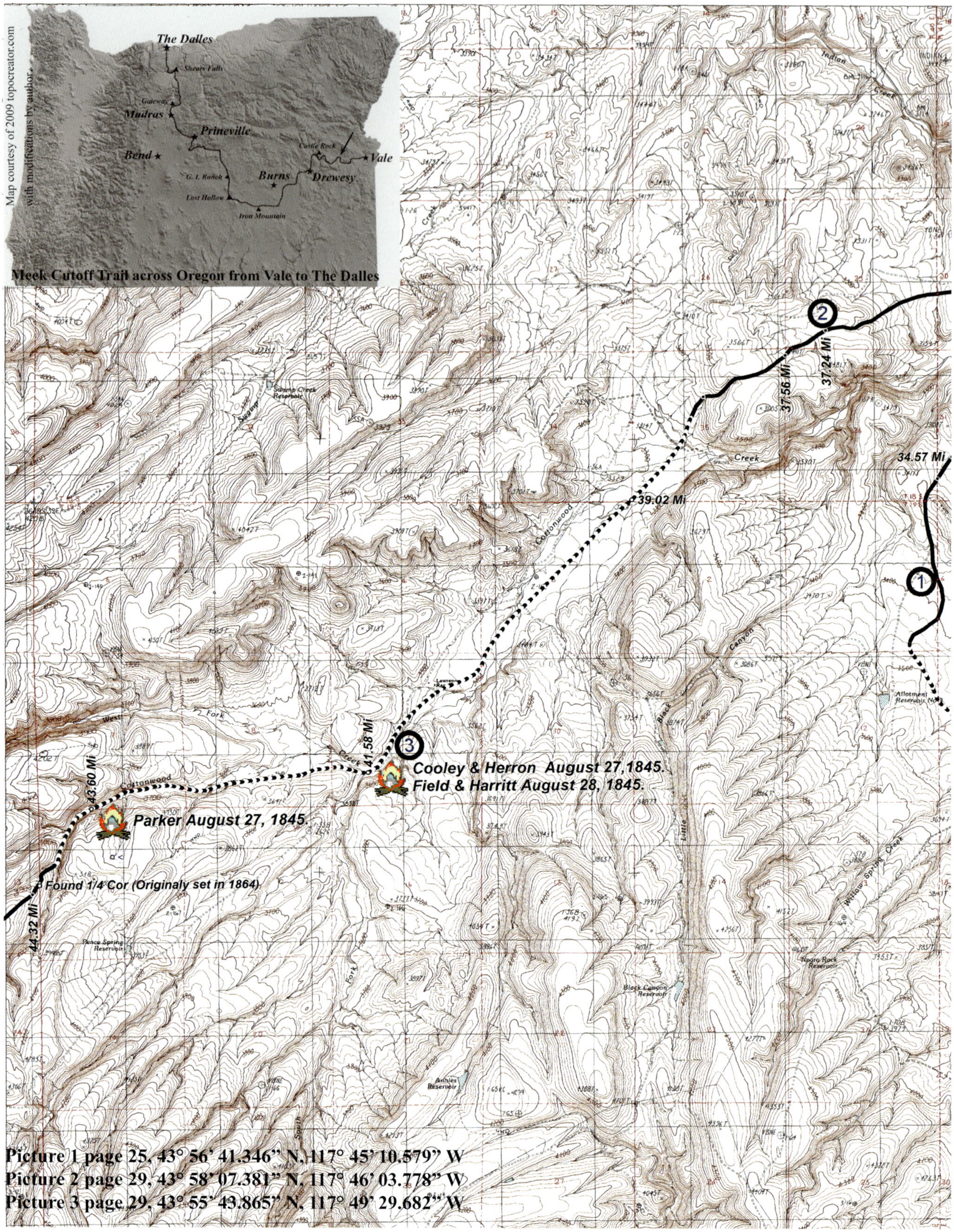

Little Black Canyon

Circles: Picture Number and Its Location.
Solid Line: Traces of the Trail. Verified on the ground by these authors.
Dashed Line: Projected Trail Location. Verified on the ground by these authors.

Traces of the Trail Leaving Their Campsite on Cottonwood Creek. This location was over the low hills before they descended back into the creek.
Location 2 viewed northeasterly on Little Black Canyon map, p. 28.

From their campsite on Cottonwood Creek, Stephen Meek led the wagons up a short ravine to bypass the long narrow defile of Cottonwood Creek. They traveled over some low hills for about two miles before descending down a steep little ravine back into Cottonwood Creek. From there they traveled up the creek bottom to the southwest until they arrived at the confluence of the Main Fork of Cottonwood Creek and the South Fork of Cottonwood Creek where they camped.

These authors continued farther up the trail, passing their campsite at the confluence of the Main Fork of Cottonwood Creek and the South Fork of Cottonwood Creek. Arriving at the upper area of the Main Fork of Cottonwood Creek at the mouth of Jones Canyon, we found many cottonwood trees growing there, and the remains of a great quantity of large cottonwood logs strewn across the floor of Cottonwood Creek Canyon. The canyon over time has experienced a number of large cloud bursts, causing a great deal of flash flooding. This is the same general area that Andrew McClure mentions "Balm of Gilead."

Confluence of the Main Fork of Cottonwood Creek and the South Fork of Cottonwood Creek
The center of the photo was their campsite on August 27.
Location 3 viewed southwesterly on Little Black Canyon map, p. 28.

SOUTH FORK OF COTTONWOOD CREEK TO AREA NEAR ANGEL WELLS

Aug Thu 28: The road to day has been verry Broken and rough to day had some rain to nite Traveled up the hollow over some verry large hills about 9 mile is a small spring near the road and about 3 mile further some out of the Way to the left whare wee Camped is a small spring and some Wood and grass Some oxen give out today. 12 miles. **Eli Cooley Diary**

28th: Made an early start this morning. Our pilot told us we had 18 miles to go to grass and water. So we traveled off at a quick pace but found no water, only a small spring that did not afford water enough to drink, so our poor oxen, cattle and horses had to suffer for water another night after a hard days travel over some of the worst road that they had traveled over yet, for it was uncommonly rocky and hilly. We passed up one mountain today that was about three miles high besides several that were ½ to ¾ of a mile high, and down some that were very near a mile slope. Passed some cedar, though they were small; grass good; course today southwest. 80 miles from Boise River. **John Herron Diary**

28: Bad road went. 7 mi. **Samuel Parker Diary**

29th: travleed 12 ms over the mountains had bad road encamped at a good spring affording plenty water for camp use none for stock found tolerable good grass and a fiew willows. **Jesse Harritt Diary**

Fri Aug 29th: Went about 12 miles today, over mountains to which those we had previously crossed were small hills, camping near a little spring in the mountains which affords sufficient water for the use of the camp, but our cattle would have been obliged to do without any had it not been for a storm of rain which came on in the evening, the first storm for months. The mountains are covered with small, black, hard, nine-cornered stones, about the size of those used to macadamize a road, and our cattle cringe at every step. **James Field Diary**

1853 Andrew McClure Diary

Monday, September 5. William Bond lost a cow this morning. On starting we travelled up the side of the ravine for two miles, when descending a hill into the ravine we came to a spongy piece of ground where we were able to get a small quantity of water for our suffering cattle. The water here is not sufficient for much stock but by digging holes and dipping with cups the teams were refreshed a little. From here the trail leads up a steep hill for one mile passing several budding aspen groves when we come near the summit the ground is more level. This part of the trail is very stony and hard on the oxen. Travelling over this ridge and crossing a valley on a ridge which I suppose is the dividing ridge between the waters of Malheur and Burnt rivers rising out of this valley and turning to the right to pass around the mountain peak and traveling three miles downhill and descending into a very steep hill where we were again able to dip a little water from holes which we gave our stock in buckets. Here we found a dead ox and a deserted wagon, boxes and other stuff. Ascending the hill out of the ravine and travelling one mile found water one mile to the right in the ravine sufficient for stock. Stopped here to graze but finding water plentiful and grass as good as usual the men came to the conclusion to camp. The road today has been very rough and discouraging. The roughness of the surface, and the crookedness of the road are sufficient to relax or increase the energies of the worried and worn-out emigrant. Some still unwell the weakness contracted on Boise still stays with us. Grass here is plentiful but very dry and the animal which eats needs water often which it has not at all times in this country. *[Camped near Becker Reservoir.]*

In addition to the Elliott Wagon Train and the Macy Wagon Train using the Meek Cutoff, it was also used in 1859 by Captain H.D. Wallen with his supply wagons. Wallen was a member of the Fourth Infantry of the US Calvary, and was making a reconnaissance survey for a military road from The Dalles on the Columbia River to the Great Salt Lake. Under his command was Lieutenant Joseph Dixon of the Topographic Engineers. Dixon was doing the mapping of the expedition. The interpretation of Dixon's map indicates that Wallen was retracing the Meek Cutoff Wagon Trail from the vicinity of Harney Lake and on to Fort Boise.

Under Cadastral Survey Contract No. 105, dated July 22, 1864, William H. Odell was surveying the Guide Meridian line between Ranges 39 and 40 East.[1] (See Location 1 on Westfall Butte Modified map page 32). He mentions "a road" in his field notes. This survey was nineteen years after Stephen Meek had led the wagons through this country, ten years after Macy had led a wagon train along this same route, and only five years since the Wallen expedition. Odell doesn't call it the Meek Trail, but he did recognize the evidence of a road. This is the only place along the Guide Meridian that

[1]Guide Meridian is defined as a line that that runs north and south from the base line at intervals of 24 miles east and west of the Principle Meridian which is the Willamette Meridian for Oregon and Washington.

he mentions any road, even though the Guide Meridian is several miles long. Under Contract No. 462, dated April 11, 1883, Rueben R. Leigh was surveying the range line between Ranges 38 and 39 East. He tells of crossing an "Old Emigrant Trail." In addition to these surveys, Cadastral Surveyor Joseph A. Ganong shows portions of the same trail describing it as an old wagon road in his field notes and map of Township 19 South, Range 39 East dated May 19, 1913. The surveys of Odell, Leigh, and Ganong help to confirm the actual location of the Meek Cutoff Wagon Trail through this area.

The companies of the wagon train are now three to four days out on the new route. Grumbling, complaining, and discontentment have begun to grow with each passing day. The main Oregon Trail was a well established wagon road. It had been used by many travelers, as well as the wagon trains of 1843 and 1844. The hard work of clearing the road had already been done; all they had to do was follow the trail. Now however, they were making the new trail themselves, and it was hard work. Large rocks had to be moved. The going was rough, stony, and difficult. James Field described the land best when he wrote, *"The mountains are covered with small, black, hard, nine-cornered stones, about the size of those used to macadamize a road, and our cattle cringe at every step."*

Aside from the stony ground and the long pull as they climbed toward the summit, Stephen Meek had led them over the very best possible route through the mountains. He had to deviate from the Old Hudson Bay Trail especially through this area, as the terrain that the old trail crossed was very rough and not conducive to wagon travel in many places. By the time they had reached the summit, they had actually gained 2500 feet in elevation in just over eight miles. Their long climb was about an average 6 percent grade. Once on the summit, they had reached the highest location of any place along the Meek Cutoff Wagon Trail. By deviating from the Old Hudson Bay Trail through this area, they had traveled an extra four miles and climbed an additional thousand feet in order to safely navigate over this range of mountains.

The emigrants had been traveling in a southwesterly direction for the last 13 miles since leaving their first campsite on Cottonwood Creek. Interpreting Andrew McClure's words, *"crossing a valley*

TRAIL UP JONES CANYON RIDGE. Notice traces of the trail in foreground along ridgetop. Jones Canyon is in the background. The area is very stony and hard on the animals feet. Location 1 viewed easterly on Westfall Butte (Modified) map, p. 32.

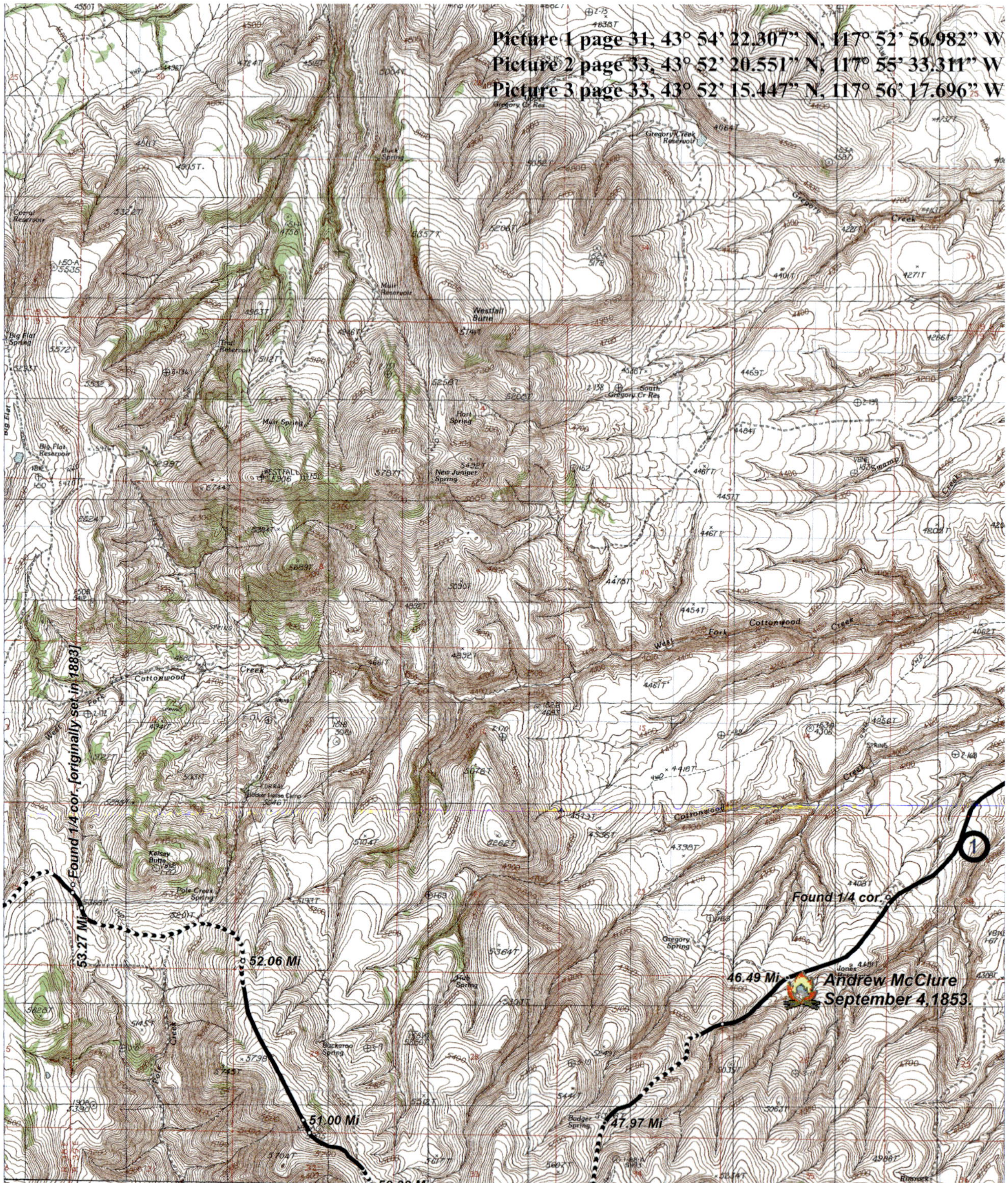

Westfall Butte (Modified)

Circles: Picture Number and Its Location.
Solid Line: Traces of the Trail. Verified on the ground by these authors.
Dashed Line: Projected Trail Location. Verified on the ground by these authors.

on a ridge" is actually the wide summit of the mountains where the drainages divide running south into the Malheur River and north into the main fork of Cottonwood Creek, not Burnt River as Andrew McClure supposed due to his lack of knowledge about the country. When they reached the summit of the mountains after leaving Cottonwood Creek, John Herron, who came from Kentucky, was awe struck at the view he saw. His comment, *"We passed up one mountain today that was about three miles high..."* is exaggerated somewhat, but when one is at the summit, it does seem very high when looking back to their last camp. James Field also expresses this same thought; the mountains they had previously crossed and called mountains were only small hills when compared to the mountains that they were now on.

Here at the summit, the trail turns west for about one mile before turning northwesterly about four miles to a spring. At this spring, Andrew McClure mentions finding a dead ox, a deserted wagon, and personal effects and belongings of some unfortunate emigrant. Most likely these were from members of the advanced companies of the Elliott Wagon Train. Just 30 years later and a few feet beyond this spring location, the trail location was confirmed by the surveyor, Rueben R. Leigh. He states he crossed the "Old Emigrant Trail" 4 chains (264 feet) south of a quarter corner he set along the line. This corner was a 16" x 12" x 10" stone placed in the ground and marked ¼ on the west side of the stone with a mound of stone placed alongside. Today, this corner has been found and verified. Now it has a permanent brass cap monument in place. Although the traces of the trail are no longer visible, the trail's location can easily be determined from Leigh's notes.

Traveling westerly from this spring about a mile and a half over a couple of small ridges, they come to a spring *"some out of the way"* south of their trail as Eli Cooley described it, where they camped. Today, this spring doesn't have a name, but it is about half a mile south of Angel Wells Reservoir.

Over the years, this mountain range has acquired a number of names such as Lake Ridge, De Armond Mountains, Westfall Butte, and Bendire Mountains, all being prominent locations along this range. Many writers have incorrectly assumed the Meek Cutoff Wagon Trail left the Oregon Trail at Vale, Oregon, leading to Harper Valley and on to Westfall, Oregon, and then to Westfall Butte. There it is alleged that the trail followed along to the north end of Bendire Ridge and then on down through the south end of Willow Basin. Continuing on to the south end of Bendire Mountains and on into Agency Valley. However, this route would not be conducive to wagon travel.

Aspen Groves. *"...the trail leads up a steep hill for one mile, passing several budding aspen groves..."*. Andrew McClure Diary, September 5, 1853. Location 2 viewed southwesterly on Westfall Butte (Modified) map, p. 32.

Valley on a Ridge. *"...small, black, hard, nine-cornered stones..."* James Field. *"Travelling over this ridge and crossing a valley on a ridge..."* Andrew McClure Diary. To the left of the present-day traveled road, the drainages run south into Malheur River. To the right the drainages run north into the Main Fork of Cottonwood Creek. Location 3 viewed westerly on Westfall Butte (Modified) map p. 32.

Spring Half a Mile South of Angel Wells Reservoir
"... some out of the Way to the left whare wee Camped is a small spring..." Eli Cooley on August 28, 1845. Location 1 viewed southerly on De Armond Mountain map, p. 36.

ANGEL WELLS AREA TO WARM SPRINGS CREEK

Aug Fri 29: The road to day has been quite Broken and rough to day Weather fine road quite crooked Come about 6 miles and Camped on a Hill fork plenty of grass and Willow here West the general corse has been about. 6 miles. **Eli Cooley Diary**

29th: This morning we left our dry encampment and traveled about ¾ of a mile northwest course, then turning a northeast course, one mile, then north ¾ of a mile, then we turned northwest about 3 miles and passed up a mountain about one mile high; here we changed our course to west about one mile to the top of another mountain, here we discovered water and grass sufficient about 3½ miles off, so we turned a southwest course over some as rocky road as ever I want to travel, for our wagons were off one rock on to another all of the way down the slope of the mountain, which occasioned a mighty jolting and rumbling with old wagons, for both men and cattle were in a hurry to get to water. We found a beautiful little stream of excellent water and plenty of grass, and willows that were dry and some cedar to make a fire with. We passed considerable cedar timber, but it was low and scubby. We had considerable rain this evening. Distance nine miles. **John Herron Diary**

29: Very bad road Broke 3 wagons today. 5 mi. **Samuel Parker Diary**

30th: had a fine shower of rain last night this morning the fog was so thick that we had great difacult in collecting our catel made a start at 7 oclock travled 10 ms over huge mountains and encamped on hill fork a butiful little branch found good grass and willows a fiew rods from us ware a warm spring bursting from the side of a lofty mountain a little above bloodheat **Jesse Harritt Diary**

Sat Aug 30th: Went about 12 miles today, over mountains as high as any yet met with, but some of them were grassy without rocks, while others were covered with big, round stones so nice to jounce wagons over, spoken of back toward Ft. Hall. We camped upon a small branch and found grass and water both plenty and good, which was what our cattle stood in much need of, as for several days we have had hard roads and bad camps, which has cut down stock lower than at any time. Three or four oxen have laid down in the road and given out every day for the past few days. **James Field Diary**

Trail is ascending a long gentle slope out of the North Fork of Warm Springs Creek. Traces of the trail are evident as rocks were rolled aside to the left of the trail. Existing jeep road on the right. Location 2 viewed northerly on De Armond Mountain map, p. 36.

1853 Andrew McClure Diary

Tuesday, September 6. Left an ox near camp worn out by fatigue and want of food and rest. The prospect before us this morning looked nor did we find it at all deceptive in appearance. Instead of following the trail broken by Elliott our men took the hill on the north and struck the trail two miles from camp.

Travelling about twelve miles over a very rough road and found no water. The road is the worst trail this side of Missouri and the worst I ever saw. I think we have not travelled over one hundred feet of level ground today and the hills are covered with very large stones principally of Basalt. The descent

> from the top of the hill to Malheur River I judge to be not less than three thousand feet and that in the short space of four miles while the road is the most stony that is found in these parts and more easily imagined than expressed.
>
> Encamped at the foot of the hill on a small creek which flows into Malheur. Water tolerably good dry grass plentiful.
>
> Our cattle are weak and nearly exhausted and from no other visible cause but fatigue and hard roads. There are no loads upon the wagons, and the grass, such as we find is plentiful.
>
> Some of the men killed a cow this evening for meat. She was the fattest and we thought made fine meat. The mountains before us look to be impractible for wagons. They are higher, look steeper and more rugged than those passed over.
>
> Mr. Elliott is thought to be about twenty miles ahead and seems to follow as nearly as possible the footsteps of Meeks. The road is said to have been surveyed across the Cascades is the only assurance. *[Camped on Warm Springs Creek.]*

Leaving their camp at Angel Wells on August 29th, John Herron gave a somewhat detailed description of the next day's journey. They traveled down what is called the North Fork of Warm Springs Creek which in recent times has had severe cloud bursts, uprooting trees and placing boulders almost the size of cars on top of the fallen trees. Then the trail turns up a dry draw continuing north, crossing the head of Willow Basin Creek and passing Morton Spring.[1] Morton Spring is where Samuel Parker's Company camped and repaired three wagons. The rest of the train traveled on, crossing the ridge between De Armond Mountain and Bendire Mountain. Then turning to the west, it crossed over Emigrant Hill, which was named by the early settlers and is still recognized by the local ranchers today. The trail then descends into Warm Springs Creek near the vicinity where Richard De Armond settled in 1891, and today, is a part of the William Butler Ranch. The trail through this area was very rocky.

Trail Crossing Emigrant Hill. The trail in the distance is depicted by the arrows. It continues on a westerly course through a prominent saddle before descending into Warm Springs Creek. The inset photo is the remains of what appears to be a saucer which was found near the location of the left arrow in the photo. Location 3 viewed northerly on De Armond Mountain map, p. 36.

[1]A dry draw is defined as a draw that does not have any water in it.

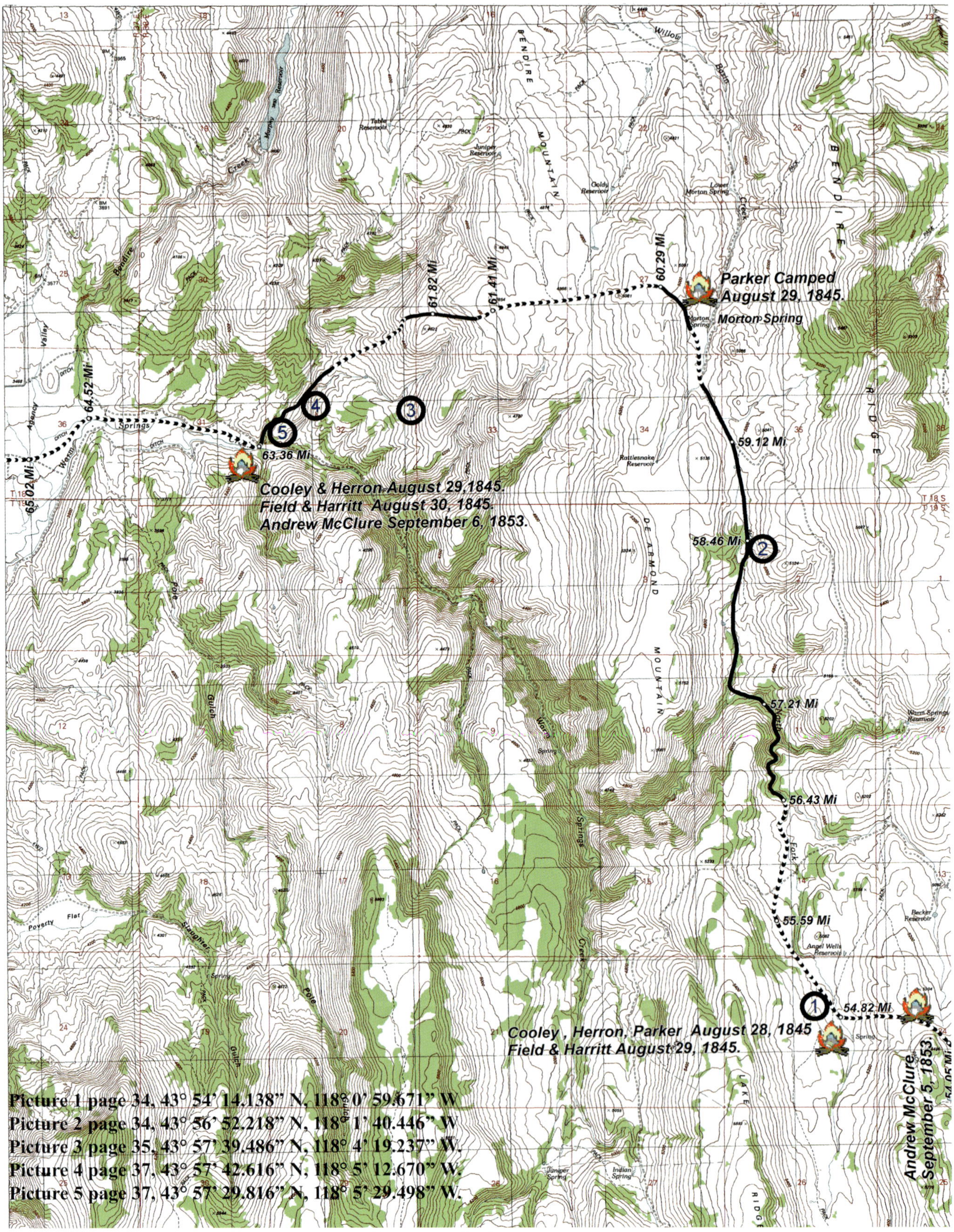

De Armond Mountain

Circles: Picture Number and Its Location.
Solid Line: Traces of the Trail. Verified on the ground by these authors.
Dashed Line: Projected Trail Location. Verified on the ground by these authors.

Trail Descending Emigrant Hill. Traces of the trail are evident just left of the center in the photo. The trail continues on down the small ravine descending into Warm Springs Creek. Location 4 viewed southwesterly on De Armond Mountain map, p. 36.

The past two days were long and hard on the livestock. Upon descending Emigrant Hill, John Herron writes, *"...we turned a southwest course over some as rocky road as ever I want to travel, for our wagons were off one rock on to another all of the way down the slope of the mountain, which occasioned a mighty jolting and rumbling with old wagons, for both men and cattle were in a hurry to get to water."* They camped on Warm Springs Creek above where the cattle were grazing.

Jesse Harritt, diarist and one of the cattle drovers, described the spring as *"a little above blood-heat."* This hot spring continues to flow just a short distance west of the present county road that runs through Agency Valley.

Entering the Valley of Warm Springs Creek. *"We found a beautiful little stream of excellent water and plenty of grass, and willows..."* John Herron, Aug. 29, 1845. This is the general area the wagon train camped on Warm Springs Creek after coming down Emigrant Hill. Location 5 viewed southwesterly on De Armond Mountain map, p. 36.

WARM SPRINGS CREEK TO NEAR THE BACKWATERS OF BEULAH RESERVOIR

Aug Sat 30: The road to day has been Broken but Tolerable good a sprinkle of Rain this Evening Come about West crossed a small Branch for about 4 miles and Struck Mallaer River and Camped plenty of grass and Wood here Traveled down the creek wee camped on last nite about 1½ and left it on our left Come to the left of a verry high Mountain leaving it on our rite. 4 miles. **Eli Cooley Diary**

30th: This morning very wet and rainy, late breakfast. 9 o'clock before we collected our oxen together, 10 o'clock all of the wagons on the roll again. Traveled about 5 miles a west course to the stream that we left the 26th. Here we encamped for there are mountains all around us, and we have the Blue Mountains to climb over again tomorrow that are said to be 25 miles across. Grass very good and plenty of willows, elder, and balm on the mountains. Some cedar but they are small and low; the mountains where we are now are covered with grass; it grows up under the snow in winter and dries up with the heat of summer, but does not rot like it would farther east where it rains through summer, for it seldom ever rains here in the summer. The cattle and horses eat it as well as they would well cured hay. Wild sage growing. Scarce 100 miles from Boise river. **John Herron Diary**

30: Rock all day pore grass more swaring than you ever heard. 11 mi. **Samuel Parker Diary**

31st: Rode tolerable good made an advance of 5 ms and encamped on a stream affording the best of water grass and timber in abundence. **Jesse Harritt Diary**

Sun Aug 31st: Went about five miles this morning and camped one more on Malheur River near a peak in the Blue Mts, called Fremont's Peak, the highest point of land in this part of the country, and easily distinguished at a great distance by a large conical rock upon its summit, having one perpendicular side to it. Found an excellent encampment again here. **James Field Diary**

1853 Andrew McClure Diary

Wednesday, September 7. Started as soon as we could collect our cattle and for four miles the road led down a gradual descent, touching the creek in several places crossing a spring branch of good water and passing through a fine bottom of grass. From here the trail takes a northwesterly direction for six miles and rises over the point from the mountain peak on the right. This part of the road is rough, rising very fast. The descent is long and steep, but tolerably smooth, being gravel. After descending this hill we again come to Malheur, but not the dull stagnant unhealthy stream that we found when we first saw it, but a bright clear sparkling mountain stream running with rapid current. About ten feet wide and two feet deep. Cool good water for use. The mountains before us look to be impracticable for wagons, but Meeks and Elliott have both ascended and "what man has done man can do". The valley here is covered with fine grass, the grass being three or four feet high, and the wild rye as much as six feet the former affording fine food for animals. The valley is from one to three hundred yards in width and bounded by high hills. Some sickness in the train. No animals lost today. *[Camped on Malheur in valley near Sarah Chambers grave.]*

Levi Scott Gravemarker
In Agency Valley Cemetery. Oregon California Trail Association has placed a memorial plaque describing his life.

Bill Cooley Gravemarker
In Agency Valley Cemetery.

From their camp on Warm Springs Creek, the trail turns west and follows the creek for about a mile where it enters a valley called Agency Valley crossing Bendire County Road. It was named after the Malheur Indian Agency that was located there between 1872 to 1879, at which time the agency was closed and abandoned. After crossing the northeastern portion of Agency Valley, the trail ascends a small ravine and passes by Agency Valley Cemetery, which lies to the north of the trail about 900 feet. One of the Agency Valley Cemetery's oldest looking headstones is that of Bill Cooley. There are no dates on it. A notable stone is that of Captain Levi Scott.[1]

Half a mile up this ravine the trail goes through a saddle and descends southwesterly to the backwaters of Beulah Reservoir. Crossing the valley, they came to the North Fork of the Malheur River where they camped. The companies began arriving at this vicinity on August 30.

On the 30th, Parker had to travel almost twice as far as Cooley and Herron to catch up and camp with them at the backwaters of Beulah Reservoir.

[1]Levi Scott played a major role in opening up the Applegate Trail into the Willamette Valley in 1846.

BACKWATERS OF BEULAH RESERVOIR TO NORTH FORK OF THE MALHEUR RIVER

Aug Sun 31: The road to has been verry Broken and some rock Crossed the River this morning 2 then turned to the rite over the hills and in about 1½ miles come near the River then left it again went over the hills again here a verry steep hill then struck the river again and come about 1 mile up it and camped plenty of grass and Wood here. Weather fine Freemonts peak. 5 miles. **Eli Cooley Diary**

31: Went up the Creek. 5 mi. **Samuel Parker Diary**

31st: Started about 8 o'clock with the expectations of crossing the mountains today. 7 oxen were missing, so we had to leave 5 wagons that did not come up with us until 2 o'clock and would not have overtaken us then if we had not laid by for them, so we traveled only 5 miles today and encamped south of a peak of the mountain that is about 2 miles high. We could see it five days before we came to it. There is on its summit a rock that is about one hundred feet high and has on its top some beautiful young pine. Our course today was about west over some very steep hills, and some rocks. Grass good and plenty of dry willows and alder. **John Herron Diary**

Sept 1st: made a small move of 5 ms over bad road and encamped on the same stream oposite Fremounts peak one of the loftyest points of the blue mountains found good grass and aulder timber in abundence. **Jesse Harritt Diary**

Mon Sept 1st: Went about 5 miles camping again on the Malheur. The road today, for short turns, sidling places, hard pulls, and jolting stones was rather ahead of anything we have had in the same distance, but the camping is first rate. **James Field Diary**

1853 Andrew McClure Diary

Thursday, September 8. From Camp the road again led up the bluff on the right east bank of the river. The road here nears the mountain peak on the left. The river on our left running through rocky canyons. Some distance onward the trail turns to the left, passing down a ravine and over some very rough points we came to the river and gorge. Made about four miles in the forenoon. Found good grass. Here the leader of our train formerly took two men with him and went ahead to examine the road. The teams were yoked and followed. We passed on came to this crossing. Which is about S 60° West from the mountain peak with a rocky top. The crossing is good. Mr. V. McClure passed on ascending the rising ground but after going some distance he sent a man back to stop the train while he went ahead. When they returned they stated that the worst was yet to a hill destitute of everything but rocks and seems to be striking directly across the range ahead. There is here and there a cedar which springs from among the large rocks on the sides of the mountain. This country is a little the most discouraging we have met each ridge or range which we cross is but to bring another rougher, higher and more difficult to our sight.

NEAR THE BACKWATERS OF BEULAH RESERVOIR. Modern-day covered wagons are camped near the location where the wagon train camped when they arrived at the North Fork of the Malheur River. Location 1 viewed southeasterly on Castle Rock (Modified) map, p. 40.

NORTH FORK OF THE MALHEUR RIVER. The foreground is the location where the wagons crossed the river twice. *"Crossed the river this morning 2 [twice]..."* Eli Cooley. *"...the valley is one hundred to three hundred yards in width..."* Andrew McClure. Location 2 viewed northerly Castle Rock (Modified) map, p. 40.

From this campsite location, the trail turns northwesterly up the North Fork of the Malheur River crossing the river twice. About a mile and a half up the river from their camp and to the east of the trail, is where Sarah King Chambers' grave is located.[1] Her grave is just above the Castle Rock

[1]According to correspondence, Sarah Chambers was the first person of record who died on the Meek Cutoff Wagon Trail. The Chambers and King families were at least three or four days behind the lead wagons. None of the diaries mention her passing.

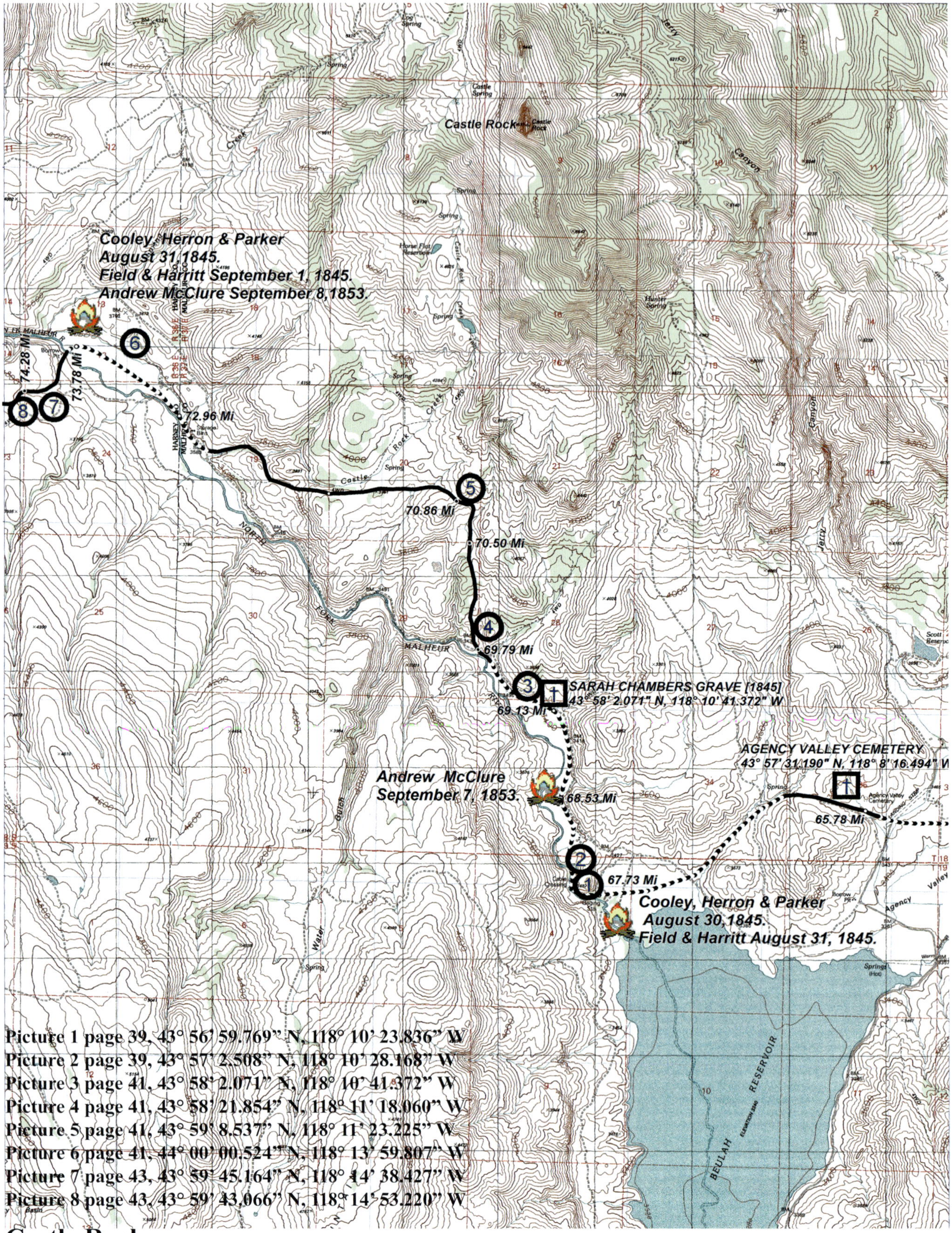

Castle Rock (Modified)

Circles: Picture Number and Its Location.
Solid Line: Traces of the Trail. Verified on the ground by these authors.
Dashed Line: Projected Trail Location. Verified on the ground by these authors.

SARAH CHAMBERS GRAVESTONE
Mrs. S. Chambers, September 3rd, 1845. Location 3 viewed easterly on Castle Rock (Modified) map, p. 40.

TURNING AWAY FROM THE RIVER AND HEADING NORTH TOWARD CASTLE ROCK. Location 4 viewed northerly on Castle Rock (Modified) map, p. 40.

ASCENDING SOUTHWEST OF CASTLE ROCK PEAK
Portion of the trail on steep side slope that had to be built. Cattle use it today. Location 5 viewed northwest on Castle Rock (Modified) map, p. 40.

CASTLE ROCK RANCH. This is the location where the emigrants camped for the last time on the North Fork of the Malheur River. Location 6 viewed southwest on Castle Rock (Modified) map, p. 40.

Ranch, formerly the Beal Ranch County Road. Advancing up the river ¾ of a mile, the trail turned northerly away from the very rocky, narrow canyon where the river flowed, heading toward the prominent landmark Castle Rock. John Herron describes it saying, *"...a peak of the mountain that is about 2 miles high. We could see it five days before we came to it."*

The traces of the wagon swales are clearly visible ascending the hill to the southwest of Castle Rock. James Field describes the trail as, *"...short turns, sidling places, hard pulls, and jolting stones...."* At the top of a small ridge 2½ miles south of the peak, they turned westerly crossing Castle Rock Creek and descended over large rocks back to the North Fork of the Malheur River. They followed up the river for one mile and camped.[1]

On September 8th, Andrew McClure writes that they had came to the crossing which was S 60° W from the mountain peak. It must be emphasized here that in one transcription of McClure's diary, a flagrant error was made of this bearing. McClure made it very clear that they were following the Meek Cutoff Wagon Trail as closely as possible. Therefore this diary has been used by researchers in trying to locate where the Meek Cutoff Wagon Trail crossed the North Fork of the Malheur River. Upon arriving at the Malheur River crossing, he writes very clearly in his diary that the crossing bears S 60° W, from the mountain peak with a rocky top (Castle Rock); NOT the bearing of S 80° W, as has been erroneously relied upon.This error has caused misinterpretation, misunderstanding, and confusion as to the trail's true location. Using the original diary entry of S 60° W, the trail crosses the Malheur River at a good location and continues up a rocky hill to the mouth of a very rocky ravine. Traces of the wagon trail can be seen on this rocky hill, in this ravine, across the plateau, into the second ravine, and on up the hill to the summit. This location is confirmed by all of the diarists.

Contrary to the beliefs of some, the trail could not and did not physically encompass Castle Rock Mountain and then descend into the upper reaches of the North Fork of the Malheur River, crossing the river supposedly somewhere just south of the mouth of the Little Malheur River. This crossing has been alleged by many writers using the erroneous bearing S 80° W. In addition, this would have caused the emigrants to travel at least a distance of ten miles for that day over terrain that would have been difficult, if not impossible, for a wagon to travel over. All the diarists write that they traveled only about five miles that day to return back to the river.

---

[1]Today, that location is on the Castle Rock Ranch.

NORTH FORK OF THE MALHEUR RIVER UP ROCKY RAVINES OVER TO COTTONWOOD CREEK THEN TO OTIS CREEK

Sept Mon 1st 1845: Weather fine to day Road verry rough and Broken crossed the creek this Morning and come up a hollow which is verry Rockey come about 4 miles and struck a Branch only water in holes Come about 1 mile Down it and after crossing it 3 times left it to our left and Turned up a hollow and in about 5 miles further struck a Branch and Camped plenty of grass and Willow here plenty of wood and grass on the Branch wee crossed 3 times the corse has been a little West of South. 10 miles. **Eli Cooley Diary**

September 1: The worst road you ever seen 5 Wagons Broak. Missis But worse. 17 mi. **Samuel Parker Diary**

Sept. 1st: Made an early start. 7 o'clock all on the move again, about a southwest course. Soon crossed the little stream called Malheur for the last time. I expect that I shall ever see it and unless it was better travelling on its banks than it is, I hope that no other emigrants will ever be gulled as we have been. On leaving this stream we traveled up a hollow or gulch that was I expect as rough a way as ever a wagon traveled. We had to remove some ten thousand stones before we could pass near the head of this ravine. We changed our course to south and turned down a dry hollow about 2 miles to where we found first rate water. Some took dinner here, and then continued our course south down the branch about 1 mile, then we began to climb the mountains again, passed over some very high ones until late in the evening we came into a valley and passed through it to a small stream running southeast and encamped about half past six; found plenty of grass and some dry willow. Distance today 15 miles. **John Herron Diary**

2nd: made an erly start over bad road for 8 ms broake one axeltree which detained us about 2 hours balance of the road tolerable good traveled 12 ms and encamped on a small rivulet winding its way through a level valley with its margin butifully adorned with small willows. **Jesse Harritt Diary**

Tues Sept 2nd: Traveled about 15 miles today, in a direction but little west of south, camping upon a small branch of the Malheur which puts into the South fork. About 4 miles of our road this morning rather exceeded anything we have passed over yet for rock, they being both large and sharp, lying in a narrow ravine where there was no shunning them. We got through, however, with only one broken axel tree [sic] and two wagon tongues, together with some other little fixings, which was really a favorable come off.[1] **James Field Diary**

1853 Andrew McClure Diary

Friday, September 9. The crossing here is good, bottom solid and banks tolerably so. From the ford the trail leads up a rocky hill to the mouth of a ravine which is extremely rocky. One mile from the ford we came to a plain which gradually ascends to the mountain. One mile further we entered a ravine which if possible is more rocky than the former and being an ascent made it very hard on the teams. Two miles up this ravine which runs an easterly direction. Two miles from the head of this ravine over a better country and down hill we came to a dry branch with water in pools and is running in some places. This stream runs about S 10° E. The road follows down this stream one and a half miles and turning to the left up a ravine ascends the bluff the ascent rocky when on the hill the trail takes a direction of about S. 30° West for about six miles when it descends a hill and enters the valley formed by several

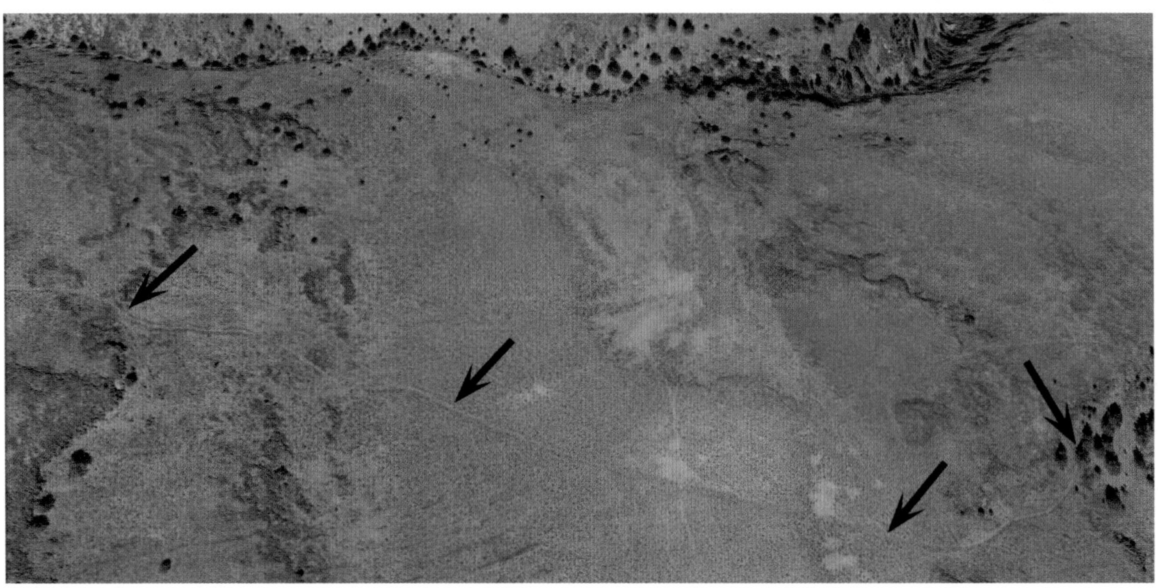

"Map data: Google Earth" 1994 Imagery Date: 9/11/2012, 43° 59' 42.94" N 118° 15' 09.08" W elev 3854 ft eye alt 9503 ft.

SATELLITE IMAGE. Image shows the trail route across the *"plain"* as described by Andrew McClure, Sept. 9, 1853, *"One mile from the ford we came to a plain which gradually ascends to the mountain...."* Andrew McClure.

[1]Axletree is defined as a crossbar of wood holding the wheels onto the wagon.

First Ravine. *"The worst road you ever seen..."* Samuel Parker. After crossing the North Fork of the Malheur River and ascending the hill a short distance, the trail entered a very rocky ravine. Location 7 viewed southwest on Castle Rock (Modified) map, p. 40.

Near the Head of the First Rocky Ravine Just Before the Trail Comes Out on a Plateau. Today, a large juniper is growing in the middle of the trail. Location 8 viewed southwest on Castle Rock (Modified) map, p. 40. On the satellite image on page 42, see arrow on the right side of image for the location.

> branches. One mile onward brought us to water where we encamped, having travelled about twelve miles. The trail this evening passes over a country gradually descending and much less stony. We called it a good road. Good grass here and water in some of the ravines. A stream ahead which I suppose is the South Branch of Malheur. The country looks better here the soil blacker, richer and more productive. *[Camped in Otis Creek area.]*

The emigrants left their campsite, crossed the Malheur River, ascended a rocky hill, and entered a very rocky ravine. When walking up the first ravine, these authors were amazed at seeing where all the rocks had been thrown aside to clear the wagon road. Coming out of this ravine onto a plateau or plain, the trail is easily seen due to the difference in vegetation which highlights the trail in addition to the rocks thrown aside. After they crossed the plateau, they entered into a second ravine, which required even more work than the first ravine. It was steeper, brushier, and if possible, had more rock.

From this second ravine, the trail tops out across the ridge and descends to another second Cottonwood Creek that is along the trail. John Herron in his diary entry of September 1st describes traveling down Cottonwood Creek, *"We changed our course to south and turned down a dry hollow*

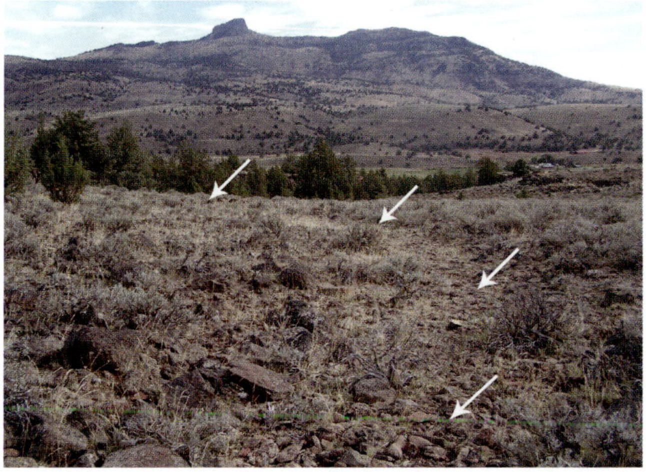

Crossing the Plateau. View looking back on the trail. Castle Rock is in the background and Castle Rock Ranch at far right. Location 1 viewed northeast on Cottonwood Reservoir map, p. 44. On the satellite image page 42, see second arrow from the right for photo location.

Crossing the Plateau. Looking ahead on the trail and into the second ravine. Notice the rocks piled along both sides of the trail. Location 2 viewed westerly on Cottonwood Reservoir map, p. 44. On the satellite image on page 42, see arrow on the far left side for photo location.

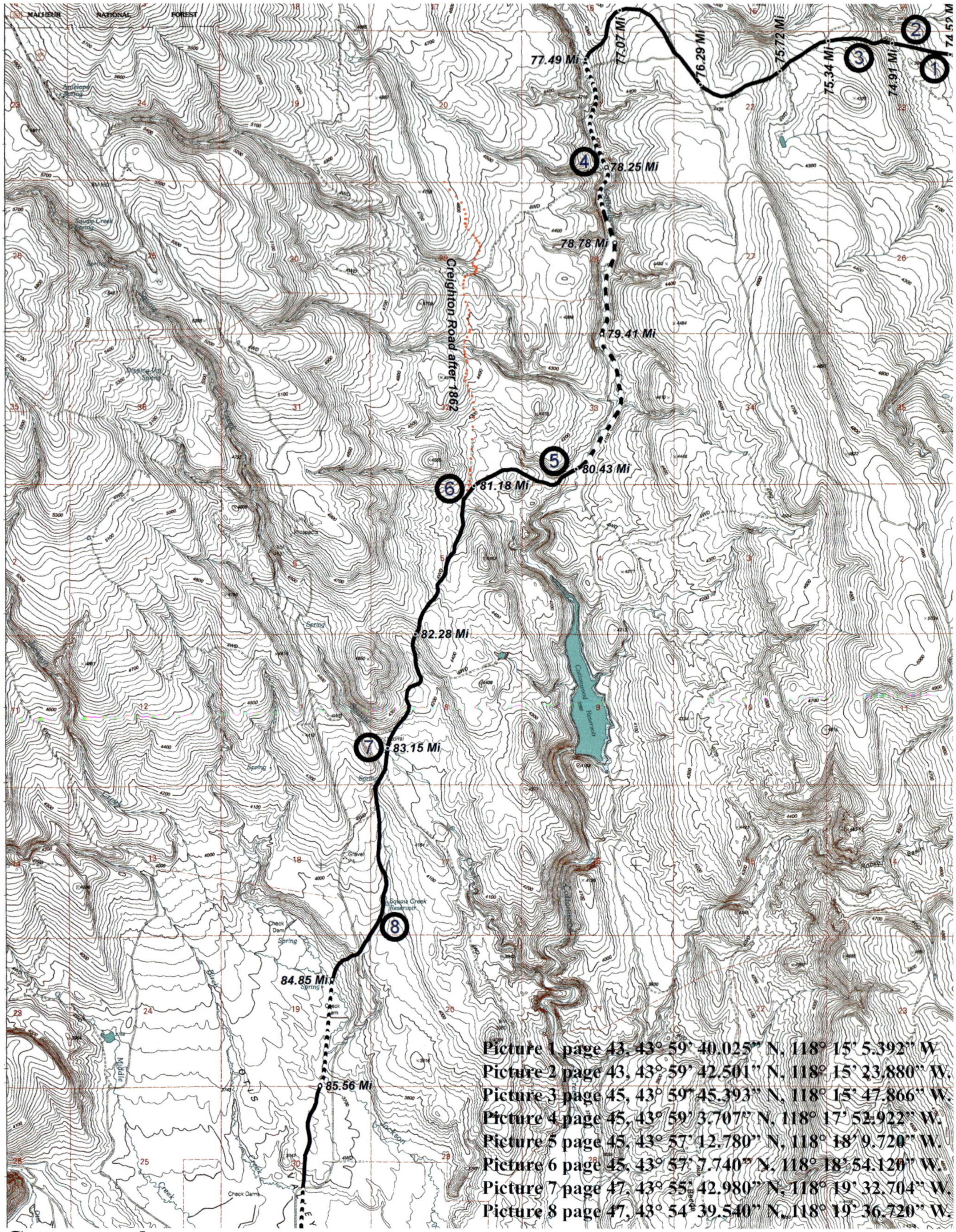

Cottonwood Reservoir

Circles: Picture Number and Its Location.
Solid Line: Traces of the Trail. Verified on the ground by these authors.
Dashed Line: Projected Trail Location. Verified on the ground by these authors.

Second ravine from Malheur River and After Crossing the Plateau. Location 3 viewed westerly on Cottonwood Reservoir map, p. 44.

These Authors' Camp on the Trail Along Cottonwood Creek
Location 4 viewed easterly on Cottonwood Reservoir map, p. 44.

about 2 miles to where we found first rate water. Some took dinner here, and then continued our course south down the branch about 1 mile, then we began to climb the mountains again, passed over some very high ones..."

It has been purported by some writers that the trail turned to the left when leaving Cottonwood Creek, placing it on the east side of Cottonwood Creek. From here, it was alleged to go toward the large springs at the head of Warm Springs Creek. Eli Cooley's diary entry of September 1st clearly determines the trail's direction when he writes, *"...crossing it [Cottonwood Creek] 3 times left it [Cottonwood Creek] to our left and Turned up a hollow..."* This diary entry has been misinterpreted in thinking that the trail went east from the Cottonwood Creek. After crossing Cottonwood Creek three times, they left it on their left. His manner of speaking in past diary entries confirms this conclusion. Andrew McClure in 1853, also writes in his diary on September 9th, "... *turning to the left up a ravine ascends the bluff the ascent rocky when on the hill the trail takes a direction of about S. 30° West for about six miles...*" He does not mention leaving Cottonwood Creek because the trail had followed along the toe of the slope where the canyon floor was wide and the creek flowing some distance to the left. Had they continued on down Cottonwood Creek, the canyon narrows and becomes steep and rocky, forcing the wagon train to climb out onto benched land.[1] These authors found traces of the trail very visible. It can be followed

Trail Leaving Cottonwood Creek
Location 5 viewed southwesterly on Cottonwood Reservoir map, p. 44.

Summit South of Cottonwood Creek. Creighton Road coming in from the left joining the Meek Cutoff Wagon Trail coming in from the right. Location 6 viewed northeasterly on Cottonwood Reservoir map, p. 44.

[1]The trail was later used by the early settlers along Cottonwood Creek, particularly John Palmer who proved up on his homestead in 1920. Today, this area is referred to as the Palmer pasture.

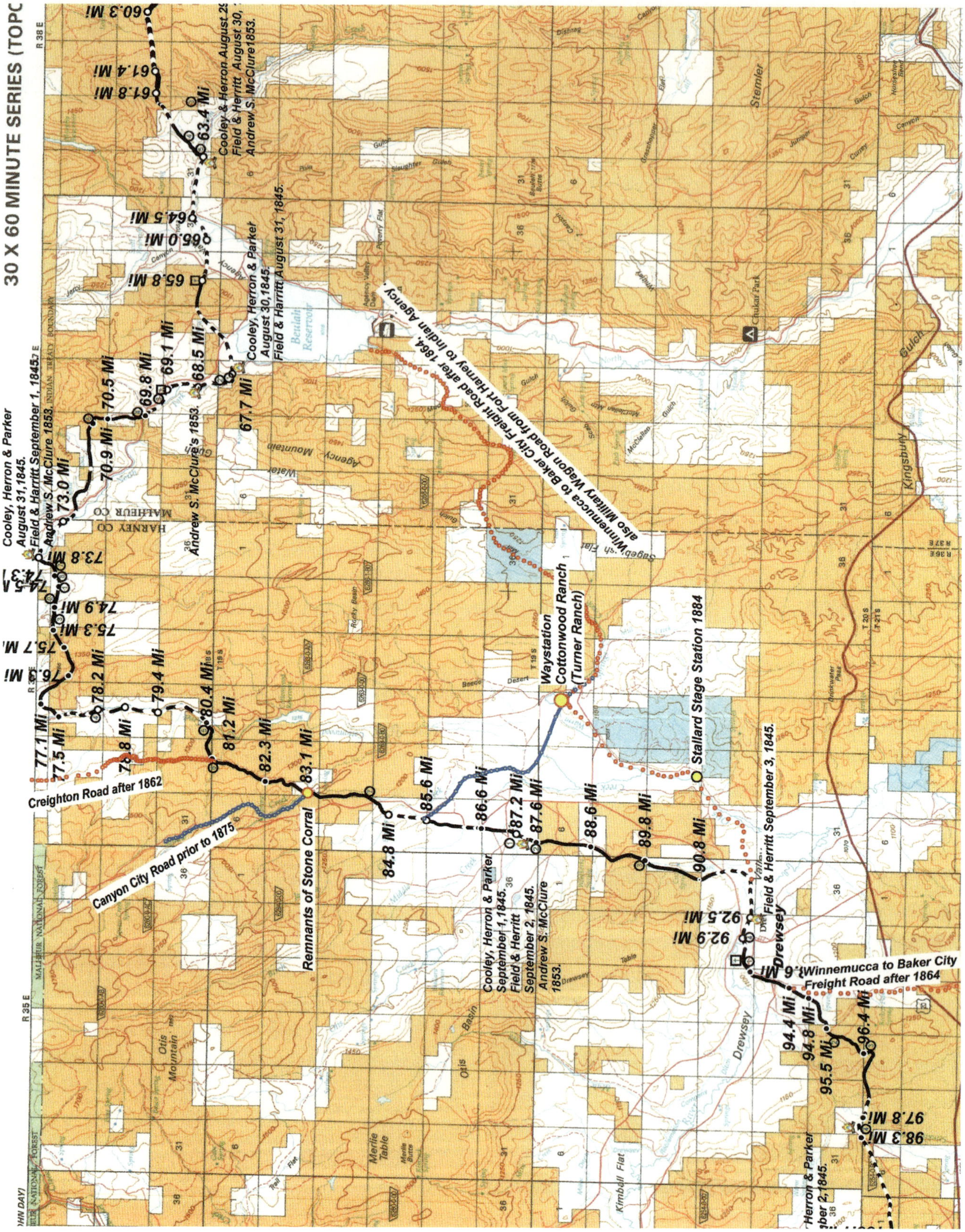

Black Line: Meek Cutoff in 1845
Red Dots: Winnemucca to Baker City Freight Road Established After 1864
Blue Dots/Line: Canyon City Road Established After 1875

STONE CORRAL AT SQUAW CREEK. Stage stop located later at the junction of the Meek Cutoff Wagon Trail with Canyon City Wagon Road. Location 7 viewed northeasterly on Cottonwood Reservoir map, p. 44.

TRACES OF THE TRAIL BEFORE DESCENDING INTO OTIS VALLEY Section Corner that Meldrum and Thompson set in 1875 is to the left of the trail. Otis Valley County Road is directly ahead ¼ of a mile. Location 8 viewed South on Cottonwood Reservoir map, p. 44.

easily today as it climbs up the slope to the southwest out of Cottonwood Creek. McClure had already gradually left the creek and was about 400 feet west of the creek at the mouth of a ravine. At that point, he ascends the ridge to the left of the ravine following up the ridge top. The bearing McClure gives the trail at this point is absolutely correct with the traces of the trail on the ground. At the summit, these authors found traces of the Creighton Road coming in from the north.[1] At this location, the companies in the wagon train had traveled about 7½ miles from their last camp that was located near the base of Castle Rock along the banks of the North Fork of the Malheur River. Their course now turns slightly southwest for approximately 6 miles.

These authors found traces of wagon swales continuing on into Squaw Creek. There we found the remnants of a large stone corral. This location was at an old stage stop that had been developed sometime after 1875. At this old stone corral, there was a junction with a wagon road coming in from the northwest called the Canyon City Wagon Road which was used as a stage line, as well as for freight wagons. The Canyon City Wagon Road follows the Meek Cutoff and skirts along the northerly side of Otis Valley for about the next two miles. There the Canyon City Wagon Road turns to the southeast leaving the Meek Cutoff. The Canyon City Wagon Road terminates at a way station located at the large springs at the head of Warm Springs Creek.[2,3] The Canyon City Wagon Road was also called the Harney Military Road to the Malheur Indian Agency. The Indian Agency was located in Agency Valley. The springs at this location have been incorrectly assumed by other writers to be the location where the Meek Cutoff Wagon Trail passed through continuing on to the Middle Fork of the Malheur River.

The trail continues on passing near a section corner set by Cadastral Surveyors, John Meldrum and David Thompson, in 1875. (See right photo above). They made reference to the trail as being the Creighton Road. The trail here crosses the Otis Valley County Road. Evidence of the trail is clearly visible all along this area. This area is quite rocky so the emigrants had to throw rocks aside as they made their way to their next campsite on Otis Creek in Otis Valley.[4] They actually covered about 13½ miles in this day's travel.

---

[1]The Creighton Road was a military and freight road that joined into the Meek Cutoff in about 1862.

[2]A way station was a place where travelers could stop over for the night. It had been established there along the Winnemucca to Baker City Freight Wagon Road.

[3]These springs are located on the ranch formerly referred to as the Turner Ranch; it is now called the Cottonwood Ranch and owned by John Moon.

[4]Their campsite was located just below the home of Jeff and Sheri Hussey.

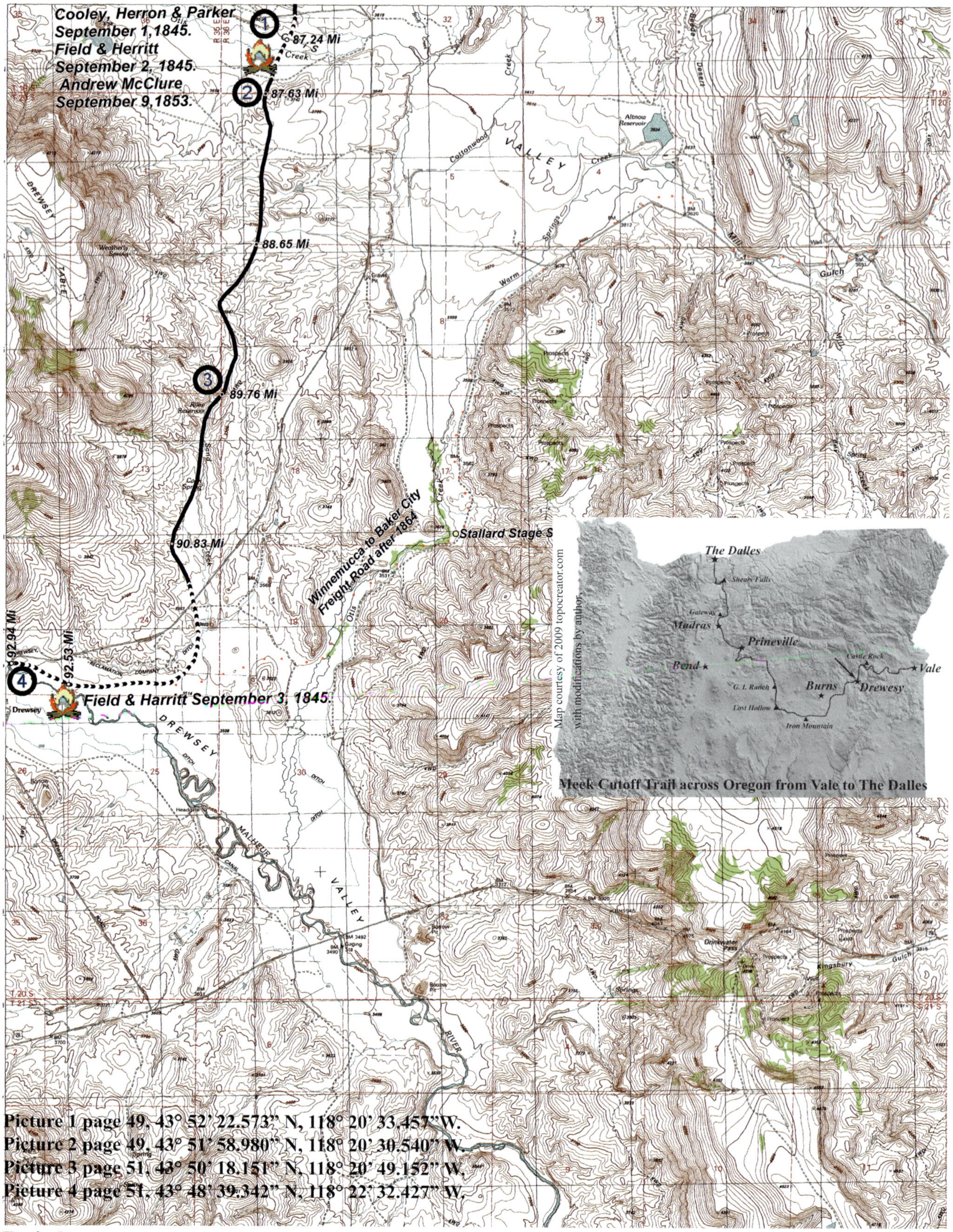

Drinkwater Pass

Circles: Picture Number and Its Location.
Solid Line: Traces of the Trail. Verified on the ground by these authors.
Dashed Line: Projected Trail Location. Verified on the ground by these authors.

OTIS CREEK TO STINKINGWATER CREEK

Sept Tue 2: The road to day has been broken Weather fine Crossed the Branch this Morning and Traveled about South for about 5 miles and Struck a Creek and Traveled up it a short Distance and crossed it then left it to our rite and in about 5 miles struck a Drean of the creek and camped the Drean has only Water in holes plenty of grass and Willow on the Creek and also here the road for about 7 miles is clear of rock it then is somewhat Rockey to the Bottom of the Drean on which wee camped. 10 miles. **Eli Cooley Diary**

2nd: Started about 8 o'clock and traveled about a south course 7 miles to the south branch of Malheur, and waited for one wagon that had the tongue broken out of it. 2 o'clock wagon up with the company. Here we turned a southwest course to a branch of the same stream we left at noon. It had nearly dried up. Grass very good on its banks, and a few willows. Our road in the forenoon was very hilly and some stone. The mountains still continue covered with grass and some scrubby cedar, but a tree three feet in diameter will not be over 25 feet high. The country appears to be getting more level. Distance today about 12 miles. **John Herron Diary**

2: Went to a small creek down the worst you ever seen a wagon go Stony. 10 mi. **Samuel Parker Diary**

4th [sic]: Made a new axeltree. Started late. Had good road. Travleed 7 ms and encamped on the south fork of Malhulen R. Found good grass and willows. **Jesse Harritt Diary** *[Camped on Middle Fork Malheur River near Drewsey.]*[1]

Wed Sept 3rd: Went only about 6 miles today, as we were obliged to put in a new axle tree. Camped upon the South fork of Malheur again. It is now pretty evident that Meek, the pilot who is leading the company this route instead of the old one, does not intend to fall down to the Columbia via the John Day river at all as he told them on leaving Fort Boise, for we are evidently now through the Blue Mts., and still making a southwest course. It is now said that Meek's intentions is to take us over onto the head of the Willamette if he can find a place along the Cascades which will admit of the passage of wagons through, and if not we go down the Deschutes River to the Columbia. **James Field Diary** *[Camped on Middle Fork Malheur River near Drewsey.]*

Leaving their campsite, the emigrants crossed Otis Creek and ascended the ridge in a southerly direction. The wagon swales are visible today because erosion has left a deep scar on the hillside. The trail crosses over the flat ridge top and descends into Sand Creek. Throughout this area, expecially in Sand Creek, extensive erosion has taken place over the past 169 years. There is evidence of two other traces where the road was moved over as erosion on the earlier route made travel impassable. Arriving in Drewsey Valley, crossing the Otis Valley County Road, they turned west toward the Middle Fork of the Malheur River. Mistakenly, the emigrants refer to it as the South Fork of the Malheur River. The St. Joseph Company camped in this area.

The emigrants have been on the Meek Cutoff Wagon Trail for eight days and have traveled about 90 miles over terrain that is unlike any that they have encountered up to this point. Impatience has

Otis Creek in Otis Valley. Arrow points to the eroded trail. Location 1 viewed South on Drinkwater Pass map, p. 48.

Leavng Otis Valley. This photo is a closeup of the eroded trail. Location 2 viewed South on Drinkwater Pass map, p. 48.

[1]Harritt made incorrect date entries up to September 7th.

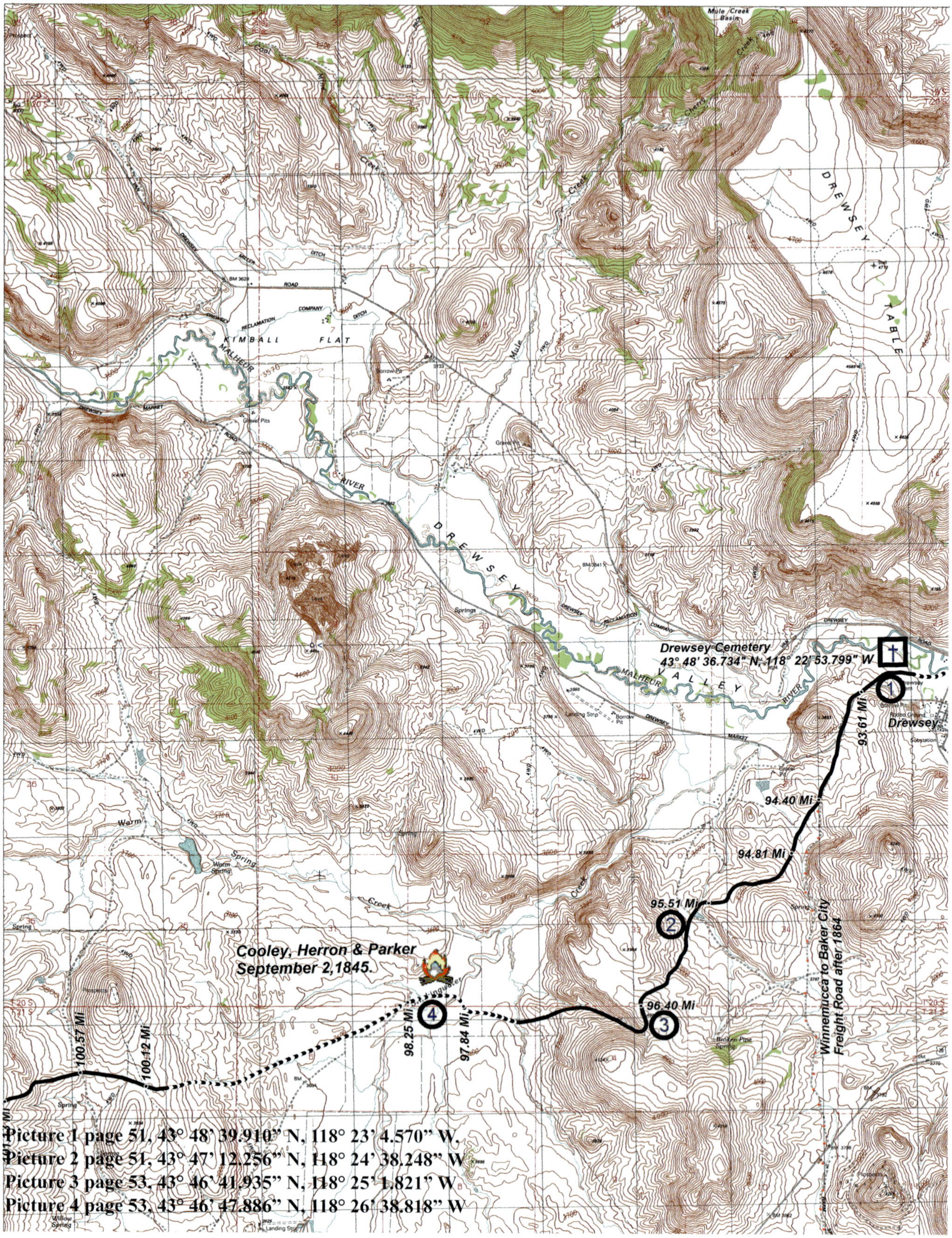

Circles: Picture Number and Its Location.
Solid Line: Traces of the Trail. Verified on the ground by these authors.
Dashed Line: Projected Trail Location. Verified on the ground by these authors.

Drewsey

Sand Creek Vicinity. Traces of the heavily eroded trail in the Sand Creek vicinity. Location 3 viewed northerly on Drinkwater Pass map, p. 48.

Middle Fork of the Malheur River Near Drewsey, Oregon Members of the wagon train mistook this location, calling it the South Fork of the Malheur River. Photo taken from Drewsey County Road. Location 4 viewed easterly on Drinkwater Pass map, p. 48.

begun to fester and there is a low tone of grumbling taking place among the less willing pioneers. Talk is beginning to mount that the guide, Stephen Meek, is leading them astray, even though they have no clue as to where they are or where they are going; they still have an opinion and are willing to exercise it at the expense of their guide. It is these authors' firm belief that Stephen Meek knew where he was going. He had been leading the wagon train along an old Indian trail, as closely as the terrain would allow wagons to safely travel, in a southwesterly direction toward the lakes in Harney Valley.

Historically, there had been lots of Indian activity throughout this area long before the area ever became the Malheur Indian Reservation. Common sense alone would indicate there would be an Indian trail crossing the country. It would be natural to follow this trail as a path of least resistance. The old Indian trail was used by the Hudson Bay trappers, by Stephen Meek when he led his wagon train through this part of the country, and later by other wagon trains, homesteaders, freighters, as well as the military as an access that aided in their travels for many years.

Trail Leaving Drewsey Valley. After crossing the Middle Fork of the Malheur River, the trail is in the foreground leaving the valley and going southwesterly, crossing Market Lane County Road and over the hills. Location 1 viewed northeastely on Drewsey map, p. 50.

Traces of the Meek Cutoff Wagon Trail. Located about a mile south of Patrick O'Toole's homesite. This point is just south of the junction with the later Winnemucca to Baker City Freight Wagon Road. Location 2 viewed south on Drewsey map, p. 50.

Patrick O'Toole and Oxen Shoes. Patrick O'Toole is a rancher that grew up just southwest of Drewsey, Oregon. He is holding oxen shoes that he found along the Meek Cutoff Wagon Trail that crosses his property.

Meek Cutoff Wagon Trail on Patrick O'Toole's Land. Photo is taken looking back on the trail towards Drewsey. Location on the Drewsey map, p. 50 is just before location 2.

The advanced wagons of the train crossed the Middle Fork of the Malheur River and continued on, passing just north of Drewsey, Oregon. The trail leaves Drewsey Valley near Drewsey Cemetery, traveling over the hills in a southwesterly direction crossing over Patrick O'Toole's property.

When these authors visited with Patrick O'Toole, he was very aware that the Meek Cutoff Wagon Trail had crossed his property. He said he had found oxen shoes on the Meek Cutoff and told us where to go across his property so that we could find and walk the trail. In addition, he also told us that when gold was discovered in eastern Oregon, the Winnemucca to Baker City Freight Wagon Road joined the Meek Cutoff about a mile east of his home. The Winnemucca to Baker City Freight Wagon Road had an extreme amount of use as is clearly evidenced by the lower right photo. This picture was not taken on the O'Toole land, but it clearly shows the heavy use. These authors drove to the location following his directions in order to find the Meek Cutoff Wagon Trail. The trail was very evident as we followed it up to the top of the ridge and down into the valley of Stinkingwater Creek.

Crossing the Summit of a Finger Ridge Before Descending into Stinkingwater Creek. Looking up the trail. Location on the Drewsey map, p. 50 is just before picture location 3.

Winnemucca to Baker City Freight Wagon Road Ruts in Solid Rock. These wagon ruts are about 5 miles nearly due north of the Meek Cutoff Wagon Trail located in Agency Valley.

Looking Back on the Trail to Drewsey Valley. The swale shows the heavy use of the trail throughout this area.

The left photo below shows their descent down the ravine and into Stinkingwater Creek. Cattle have used the trail going to and from water which helps to highlight it at a distance. However, when these authors walked on it, there was clear evidence of rocks tossed aside for the passage of the wagons. The right photo below shows a low saddle located in the center of the photo along the skyline where the trail came over the ridge, down the ravine, and into Stinkingwater Creek. Once the rest of the emigrants reached Stinkingwater Creek, they camped with plenty of water and grass.

Looking Westerly to the Stinkingwater Mountains. One can see traces of the trail as it goes down the ravine towards Stinkingwater Creek. Location 3 viewed westerly on Drewsey map, p. 50.

Stinkingwater Creek. This is the general location where some of the wagon train camped on Stinkingwater Creek. Location 4 viewed easterly on Drewsey map, p. 50.

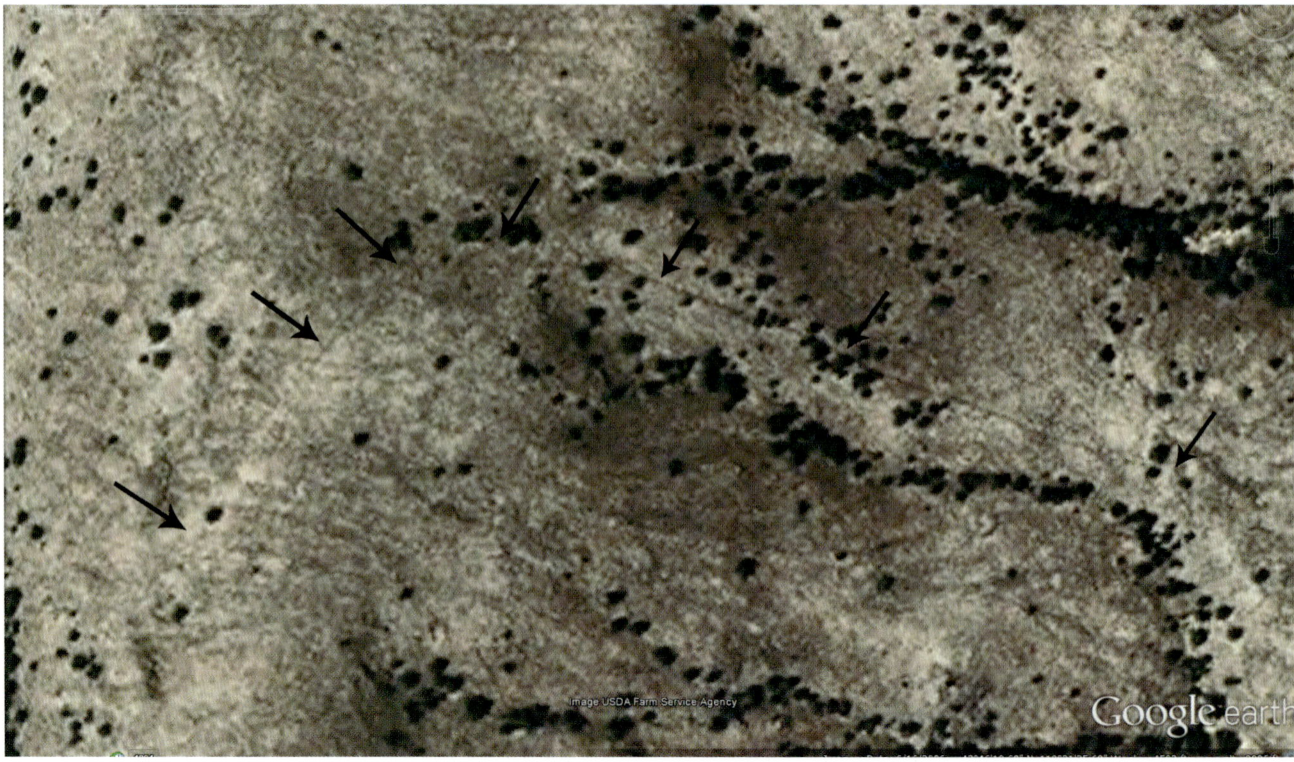

"Map data: Google Earth Image USDA Farm Service Agency" 1994 Imagery Date: 6/16/2006, 43° 46' 10.68" N 118° 31' 25.69" W elev 4502 ft eye alt 9006 ft.

SATELLITE IMAGE WITH ARROWS SHOWING THE TRAIL ROUTE ASCENDING THE SUMMIT OF STINKINGWATER MOUNTAINS

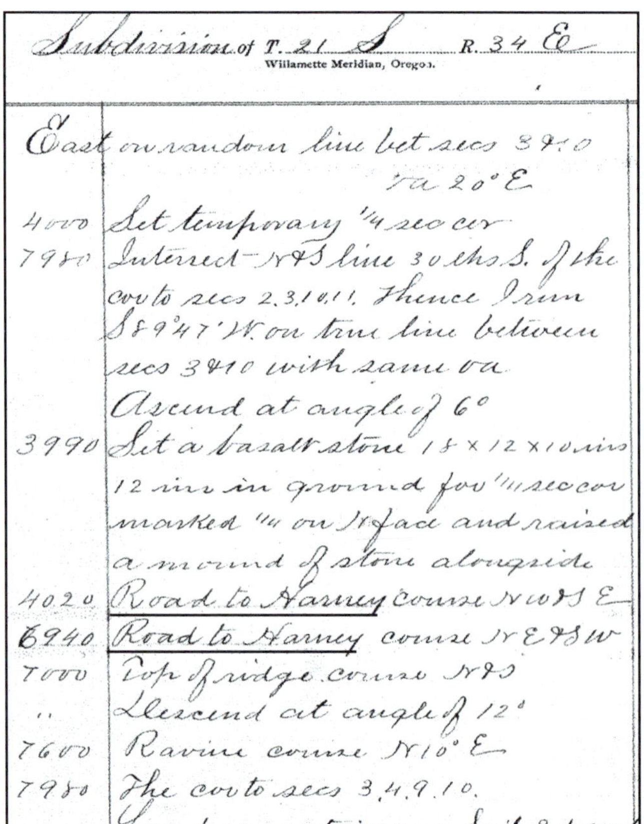

Subdivision of T. 21 S R. 34 E
Willamette Meridian, Oregon.

East	on random line bet secs 3 & 10
	Va 20° E
4000	Set temporary ¼ sec cor
7980	Intersect N & S line 30 chs S. of the cor to secs 2, 3, 10, 11. Thence I run S 89°47' W. on true line between secs 3 & 10 with same va
	Ascend at angle of 6°
3990	Set a basalt stone 18 × 12 × 10 ins 12 ins in ground for ¼ sec cor marked ¼ on N face and raised a mound of stone alongside
4020	Road to Harney course N W & S E
6940	Road to Harney course N E & S W
7000	Top of ridge course N & S
..	Descend at angle of 12°
7600	Ravine course N 10° E
7980	The cor to secs 3, 4, 9, 10.
	Land mountainous Soil 3d rate

HENRY COOK'S SURVEY NOTES. S 3 & 10, T 21 S, R 34 E, W.M.

QUARTER CORNER STONE AND MOUND OF ROCK. This corner is between Section 3 and 10, T 21 S, R 34 E, W.M. as described in the accompanying survey notes. For location of this corner see arrow to the right on the above satellite image. Survey was done by Henry Cook in 1884. Corner is alongside the trail on Stinkingwater Mountains.

STINKINGWATER CREEK OVER STINKINGWATER MOUNTAINS

As these authors started to ascend the long slope toward the top of the Stinkingwater Mountains, the location of the wagon trail was evident due to the difference in vegetation as shown in the photos below. As we walked along, we passed the quarter corner between Section 3 and 10, T 21 S, R 34 E, W.M., lying to the right of the trail. By the time this area was surveyed in 1884, the Meek Cutoff Wagon Trail had been renamed the Road to Harney as it was being used as a military and freight road from Fort Harney to the Indian Agency in Agency Valley. This is where the Beulah Reservoir is located today. When we reached the top of Stinkingwater Mountains, the trail was clearly defined by rocks that had been tossed aside.

Leaving the summit of the Stinkingwater Mountains, the trail descends over rocky bluffs, where work was required rolling large rocks aside to clear a path for the descent. When the trail turned straight off the slope, the descent was steep and rocky; a great amount of erosion has taken place over the years, leaving what appears to be a gully, but it is the eroded trail. The trail descends into the valley near where Rimrock Reservoir is located today.

Trail Ascending the Slope on the Stinkingwater Mountains. Differences in vegetation highlights the trail. Location 1 viewed westerly on Stinkingwater Pass (Modified) map, p. 56.

Vegetation Highlighting the Trail. The wagon road is 20 feet west of the found quarter corner. See arrow to the right on the satellite image page 54. The "Harney Road," as described in the survey notes of 1884, was the Meek Cutoff Wagon Trail. Location 2 viewed westerly on Stinkingwater Pass (Modified) map, p. 56.

Trail Across the Summit of the Stinkingwater Mountains. Location 3 viewed northerly on Stinkingwater Pass (Modified) map, p. 56.

Eroded Trail Descending the Summit of the Stinkingwater Mountains. Location 4 viewed northeasterly on Stinkingwater Pass (Modified) map, p. 56.

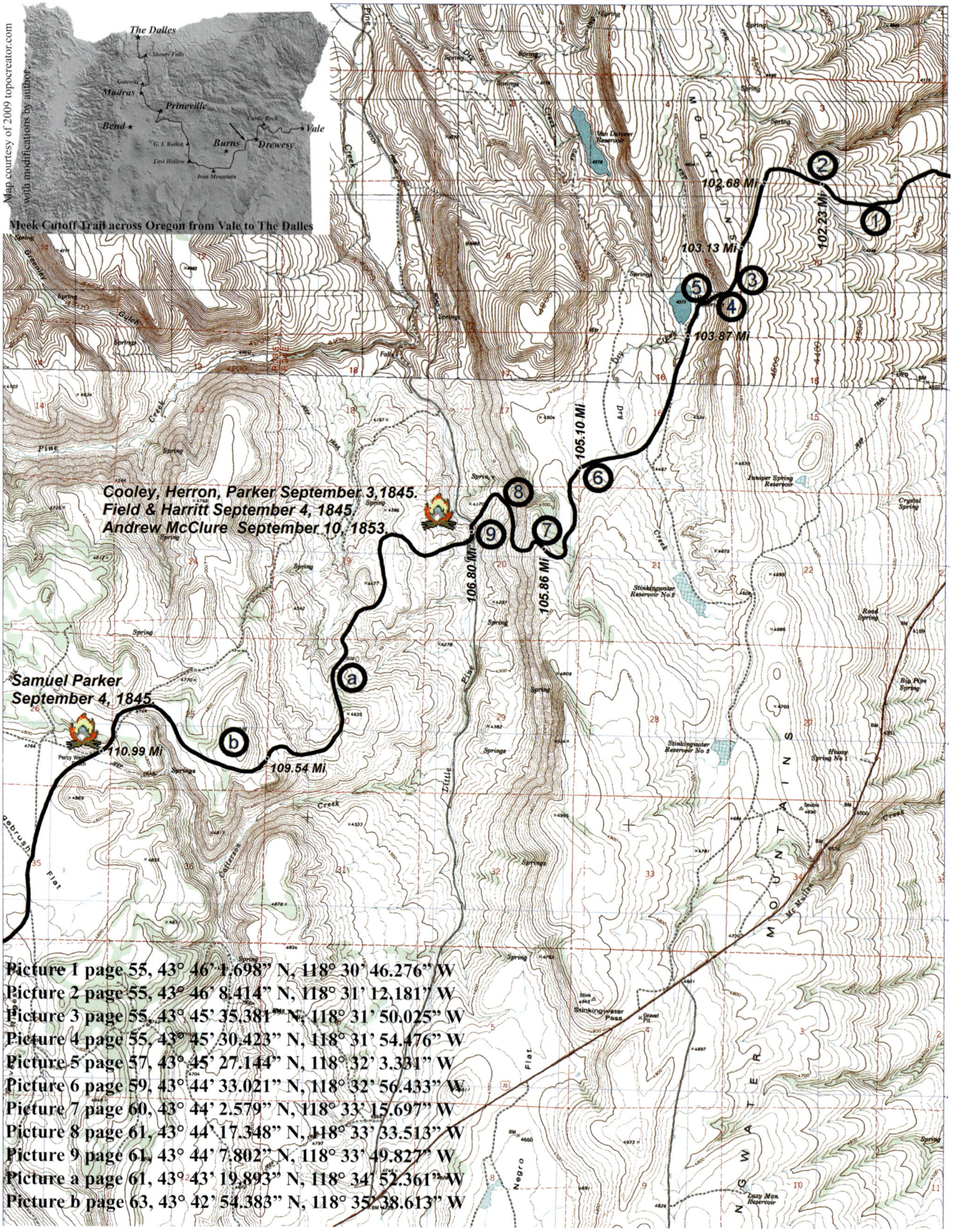

Stinkingwater Pass (Modified)

Circles: Picture Number and Its Location.
Solid Line: Traces of the Trail. Verified on the ground by these authors.
Dashed Line: Projected Trail Location. Verified on the ground by these authors.

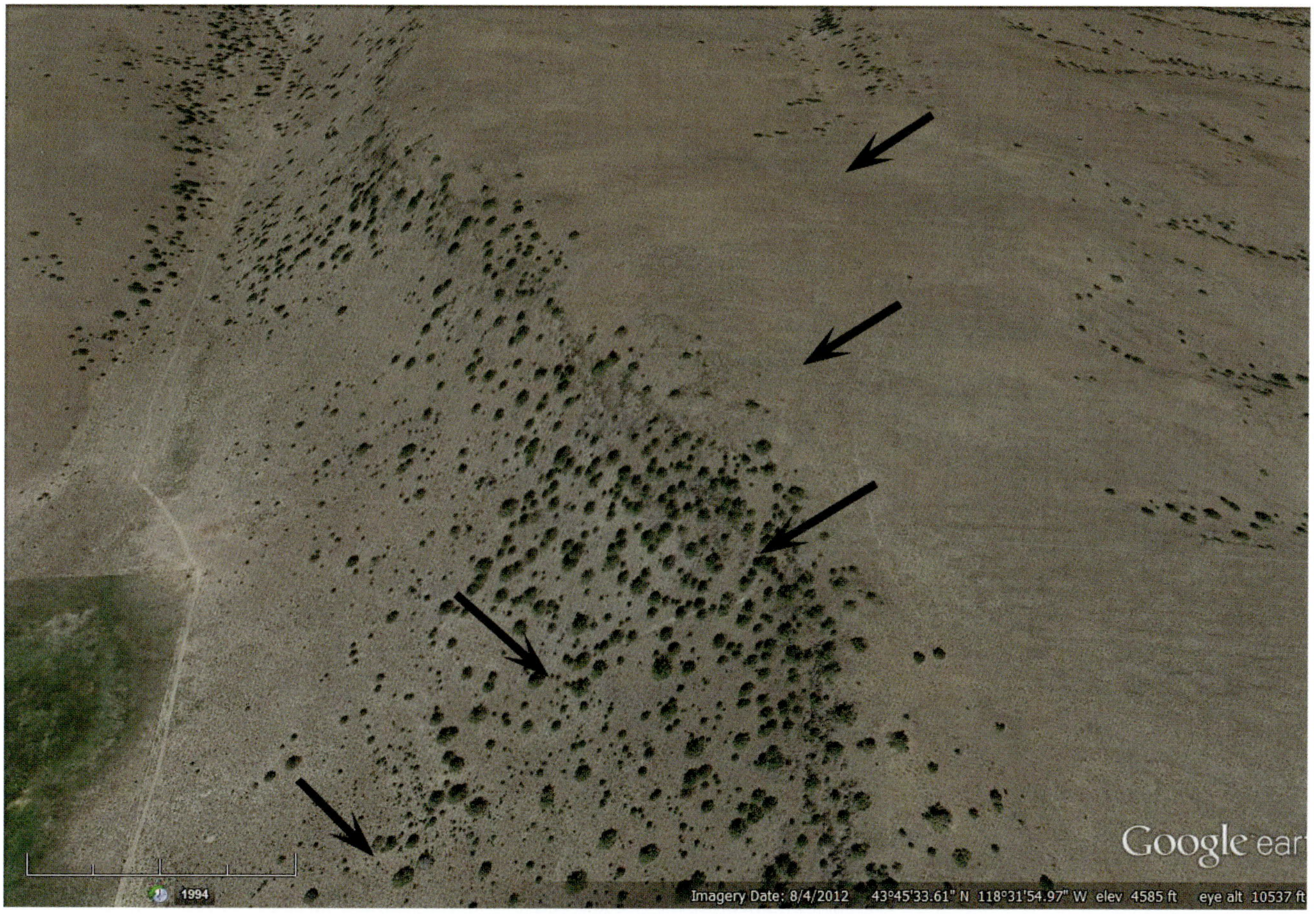

"Map data: Google Earth" 1994 Imagery Date: 8/4/2012, 43° 45' 33.61" N 118° 31' 54.97" W elev 4585 ft eye alt 10537 ft.

SATELLITE IMAGE ACROSS THE RIDGE OF STINKINGWATER MOUNTAINS. Arrows show the trail route across the ridge and descending the slope toward present-day Rimrock Reservoir.

TRAIL DESCENDING THE STINKINGWATER MOUNTAINS BEFORE RIMROCK RESERVOIR. Photo location is between the 2nd and 3rd arrows from the left on satellite image above. Location 5 viewed northeasterly on Stinkingwater Pass (Modified) map, p. 56.

STINKINGWATER MOUNTAINS TO LITTLE PINE CREEK

Aug [sic] Wens 3: The road to day has been verry broken and rockey Weather fine Crossed the Drean this Morning and have Traveled about a South west corse in about 7 miles crossed a Drean after coming down a verry steep hill some grass and Wood Water in holes and in about 1 mile furthur Crossed a Branch and Camped Some grass and Wood here some scattering seder on the hills now for about 30 or 40 miles. 8 miles **Eli Cooley Diary**[1]

3: Stony all day fore miles you Codent see the ground. 10 mi. **Samuel Parker Diary**

3rd: We started this morning about 8 o'clock, and traveled a southwest course over some very rough mountains and rocky roads to another branch of the Malheur that afforded us good water and some grass, though not sufficient, and plenty of dry willows for fire wood, and some small cedar. We passed some pine timber today. Weather very warm and dry. There is nothing here to cheer our drooping spirits. We are making slow headway, the country here is so broken and rocky that we cannot get along fast and we are rather doubtful that our pilot is lost for he has been seven days longer getting to the waters of Jay's river than he told us he would be. Some talk of stoning and others say hang him. I can not tell how the affair will terminate yet, but I will inform you in its proper place; 5 miles today southwest and 5 miles west. Total today, 10 miles. There is considerable cedar on the mountains here, but it is low and has limbs to the ground. **John Herron Diary**

5th: made an advance of 11 ms and encamped in a deep hollow out of which proceded a number of fine springs affording us good water as ever run with a fiew small willows. **Jesse Harritt Diary**

Thur Sept 4th: Went about 18 miles, the latter part of the road being rough and rocky. Camped upon the head of a small branch of the South fork of Malheur. The mountains where we first struck them were naked and perfectly destitute of timber. Near Fremont's Peak we began to see some timber upon them, and since passing that point the hills have all had more or less timber upon them, it being generally low cedar, and on reaching the top of the last hill before descending into the hollow, tall pines appear to crown the hill tops before us. **James Field Diary**

1853 Andrew McClure Diary

Saturday, September 10. This morning according to previous arrangement four men were sent ahead to examine the country and see those ahead. Left camp at about half past 7 o'clock and in four miles, crossing the point between the valleys came to a brisk running branch, tolerably good water. This part of the road is quite stony. From this we passed over several points of ridges pretty good road and six miles brought us to the South Branch of Malheur. Here we found the grass on fire which had caught from the fire of some of the emigrants ahead and as it was near noon we turned our horses loose and set about extinguishing the fire this being accomplished we unrolled our budgets and made a hearty meal of hard bread and beef with a little bacon.

After one hours delay we mounted and following the trail, which ascends the bluffs and leads off in a southwesterly direction crossing the point of the mountains came to a long hill. Here a council was called and it was agreed that Mr. V. S. McClure and Mr. Dening should return and Mr. Owen and myself proceed as far as we deemed expedient and enter into such arrangements as we could to form a company to go to the settlements in advance of the train.

From the top of a hill the trail leads down a ravine and crossing the valley of a dry branch. Some stagnant water in pools, which is five miles from the crossing of South Branch.The grass is pretty good here, but the water is very poor. From the crossing of this stream the trail takes a southwesterly course and passing round a point again turns to the west and winding over stony ground in ravines and on ridges it descends a hill and passes down a smooth valley to a very steep hill which we descended and came into the valley of several small branches. Encamped on the second, which is about seven miles from the last water. Tonight we encamped near Mr. Kinny's train. They have offered us hospitality, but not being in need we declined.

The trail turned southwesterly from Rimrock Reservoir and crossed through Dry Creek. Near that location was a huge old juniper tree that had grown up around a stump. Ax marks indicate the tree was chopped on at various times but continued to grow around the chopped parts. When these authors first walked by the tree in 2007, it was alive and growing; it measured 11 feet in circumference. In 2010, the tree was destroyed by lightning. In the photo on page 59, the author is pointing to another place where the tree had actually been cut down completely but continued growing.

These authors made our way toward the Little Pine Creek drainage by using the survey notes of Henry W. Cook, US Deputy Surveyor, under contract number 518, dated October 1, 1884. We were able to follow the dim traces of the wagon swales. Henry Cook surveyed this area 39 years after the

[1]Cooley made an incorrect month entry for this date.

Huge Old Juniper Near Trail on Dry Creek
Photo taken October 2007.

Same Old Juniper Hit by Lightning. Photo taken August 2010. Location 6 viewed easterly on Stinkingwater Pass (Modified) map, p. 56.

Meek Wagon Train had followed this old historic Indian trail. He now called the trail the Road to Harney. Clearly, this trail had been used continually for many years.

These authors walked out the trail to where we could look down into the Little Pine Creek drainage. When we turned around to walk back to where our vehicle was located near Dry Creek, we took the photo shown below. Traces of the Meek Cutoff Wagon Trail are visible through the center of the photo from bottom to top, and is just to the right of another old juniper just left of the center of photo.

Trail Evidence on Slope into Dry Creek. Looking northeast on the trail.
Photo is taken between picture locations 6 and 7 on Stinkingwater Pass (Modified) map, p. 56.

Faint Traces of the Trail are Evident as the Emigrants Crossed the Ridge. This is just before descending into Little Pine Creek. White arrows show the trails' location. Location 7 viewed northwesterly on Stinkingwater Pass map, p. 56.

As these authors reached the summit of a finger ridge along the easterly slope of Little Pine Creek, we came to an old ancient juniper standing along the trail which is pictured below. This is the same tree that appears on Plate V in the book, *The Terrible Trail: The Meek Cutoff of 1845* by Keith Clark and Lowell Tiller in 1966. This juniper felt the ax many years ago, as several limbs have been removed over time. The tree still lives today.

This author (see above photo) is standing on the trail just before it descends into Little Pine Creek. Little Pine Creek is a tributary of the Middle Fork of the Malheur River. Other researchers have assumed that the large juniper tree (the third tree to the left of the author) was used by the emigrants by tying ropes to it to let the wagons down over a steep bluff. Actually, this tree lies to the left of the trail and about 350 feet to the southeast from where the trail makes its way through the rimrock and descends into Little Pine Creek. The tree lies too far from the trail to be of any use in that manner. The trail was steep but it was not necessary to use any ropes making the descent. The trail continues along a sidling cross slope where erosion has taken its toll on the wagon swales rendering them into a deep gully. The trail then reaches a large flat before turning down the slope into Little Pine Creek where we found remnants of a stone structure as shown on page 61 in the top right photo. The remnants are all that remain of a way station. Adjacent to the stone structure is what appears to have been a spring or well. There is evidence that water has flowed from this site for many years making a boggy area below the spring and structure. Little Pine Creek is about 600 feet beyond the spring and down a gentle slope. Eli Cooley writes, *"...crossed a branch and camped."*

Tree on Summit Above Little Pine Creek
Juniper tree along the trail showing old ax cuttings. Photo was taken in October 2007.

The Trail Coming Down the Steep Hill into Little Pine Creek Location 8 viewed southeasterly on Stinkingwater Pass (Modified) map, p. 56.

Remnants of a Way Station Above Little Pine Creek
Pine Creek County Highway is about 500 feet below spring and remnants of way station.

LITTLE PINE CREEK TO HARNEY VALLEY

Sept Thu 4: weather fine to day and the road has been broken for a pease and then first rate crossed the main divide to day which is about 7 mile from whare wee camped and about 3 miles further to a Valley this far the road is verry Broken an rough and some seder and pine timber after wee got in to the valley the road was first rate to whare wee camped which was on a small Drean about 4 miles from whare wee struck the valley Some willow and plenty of grass here as wee come over the Divide wee saw the Caskade Mountains at a considerable Distance here the valley appears to bee perfectly level as far as the Eye can reach Saw some Indians here the corse is about South west to day. 14 miles. **Eli Cooley Diary** *[Camped on Cow Creek where it crosses Harney Valley.]*

4th: We started about 8 o'clock and traveled a south course about 4 miles, then turned southwest about 2 miles and passed down a very rocky hill or mountain into the valley of Jay's River, here we turned a west course about 8 miles to a beautiful little rivulet of water but no wood except small willows. Grass is very good. This valley is on the river that we have been looking for the last seven days. I hope the grumbling will cease now as our course appears to be west and the peak at the mouth of Jay's river near the Columbia is visible, and our pilot says it is about one hundred miles distance. Today 14 miles. **John Herron Diary** *[Camped on Cow Creek where it crosses Harney Valley.]*

4: To A Spring. 5 mi. **Samuel Parker Diary** *[He fell behind and camped at a location in Sagebrush Flat.]*

Area Where the Emigrants Camped on Little Pine Creek
Area is south of the Pine Creek County Highway. Location 9 viewed northerly on Stinkingwater Pass (Modified) map, p. 56.

Traces of the Trail Leaving Little Pine Creek
Location "a" viewed southwesterly on Stinkingwater Pass (Modified) map, p. 56.

Fri Sept 5th: Went 15 miles. Camping upon Lake fork of John Day's river. I was mistaken about our being through the main range, yet the road for the past few days has led across low mountains which, having their steepest descent toward the west, did not appear high until we ascended them. The map of the country we had with us also indicated that we had passed the head of the John Day River, as the Malheur was made to head much further south than the John Day, and yet we have held a southwest course from the Malheur, and we are now upon the head forks of the John Day river.[1] **James Field Diary**

6th: as we advanced we gradually ascended a butiful mountain gained the top upon which grew a number of pine and seder trees a fiew miles further a butiful land scape appeared to sight to the west a large valley to the southwest the Caskade mountains to the Northwest ware the Columbia river we gradually descended this lofty mountain entered the valley down which we proceded 5 ms came to a butiful little rivulet with its banks shaded by a fiew small willows where we encamped haveing came 12 ms. **Jesse Harritt Diary**

5: Crossed the Divide to the head waters of the diggers lakes in the nite. 11 o clock. 23 mi. **Samuel Parker Diary**

From the encampment on Little Pine Creek, the trail takes a long gradual southwesterly climb towards the summit. The trail enters areas of pine forest as were mentioned by some of the diarists. Henry Cook's survey notes were very useful in identifying the trail's location in this area as it is quite dim and difficult to follow. Erosion has helped to highlight the trail in some locations. These authors also found a very old kerosene can along the trail helping to confirm the trail. We assume this can had been discarded later by someone other than the emigrants in 1845.

When the trail reached the summit between the Malheur River drainage and the Harney Basin, one can see prominent landmarks in all directions. To the northwest, 60 miles away, is the Strawberry Mountain Range. To the northeast, and at the emigrants' back, looms Fremont Peak (Castle Rock), over 30 miles away. To the south, about 65 miles away and seen for the first time from the trail, are the snow-capped Steens Mountains. The four pictures at the top of page 63 are viewed from the same coordinate 43° 42' 54.383" N, 118° 35' 38.613" W. See Stinkingwater Pass (Modified) map page 56, picture location "b". From the summit, the trail passed a location later named Percy's Cabin, and crossed Sagebrush Flat.[2] The trail then continued in a southwesterly direction, making its way down into the Rock Creek drainage and out of the mouth of Rock Creek. Then it proceeds into the Harney Valley, crossing US Highway 20, to where they camped along the Cow Creek drainage.

Other writers believe that the Meek Cutoff Wagon Trail followed up the main fork of Pine Creek, a tributary of the Middle Fork of the Malheur River, then climbed out of Pine Creek crossing a large flat called Oard Flat, traveled down Cow Creek, and on into Harney Valley. These writers have identified traces of an old wagon road through this area. However, this particular old wagon road was the access road built to haul lumber from a sawmill located at the northwesterly vicinity of the Oard Flat area. This lumber was used by settlers as they were developing towns and homesteads. It should also be noted that Andrew S. McClure, a member of the Elliott Wagon Train of 1853, had a son, Henry F. McClure, born in 1860 in the Willamette Valley. When he was 23, he became a Deputy Cadastral Surveyor and was working under U.S. Cadastral Survey Contract Number 480, dated July 10, 1883. Under this contract, he was surveying Townships 21 and 22 South, Range 33 East which encompassed Oard Flat and the surrounding area. His field notes and maps clearly show the location of a road going down Rock Creek called the Harney and Malheur Agency Road. This is the same location described by the diarists on the Meek Cutoff Wagon Trail. In addition, his field notes and maps make no mention of any other road or trail in the vicinity of Pine Creek, the Oard Flat area, or the creek that was later called Cow Creek. Therefore, the alleged trail did not exist prior to the year 1883 as Henry F. McClure had been instructed to identify any physical features such as roads or trails or any other man-made improvements as he was making his survey. The question stands: If Henry F. McClure could not identify any traces of a trail, how is it possible to make such a positive identification over 130 years later?

[1]Apparently they had a very small scaled map of the Oregon Territory. There seems to be at least three that were available: 1833, 1838 and 1841, all of which were very inaccurate depicting the region of central Oregon.

[2]Percy's cabin is a landmark that shows up on current maps. Percy N. West proved up on a 320 acre homestead in 1917.

STEENS MOUNTAINS. Seen for the first time looking south from the trail. Right photo is a close-up view.

STRAWBERRY MOUNTAIN RANGE. Looking to the northwest toward the Columbia River.

FREMONT PEAK (CASTLE ROCK). Looking to the northeast.

All four photos from location "b" on Stinkingwater Pass map, p. 56.

Let us revisit the moment the wagons reached the summit of the mountains between Little Pine Creek and Harney Valley. Here the emigrants laid eyes upon the snow-capped mountains some 65 miles directly south of their present location. They had heard that the Cascade Mountains were snow-capped, so they assumed these mountains to be the Cascades. Some of the emigrants thought Stephen Meek was heading straight for those mountains in an attempt to cross directly over the mountains into the Willamette Valley instead of going to The Dalles. The fear that they were being led astray had been haunting them for days, and now this appeared to be a reality. As they reached the Harney Valley, those snow-capped mountains haunted them even more for Stephen Meek was actually beginning to bypass the snow-capped "Cascades" and lead them out into the vast desert that lay ahead. Where was he going? Little did

IRON MOUNTAIN. A prominent landmark seen from a location near Sagebrush Flat. Location 1 viewed southwesterly on Buchanan (Modified) map, p. 64.

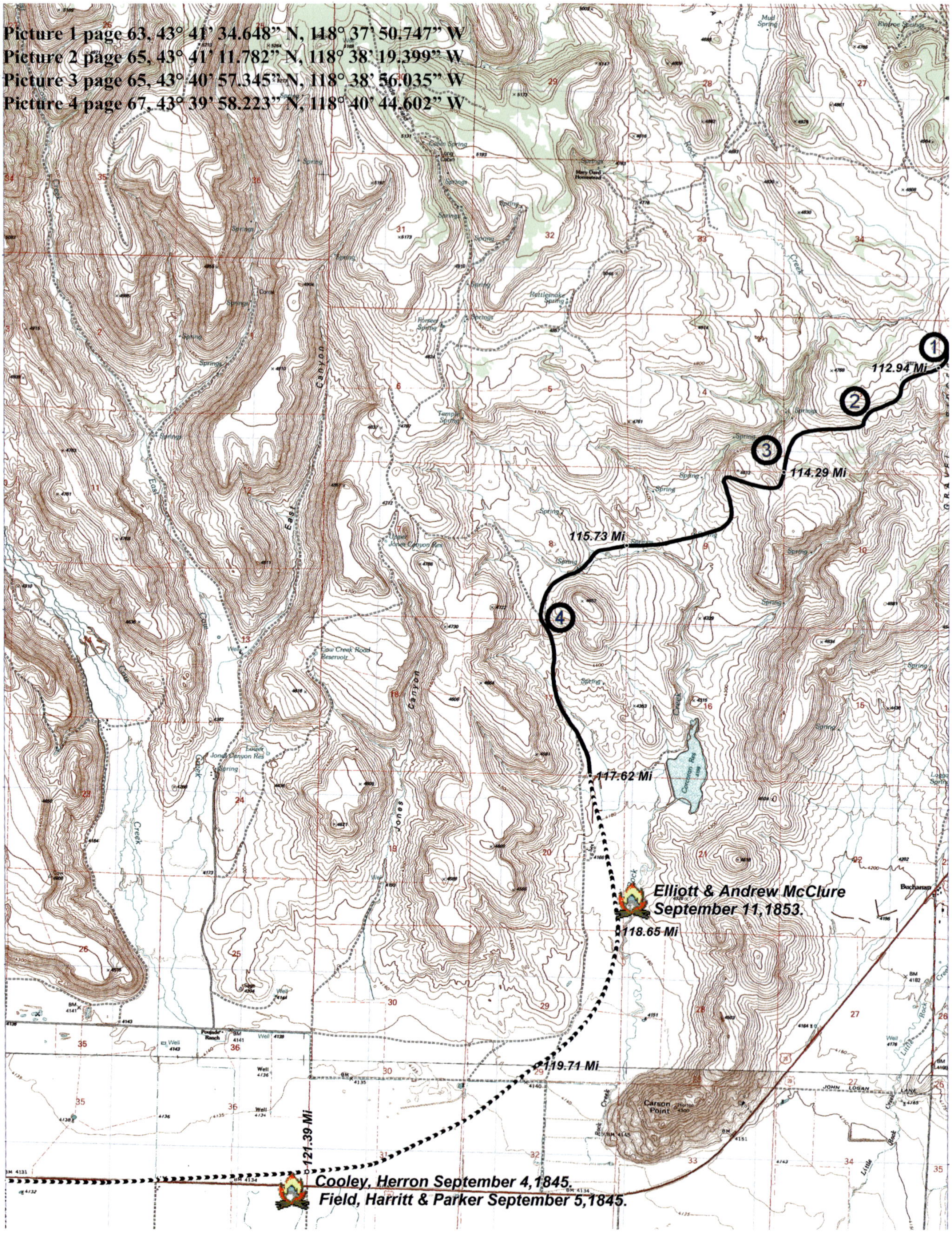

Buchanan (Modified)

Circles: Picture Number and Its Location.
Solid Line: Traces of the Trail. Verified on the ground by these authors.
Dashed Line: Projected Trail Location. Verified on the ground by these authors.

the emigrants know that Stephen Meek had explored this region and saw those mountains when he was with the Bonneville Expedition of 1834. He had no interest in these mountains. He called them by what the Indians and mountain men called them: the Snow Mountains. Today, they are known as the Steens Mountains. What Meek was really interested in was a very prominent landmark to the southwest some 50 miles in the distance called Iron Mountain.

Some of the other emigrants were pleased when he turned west upon entering the valley. On September 4th John Herron writes, *"...into the valley of Jay's River, here we turned a west course about 8 miles to a beautiful little rivulet of water but no wood except small willows. Grass is very good. This valley is on the river that we have been looking for the last seven days. I hope the grumbling will cease now as our course appears to be west and the peak at the mouth of Jay's river near the Columbia is visible, and our pilot says it is about one hundred miles distance."* Herron is saying this valley is on the Crooked River or as he called it Jay's River. He thinks they are looking at the Cascade Mountains and Mt. Hood near the Columbia River. According to the map they had with them, it looked as if they could just follow a large river through the Cascades into the Willamette Valley. It appears Ownbey was quite insistent about taking that route through the Cascades. This is where Ownbey's Company wanted to end their journey. They could care less about going to The Dalles.

The emigrants were confused, bewildered, and yes, lost. They had no idea where they were or where they were going, yet they were willing to exercise their opinion for what it was worth. This has helped create wild and unsubstantiated lost wagon train stories and has hovered over Stephen Meek like a black cloud and continues to do so. Writers have been quick to perpetuate this confusion by repeating ill-fated rumors and opinions gleaned from faded memories, poorly written letters and newspaper articles, rather than try to seek the truth of the trail.

The members of the Meek Wagon Train were very fortunate in having Stephen Meek as their guide. Meek wasn't lost; he knew exactly where they were. If they had listened to him closely and did exactly what he had wanted, there would have been fewer problems and difficulties later experienced along the trail.

TRACES OF THE TRAIL. Traces are visible across the summit of Sagebrush Flat down into the Rock Creek drainage. Location 2 viewed southwesterly on Buchanan (Modified) map, p. 64.

DEEP WAGON RUTS ACROSS THE SOLID ROCK SLAB. The military wagons, freight wagons, and settlers of the area all used the Meek Cutoff Wagon Trail in the Rock Creek area as their main access across the country. Location 3 viewed southwesterly on Buchanan (Modified) map, p. 64.

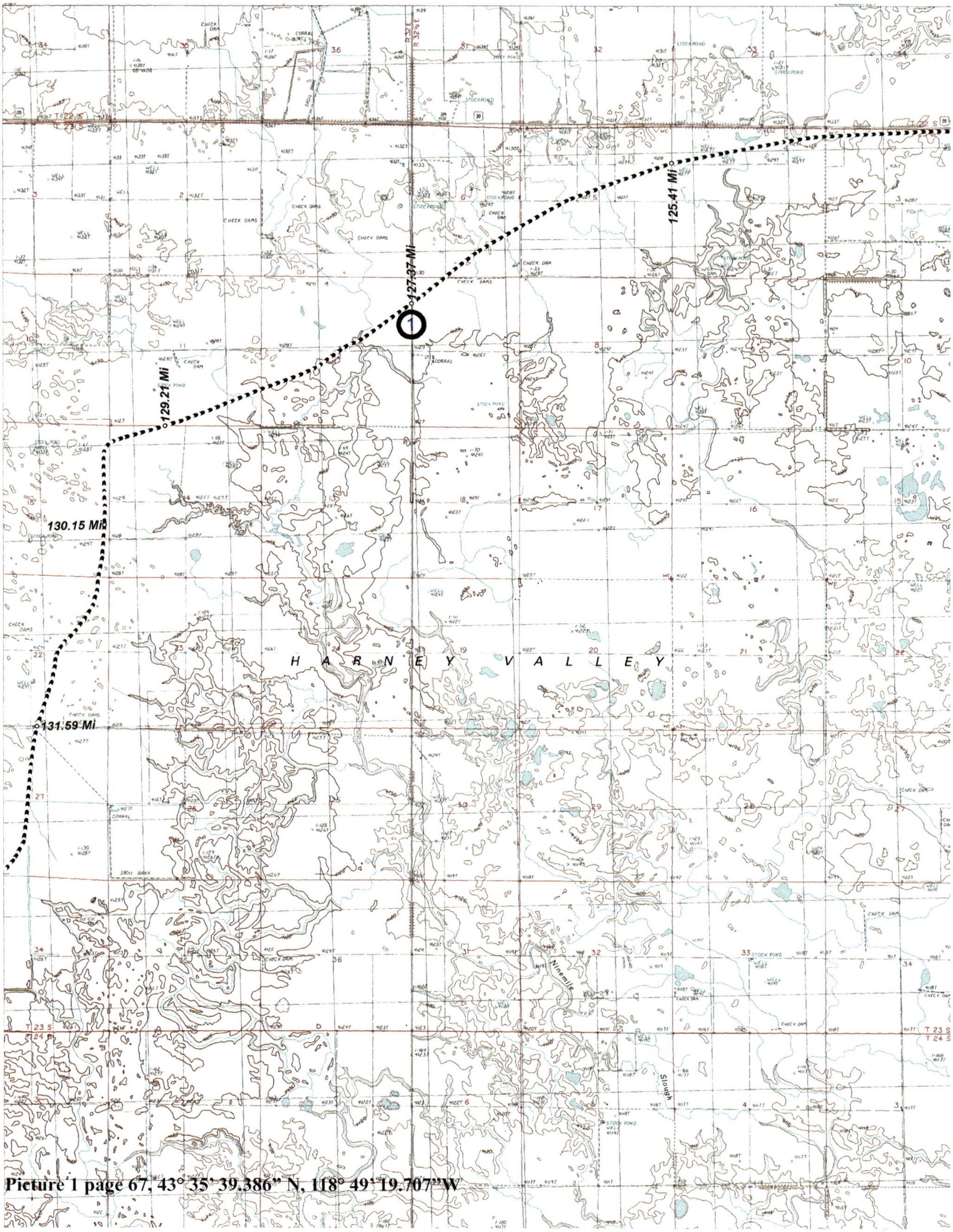

Circles: Picture Number and Its Location.
Solid Line: Traces of the Trail. Verified on the ground by these authors.
Dashed Line: Projected Trail Location. Verified on the ground by these authors.

Ninemile Slough

Rock Creek Valley at the Upper Edge of Harney Valley. Traces of the trail are visible on the last descent down into the Harney Valley that lies in the distance. The trail continues to be heavily used by cattle today as they travel to and from water. Location 4 viewed southerly on Buchanan (Modified) map, p. 64.

Plains of Harney Valley. *"...here the valley appears to bee perfectly level as far as the Eye can reach..."* Eli Cooley. Much of the Harney plain is arid and covered with sagebrush. Location 1 viewed southwesterly on Ninemile Slough map, p. 66.

HARNEY VALLEY TO THE SILVIES RIVER

Sept Fri 5: the road to day has been first rate and level Weather fine Crossed the drean this Morning and left it on our left and have Traveled about a south west corse Crossed a small Creek and Camped it runs to the left plenty of grass and Willow here Saw a few Indians to day. 15 miles. **Eli Cooley Diary**

5th: We started at 8 o'clock and traveled in a southwest course across the valley of Crooked or Jay's river, about 15 miles to a branch of Crooked river, which afforded plenty of grass and some fine dry willows for firewood; the water very bad, hardly fit for use. We passed over some very rich looking soil today but no timber. This valley is covered with wild sage. The country looks level as far as we can see to the west. We have been in sight of the Cascade mountains for the last twenty miles. The nights are very cold, days pleasant, looks like autumn had set in. **John Herron Diary**

6: Down the Bottom Sandy and Sage. 23 mi. **Samuel Parker Diary**

7th: Continued down this rich valley 14 ms and encamped on Crooked river a small murmuring stream running to the south shaded on its banks by a fiew willows as we advanced this morning the butiful ceniry increased this vally is one of the most sublime places I ever saw it is from appearance from 30 to 50 miles wide from north to south the length of which I am not able to determine the soil is rich and butifully set over with fine grass inter mixed with patches of sage the mountains to north in places is thickly set with pine and seder timber. **Jesse Harritt Diary**

Sat Sept 6th: Went about 14 miles today, camping upon another fork of Crooked River instead of John Day as stated yesterday, and we are in fact upon the waters of the Deschutes River, and steering direct toward the Cascade Mts. in order to attempt a passage through them. The tale of our going down the John Day river was a mere tale of Meeks in order to get us upon this route and then take us wherever he pleased. But if he now fails to take us across the Cascades his head will not be worth a chew of tobacco to him, if what some of our men say prove true. He is with Owensby's company which is one day's travel ahead of ours, and we make their camps every evening, where we find a note buried at the foot of a stake, stating the distance to the next camp, and the names of the streams. **James Field Diary**

They left their encampment at Cow Creek and traveled about 8 miles southwesterly across the flat Harney Valley. Then they turned south for another 5 miles, crossing State Highway 78 and continuing on two miles to the Silvies River encampment. This location on Silvies River is southeast of Burns, Oregon, approximately 10 miles.

Reading James Field's diary entry about the guide taking them across the Cascades, it appears that the emigrants are so confused that they can't even remember where their guide was going to lead them. In the beginning of the Cutoff when they hired Meek, there was not any mention about crossing the Cascades. On August 23rd, John Herron had written, *"...down to the Dalles, on the Columbia River."*

James Field comments, *"...we make their camps every evening, where we find a note buried at the foot of a stake, stating the distance to the next camp, and the names of the streams."* It is the guide's job to ride out ahead of the companies, well in advance, planning the next day's route and camp sites. Then he rides back to the camp and tells the emigrants what is to be expected the next day. Therefore, a note can then be left at the camp for the companies that will follow. These authors might mention here that in addition to Stephen Meek's wife Elizabeth, who was assistng Stephen in this duty, they have a friend along with them, Nathan Olney.

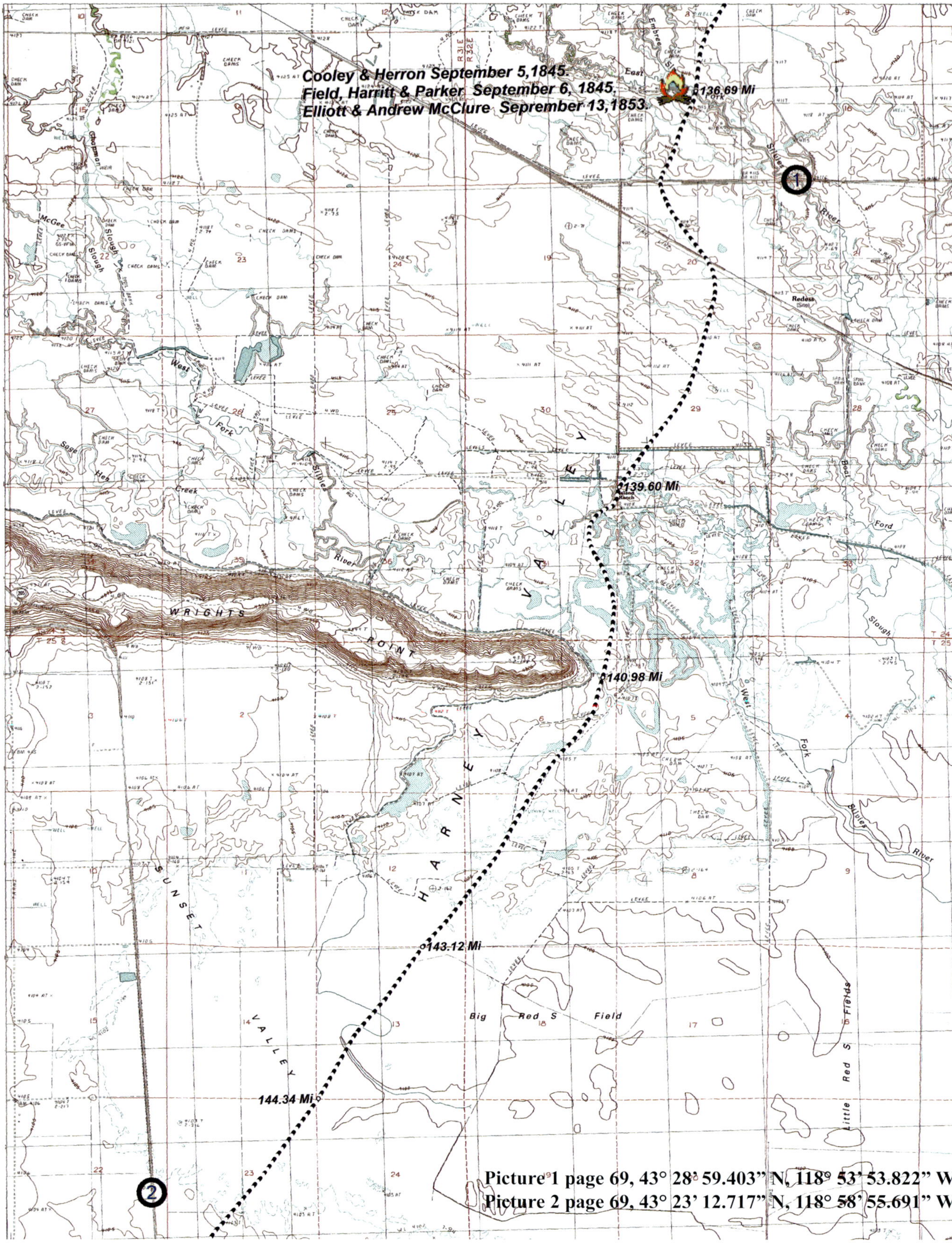

Circles: Picture Number and Its Location.
Solid Line: Traces of the Trail. Verified on the ground by these authors.
Dashed Line: Projected Trail Location. Verified on the ground by these authors.

Redess

Silvies River Near Burns, Oregon, with Wrights Point far Right. *"...branch of Crooked River..."* John Herron. Steens Mountains are faintly visible at the far left 65 miles away. John Herron writes the Steens Mountains are the Cascade Mountains. Location 1 viewed southerly on Redess map, p. 68.

Wrights Point Extending into Harney Valley *"...in about 1 mile further passed the point of a ridge leaving it to the rite and in about 14 miles further Camped by a lake..."* Eli Cooley. Photo taken from State Highway 205. Location 2 viewed northeasterly on Redess map, p. 68.

1853 Andrew McClure Diary

Sunday, September 11. This morning we were cordially invited by Mr. Kinny to eat breakfast and having but little provisions, we accepted. We were treated with much kindness. About 7 o'clock we caught our horses and bidding our kind friends of "Emerald Isles" [sic] a good morning we set out on our way. From camp the trail ascends the hill and, taking a southerly course follows up the ravine four miles then turning west it winds among the heads of the branches which form what is termed the West Branch of the South Branch of Malheur. Here are some pine trees and the cedars are quite numerous.

The mountains ahead appear to sink away and the country to become that of a small valley. We hoped for better roads. This part of the trail passes through a stony part of the country.

From this we appeared to be travelling down hill and four miles after leaving the ravine we found ourselves on the brink of a hill with a beautiful valley spread like a map before us. This we were satisfied was the water of the Deschutes or Fall River as it is sometimes called. Going down the hillside is steep and somewhat rocky. On the right is a ravine we found a small pool of water not very good. From this the trail turns to the right and following the ravine, passes round on the base of the hill and down the ravine into a broad valley. Three miles from the last water the trail comes near a creek on the left with stagnant water in pools. There we found Capt. Elliott's last nights camp. The valley is very level and when the trail is well broken will be fine travelling. From this creek the trail turns round the point of the mountain on the right and four miles brought us to a small stream issuing out of the mountain and forming a slough water rather poor, good grass and a good place to camp. Seven miles further brought us to Elliott's camp which we found to be on a fine little stream of good water coming from the mountains and running briskly through a level plain which looks like a meadow. This stream runs southward perhaps emptying into the East Branch of Fall river.

We found The Elliott Train [sic] nearly out of provisions and had just killed an animal for food. They are in good spirits and seem to care little for their situation. Mr. say he will make arrangements promising in so far to forming a crowd for relief. *[Camped on Silvies River in Harney Valley.]*

1853 Andrew McClure Diary

Monday, September 12. The arrangements being made with the Capt we mounted our horses promising to return in three days equipped for a trip to The Valley.

Riding until about 10 o'clock and retracing about 12 miles of our yesterday's travel we met Mr. V. S. McClure and Mr. Drusy. We stopped at the foot of the mountain turned our horses upon the grass and awaited the arrival of the train. They came up about 3 o'clock and we turned about and the train has gone to camp at Dry Creek at the camp of Elliott on the night of the 10th. The grass is very fine, a few willows for fuel.

We were overtaken today by some men from the trains behind who have encamped near us and intend to wait our readiness to start on the morrow.

The men of our train held a meeting for the purpose of making an arrangement for sending in for provisions. *[Camped on Rock Creek, near Harney Valley.]*

1853 Andrew McClure Diary *[Short cut across Harney Valley.]*

Tuesday, September 13. Our train was astir early and, while in commotion to get us off news was brought into camp that a lady in Mr. Miller's train died last night and would be buried some place along the road. This is the first death I have been near to since starting. We got under way about 8 o'clock and the company from our train which consisted of the following individuals: J. Denning, B.F. Owen, and myself joined five others from trains farther back on the road. On arriving at the creek we were met by a messenger from Mr. Elliott who was directed to turn the trains directly across the valley toward the point of a mountain range which sinks away in the north. From here we traveled about sixteen miles over a sandy sage plain without water when turning a little to the right we struck a creek. The water looks good and taste well. Good grass here. Stopped to graze our horses.

While here Mr. Elliott came up and recognized Mr. Charles Clark of our train. (Pack Train) The train passed us while grazing and stopped two mile down the creek. Our train. The wagon started out after us and if they followed our trail they found larger sage than they have heretofore met. They will most probably, be obliged to cut the road with axes. We replaced our packs mounted our horses and rode down to Elliott's camp. Mr. Elliott is in finer spirits than I have heretofore seen him. Grass is good beyond conception. It is from one to three feet high and of very nutritious quality. Willows for fuel.This creek seems to flow into the lake as it appears dead and does not flow as briskly as further up.

1853 Andrew McClure Diary *[Started around east side of Malheur Lake.]*

Wednesday, September 14. This morning we started about seven o'clock, and taking a course of about South 20° East for twelve miles winding through sloughs and tall grass and nooned near the mound standing on the east side of the lake which is called by some the Tule Lakes. The lake opposite this is a sheet of which presents a beautiful appearance and is throngs by bevies of geese and ducks. The grass being poor and having no water we did not stay long. After starting for again tried a course of about S 45° W but soon came to a creek which we found to contain water but so strongly mineralized that we could scarcely drink a cup of it. Facing about again we found a crossing and tried make the head of the lakes after some difficulty we succeed and being aware that we had no water ahead filled our canteens and struck straight for the hills. Encamped on the hill. Some grass no water. Made tea of the water we got from the Lake but found it so much like lye that we could not use it and drank and used water caught from a saddle blanket put up as an awning. In this way we did not suffer for water. It has rained since about three o'clock with occasional intermissions. Travelled about thirty miles today much of that distance having been consumed among the sloughs which border the lake. The low ground next the lake produces tolerable good grass but the water is unfit for use. The emigrant should avoid it as much as possible.

The Elliott Wagon Train of 1853 followed the Meek Cutoff until they reached the Harney Valley and the Silvies River. Upon seeing those snow-capped Steens Mountains to the southeast, they too, thought they were the Cascade Mountains. The Elliott Wagon Train fully intended to cross the Cascades as it was their goal to enter into the southernmost end of the Willamette Valley. Thus Elijah Elliott, without the aid of a guide that had the knowledge Stephen Meek possessed, turned down the Crooked River (Silvies River) toward those snow-capped Cascade Mountains (Steens Mountains). Elliott thought they could turn southeasterly around the lake until they reached the outlet and continue on down the river toward what they thought were the Cascade Mountains. To their dismay, there was no outlet! The wagon train was in a basin where all water flows into the lake basin and there is no outlet. Confused and bewildered, they spent several days wandering hopelessly lost. It wasn't until they finally picked up the old trail of the Meek Wagon Train that they were able to get back on their intended course. They left the Meek Cutoff in the vicinity of the Sinks of Lost Creek and made their way west to where Bend, Oregon, is along the banks of the Deschutes River. From there, they turned south toward the headwaters of the Deschutes River, finally finding the new partially cut trail that was supposed to have been prepared for their arrival. This trail later became known as the Free Emigrant Road. Following this route, they eventually were rescued by the Willamette Valley settlers before completing their unfortunate and disastrous journey into the Willamette Valley.

Writers have rightfully called the Elliott Wagon Train "the Lost Wagon Train of 1853." Many of the errors and confusion in written articles stem from the similarity in the size and nature of the Meek and Elliott Wagon Trains. There have been many stories and tales written about the Elliott Wagon Train, but many have placed the events with the wrong wagon train, thus the erroneous term "Lost Meek Wagon Train."

This ends the usefulness of Andrew McClure's diary concerning the Meek Cutoff Wagon Trail.

SILVIES RIVER TO THE NARROWS BETWEEN MALHEUR AND HARNEY LAKES

Sept Sat 6: The road to day is first rate Weather fine Come about 3 miles and crossed a small Creek plenty of grass and Willow here on the creek in about 1 mile further passed the point of a ridge leaving it to the rite and in about 14 miles further Camped by a lake leaving it to the left the creek runs to the left plenty of grass no Wood some sage here the corse has been a little West of South. 18 miles. **Eli Cooley Diary**

6th: We started about 7 o'clock and traveled about south 15 miles. Here we came to a lake which caused us to turn to the west about 10 miles; trying to get water we traveled until about 8 o'clock at night, and encamped without wood, water, fire or supper or anything to console us, so we laid down and took a good night's sleep, which revived us considerably. 176 miles from Boise river. **John Herron Diary**

7: Struck the lakes Bad water. 22 mi. **Samuel Parker Diary**

7th: road butiful and level travleed 16 ms crassed one small stream and encamped on the Northern margin of a large lake had an abundence of fine grass no wood except sage. **Jesse Harritt Diary**

Sun Sept 7th: Went about 16 miles, camping upon a lake of miserable, stagnant water, filled with ducks, geese and cranes, and surrounded with tall rushes, the borders being miry. Had excellent grass but were obliged to pack wormwood for half a mile for fuel. During the night 15 head horses and mules left us. **James Field Diary**

As they leave their encampment on the Silvies River, Stephen Meek guided the wagon train in a southwesterly direction passing the point of a long flat ridge. This is a very prominent landmark called Wrights Point that looms out in Harney Valley. It is a clear beacon that can be seen all across valley. Continuing on they crossed State Highway 205. Eli Cooley writes, "*... passed the point of a ridge leaving it to the rite and in about 14 miles further Camped by a lake....*" This lake was most likely Mud Lake, which is a portion of Harney Lake just west of the Narrows, that divides Harney Lake and Malheur Lake.[1]

A great deal of research has been done by others to prove that the year 1845 was in the midst of an extreme drought period, and because of this, Harney Lake and Malheur Lake had nearly dried up. This was used as the excuse to justify the premise that Stephen Meek became hopelessly lost since he was not able to see water impounded in this area. This research proves nothing except that the year 1845 was a dry year. The five diarists all recognized the area as a lake. There was enough water present that Eli Cooley could determine the direction of the water flowing from the Harney Lake area to the left or east into Malheur Lake. Stephen Meek also recognized the lakes as well. He had been at this location during the early winter months of 1834 when the lakes were at their lower levels and before the spring runoff had taken place.

It was at the Narrows that the emigrants could look back in the direction they had just come, seeing Fremont Peak or Castle Rock for the last time showing up on the distant skyline some 65 miles to the northeast. Stephen Meek had been relying upon this very prominent landmark for the past eleven days as he guided the wagon train to the big lakes in the Harney basin. In 1834, on his trapping expedition, Stephen Meek also could have seen Castle Rock from the Narrows. But now he was focusing his thoughts on a very prominent peak ahead of them called Iron Mountain. Therefore, he turned to the west, guiding the wagons along the northern shoreline of Harney Lake. Here the trail parallels the Double "O" Ranch County Road.

[1]It was possible to cross the Narrows at certain times of the year. Major Enoch Stein (aka Steen), commanding the 1st Dragoons, crossed the Narrows in 1859 as he made his way toward the Snow Mountains, later called the Steens Mountains after him. Today, Highway 205 has been built across the Narrows.

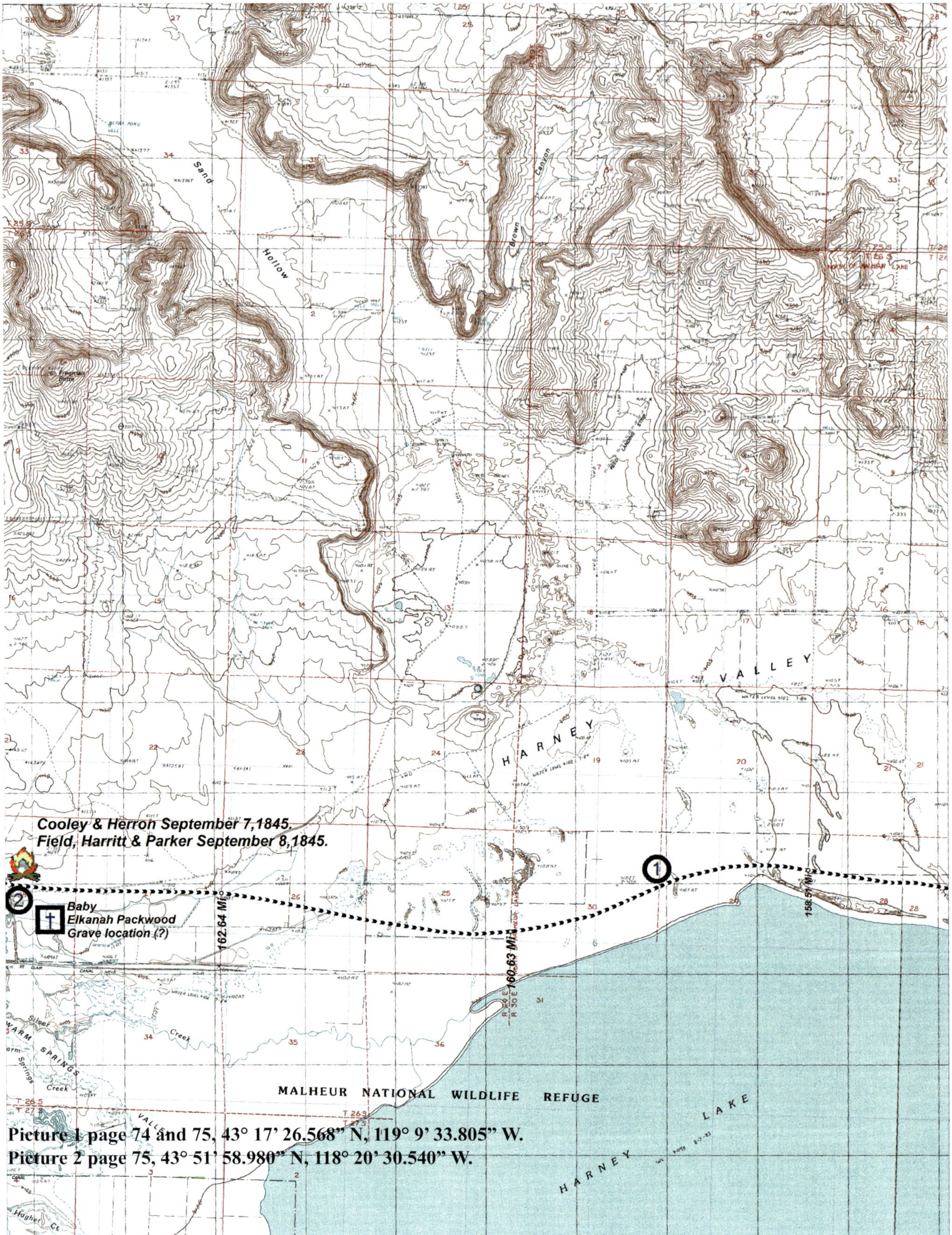

Northwest Harney Lake

Circles: Picture Number and Its Location.
Solid Line: Traces of the Trail. Verified on the ground by these authors.
Dashed Line: Projected Trail Location. Verified on the ground by these authors.

Circles: Picture Number and Its Location.
Solid Line: Traces of the Trail. Verified on the ground by these authors.
Dashed Line: Projected Trail Location. Verified on the ground by these authors.

The Narrows (Modified)

IRON MOUNTAIN. *"...Traveled allmost Towards a high point or peak and..."* Eli Cooley.
Location 1 viewed southwesterly on Northwest Harney Lake map, p.72.

NARROWS TO SILVER CREEK NEAR DOUBLE O RANCH HEADQUARTERS

Sept Sun7: The road to day has been good weather fine come about 10 miles and struck a creek and camped plenty of grass and Willow here the creek runs to the left and thrugh the lake and then round to the rite in to Jays river round the Mountains wee left holes to the rite and left the corse has been about south west or near so Traveled allmost Towards a high point or peak and to the rite is and other some Distance off Crossed a small Drean Just Before wee come to the creek. 10 miles. **Eli Cooley Diary**

7th: We started at 7 o'clock and traveled through a poor sandy valley 14 miles to a small stream of water about ten feet wide and nearly as many feet deep; water good and grass first rate; no wood only sage. Course today west. Distance 15 miles. **John Herron Diary**

8: Went down the lakes Some 5 miles then over hills to Small Creek one Child beried here. 15 mi. **Samuel Parker Diary**

8th: the road continues delightful had 13 horses stolen last night by the Indians travleed 10 ms and encamped on a small stream affording good grass and a fiew small willows. A dredful occurence a fiew minits after we ware in camp a suden deth of an infant by that disease which has been fatal before in our company the hooping caugh. **Jesse Harritt Diary**

Mon Sept 8th: Went about 13 miles, camping upon a creek which appears to feed the lake our last camp was on. We have been traveling for the last three days across a nearly dead level plain, in a southwesterly direction, and are now nearly across it, the bluffs arising abruptly from the edge of the plain, which they surround, and are in many places nearly perpendicular. Many parts of this plain, particularly where we struck it, has soil of good depth and is covered with a very fine kind of grass resembling blue grass. Much of it is covered with that same eternal wormwood mentioned so often, and there are many places that look as though they were covered with water during the wet season, now presenting a surface of naked white clay encrusted in places with a white substance resembling saleratus and answering the same purpose, as some of the women in the camp have proven by experiment. Four of the horses which left our camp were found today at a distance of several miles from it, but there is no news of the others. They probably strayed off in search of water as the borders of the lake were so miry they could not get a drink. **James Field Diary**

SQUAW BUTTE. *"...to the rite is and other some Distance off..."* Eli Cooley.
The two peaks in the left of the photo are Round Top Mountain and Glass Butte over 50 miles away.
Location 1 viewed northwesterly on Northwest Harney Lake map, p.72.

After they had traveled about 10 miles from their campsite at Mud Lake near the Narrows, they reached the mouth of what is now known as Silver Creek, as it empties into Harney Lake. The grumbling members of the train were now more convinced than ever that Stephen Meek was lost as he had turned directly away from what they thought were the Cascade Mountains.

It was at this location that several events began to unfold causing heartache, despair, discontent, dissatisfaction and an extreme lack of trust by some members of the wagon train pertaining to the guiding ability of Stephen Meek.

SILVER CREEK. The wagon train arrived in this general area along the banks of Silver Creek. It was in this vicinity that the first death that was mentioned by the diarists occurred. Elkanah Packwood, the baby of Elisha Packwood, died on September 8, 1845, very shortly after their arrival that evening. Location 2 viewed west on Northwest Harney Lake map, p.72.

The first event occurred on the evening of September 8, 1845, as the St. Joseph Company arrived on the banks of Silver Creek. Elkanah Packwood, the baby of Elisha Packwood, suddenly died of a lingering sickness thought to have been whooping cough. There was much heartache and despair in the Packwood family as they laid their child to rest in a small grave. The grave was driven over by the stock and wagons to conceal its location to prevent the Indians of that region from disturbing the grave.

The second event began at the Silver Creek camp when Stephen Meek was preparing to lead the wagon train northwesterly up the Silver Creek drainage. He had originally told the emigrants he would lead them through to the Crooked River, the Falls River (Deschutes River), and then arrive at The Dalles. Now he was ready to turn northwesterly up Silver Creek, following the old Indian and Hudson Bay trapper's trail and cross over into the Crooked River drainage. An argument ensued and some of the emigrants refused to follow Stephen Meek in the direction he wanted to guide them.[1] They felt he was lost since the "Cascade Mountains" (Steens Mountains) were clearly visible and now he was turning his back on those mountains. A very heated discussion took place in which Nicholas Ownbey, Captain of the advanced portion of the Savannah Oregon Emigrating Society, and perhaps fellow member, Joseph Cunningham, did not believe what Stephen Meek was saying about this vast region. They were insistent they should cross the "Cascade Mountains" into the Willamette Valley. Both of these companies had a large number of cattle and they had the most to gain by going that route. Due to their absolute refusal to go the direction Stephen Meek wanted to lead them, he was pressured into turning nearly due westward toward the upper reaches of the Deschutes River, leaving his original intended course of travel.

The third event that occured was described by James Field of the St. Joseph Company on September 8, 1845, when he writes *"... many places that look as though they were covered with water during the wet season, now presenting a surface of naked white clay encrusted in places with a white substance resembling saleratus and answering the same purpose, as some of the women in the camp have proven by experiment."* This experimenting was being done with nothing less than pure alkali salts, perhaps a very risky endeavor.[2] It has been said on other occasions in pioneer diaries that pioneer women had used alkali salts as a leavening in baking some breads although the final results of such a practice had not been explored. Some questions remain unanswered. How often was this done? What quantity of alkali was used? Was there any sickness attributed to the alkali? Were there long lasting effects of such a practice?

In any case, it was clear at this point that members of the St. Joseph Company were now camping together with Samuel Parker's Company also known as the Van Buren Company. The Van Buren Company, as previously mentioned, was poorly provisioned. It can only be assumed at this time, that the women of the Van Buren Company were attempting to stretch their provisions as much as possible, though James Field did not indicate who was doing the experimenting. He was only observing the practice.

Jesse Harritt, a member of the McNary family, also traveling with the St. Joseph Company, put a finger on what might be expected by breathing this white substance resembling saleratus. Jesse Harritt wrote in his diary on June 28, 1845, two months out on the Oregon Trail describing what they were encountering. He writes *"... Passed by, seen several natural curositys, the most particular was some dry salt lakes, at a distance the appearance of snow with a white sediment on its surface from 2 to 4 inches thick..."* Four days later he revisits the subject when he writes, *"Something verry astonishin a sleepy drousyness has vaded the camp ever since we came on big platte river and since we came on*

[1]James Field did not write about this argument until he recalled it on Thursday, September 11, and said it occurred at the marshy lake.

[2]Alkali salt is defined as the whitish crust formed by the evaporation of water on alkali soil. When this crust is crumbled, it feels much like common table salt.

sweet water our men have been subject to sevier pains in the head back and other parts of the cistom with cholache and cramps sore mouths and lips even the timber in our wagons has shrunk up so that one might with one hand a wheal to peecs...".[1] They were at that time in June experiencing the terrible effects of just inhaling fine alkali dust particles as they traveled along the Oregon Trail. The cattle, as well as the wagons, were stirring up this fine alkali dust. It could not be avoided; it was everywhere. Now the wagon train had advanced nearly 1000 miles in just over two months. Here they are at the Silver Creek camp encountering the same white substance resembling saleratus. They had either ignored or forgotten the previous effects of this substance, because now some of the women had began using alkali salt in their cooking as a substitute for food items that had been depleted. Some of the families were now consuming quantities of this substance directly in their diet, not realizing what the possible outcome might be.

Edwin Bryant, a medical intern of the day who chose a career in journalism, writes July 7, 1846, *"I was seized, during the night, with a violent and exhausting sickness. The soil of the country through which we are now traveling, are strongly impregnated with salt, alkali, and sulfur; rendering the use of the water in large quantities, deleterious to help, if not dangerous."*[2] By the year 1853, there was a much better understanding of just how dangerous the use of alkali salts was in the diet. Andrew McClure, from the Elliott Wagon Train, mentions the necessity of avoiding alkali on several occasions as they traveled through the country, mainly between the Platte River and South Pass and some distance beyond. On July 6, 1853, Andrew McClure says, *"the emigrant while on this stream should watch his stock closely, for should they get alkali in large quantities, they are gone past redemption."* Andrew McClure was recognizing the dangers of alkali to livestock. It is only reasonable to assume that if it will kill animals, the effects may be the same to humans.

Saleratus is described as a chalk-like powder and seems to be a general term encompassing several different substances such as pearlash and potassium carbonate. Saleratus, in its commercial form, has been distilled and purified by removing any traces of lye. People were confusing saleratus as they knew the purified substance, with alkali salts which has the same chalk-like powder characteristics. However, alkali contains lye and carbonic acid as it occurs in its natural form. The undetermined quantity of lye present makes alkali a dangerous substance. It is not known just how much salts of lye and carbonic acid any one individual human stomach can ingest and remain healthy. *The Adams Sentinel and General Advertiser* of Gettysburg, Pennsylvania, on Monday, August 15, 1853, on page 5, published an interesting article which reads, *"Saleratus is said to be injurious to the human system, and that it destroys thousands of children and some adults every year. In New Brunswick, contiguous to Maine, the physicians are wont to say that half the children are killed by the use of saleratus."*

---

[1]The wheel had dried out to a point that with one hand you could shake it apart, separating the spokes from the hub.

[2]Edwin Bryant, *What I Saw in California* (New York, 1848) Chapter 8 accessed June 2, 2014, http://user.xmission.com~octa/DonnerParty/Bryant.htm.

Stinking Lake

Circles: Picture Number and Its Location.
Solid Line: Traces of the Trail. Verified on the ground by these authors.
Dashed Line: Projected Trail Location. Verified on the ground by these authors.

DOUBLE O RANCH TO THE TOP OF A BLUFF WEST OF IRON MOUNTAIN

Mon 8 Sept: The road to day has been good Except one little Rockey place Weather fine Traveled up the creek around the head of it Towards the peak the creek runs along by the side of a Bluff and we come along by the point of the Bluff leaving it to the left here at the point of the Bluff is a Excalent Spring Some grass, no Wood Except Sage then on about a south west corse and by the Point of another Bluff leaving it to the rite then on near the peak leaving it to the left then on to an other high Bluff or Bench and camped no Water here though we found Some Water in a hole to the left up a hollow which was sufficient for cooking here Some of the oxen was Tied up all night others left out Those that was left out went Back to the Spring from whare wee camped last nite To the Spring is about 5 miles from the Spring to whare wee lay at nite is about 6. 11 miles. **Eli Cooley Diary** *[Camped on a bluff.]*

8th: We started at 8 o'clock and traveled west about 10 miles over some of the best road that we have had since we passed the Rocky Mountains, but in the evening we had some rocky road for a few miles; here we turned about two degrees north of west for about 5 miles and found no grass and had to encamp in a patch of wild sage, where it was as high as our wagons. About one mile south of where we are we found a little water, enough to cook supper with. The stream of water that we stayed on last night runs out of the side of a mountain through a hole about six feet in diameter; there is water enough within six feet of where it runs out to drown a horse. Passed some plains today that were covered. **John Herron Diary** [1] *[Camped on a bluff.]*

They left their camp near the mouth of Silver Creek, traveling up the creek about two miles where they were able to cross the creek. Then they traveled around rimrock bluffs and passed by Hibbard Spring. Eli Cooley says, *"here at the point of the Bluff is a Excalent spring."* John Herron writes, *"The stream that we stayed on last night runs out of the side of the mountain through a hole about 6 feet in diameter. There is water enough within 6 feet of where it runs out to drown a horse."* This is a very large spring and still exists today. Hibbard Spring is a part of the historic "Double O Ranch" which is now incorporated into the Malheur National Wildlife Refuge. This was another one of the landmarks Stephen Meek was relying on as he guided the wagon train. Hibbard Spring certainly helped these authors to locate the Meek Cutoff Wagon Trail.

Because of the demands made by Nicholas Ownbey of the Savannah Oregon Emigrating Society, Stephen Meek was reluctantly leading the wagon train past Iron Mountain in a nearly due west direction across basically uncharted country. Iron Mountain abruptly rises to 5380 feet. Near the base of Iron Mountain, the advanced company left the floor of the old lake bed and began to ascend a rocky slope as they made their way to the top of some bench land to make a dry encampment where sagebrush stood as tall as the wagons. They found water sufficient for cooking their meals about a mile distant to the northeast in a hollow. These authors have found and verified a spring that lies in a short canyon which is nearly a mile to the west of Iron Mountain and approximately a mile northeasterly from the general area of their campsite. There is not any other water in this general area. A large number of cattle left this campsite during the night, returning to their previous night's encampment where there was ample water to quench their thirst. The St. Joseph Company met these cattle and herded them with their own stock until the following day.

Hibbard Spring
Location 1 viewed northeasterly on Stinking Lake map, p. 78.

Thorn Spring with Iron Mountain
Location 2 viewed southwesterly on Stinking Lake map, p. 78.

[1] This is all that remains of John Herron's diary today. The diary entries thus far had been printed in an Albany newspaper, but before the rest of the diary could be printed, the original was lost in a fire at Heppner, Oregon, July 4, 1918.

Iron Mountain Flat

Dashed Line: Projected Trail Location. Verified on the ground by these authors.
Red Dashed Line: Short-cut Trail. Verified on the ground by these authors.

9: Went to a spring. 9 mi. **Samuel Parker Diary** *[Camped at Thorn Spring.]*

9th: attended to the burial of the deceased this morning before we started made a start at 10 oclock travleed 6 mis over a delightful road and encamped at a spring found no wood and but little grass. **Jesse Harritt Diary** *[Camped at Thorn Spring.]*

Tue Sept 9th: Last evening a child of E. Packwood, of Illinois, which had been ill a few days died suddenly. At presently there are a good many sick about the camp, the majority of them complaining of fever. The child was buried in the dry wormwood barrens, and as we left the camp the wagons filed over the grave, thus leaving no trace of its situation. The reason for our doing this was that the Indians in this part of the country are very fond of clothing, giving almost anything they possess in order to obtain it, and fearing that they might disturb the grave after we left, we took the precaution of leaving a beaten road across it. I cannot say that they would do anything to a grave, were they to find one, for we have passed several made by the emigrants at various times, and none of them appeared to havc been disturbed.[1] Went 6 miles camping near a spring which sinks near where it rise. **James Field Diary** *[Camped at Thorn Spring.]*

Following the advanced company of the Savannah Oregon Emigrating Society was the St. Joseph Company and Samuel Parker's Company. Having a late start, these two companies only advanced about 7½ miles to a spring. They arrived at what today is called Thorn Spring. Just as James Field describes it, Thorn Spring runs out of the base of a bluff and sinks into the ground in a very short distance.

BLUFF WEST OF IRON MOUNTAIN TO EGLI SPRING ON WAGONTIRE MOUNTAIN

Tue 9 Sept: Some rock to day weather fine Some of the Waggons started early this Morning though some of them did not get off until 10 o clock come around the Bench leaving it to the Rite. Come around and down in to the Valley along it for some Distance leaving the peak that wee saw to the rite a little to the rite Come along and went over a ridge Some Seder on it leaving 2 ridges Between us and the peak and about 2 miles through a Valley then over an other ridge with Seder on it Still having the peak to the rite then Turned to the left leaving the peak nearly behind us for about ½ or 2 mile and camped to a first rate Spring.[1] plenty of grass and some Wood here the corse is about west The road should not come so near the first peak nor over the Ridge or Bench but after leaving the Spring the road Should turn more to the rite leaving the first peak further to the left and strike across to the rite hand peak leaving it a little to the rite and strik this road again. 15 miles. **Eli Cooley Diary**

10th: made a late start travleed a west coars over a tolerable levle road tho verry stony in places found no grass nor water for 25 ms at one oclock this morning we gradually decended a long slope found a good spring affording an abundence of water and grass with a fiew willows. **Jesse Harritt Diary**

Wed Sept 10th: The ground about our encampment is encrusted with salt, which in some places may be scraped up with the hand in nearly pure state. Went about 30 miles today, over a road pretty well strewn with the hard, round . . . heads frequently mentioned after leaving Ft. Hall, and camped after midnight at a spring where we found Owensby's company, which had arrived 24 hours before us. Their last camp was about seven miles this side of ours and it was a dry one in the midst of wormwood barrens, so that they were nearly two days without water. We found about a hundred head of their stock between the two encampments, apparently nearly famished for water, and drove them on with us, but few of them giving out by the way although they looked miserable. **James Field Diary**

10: Went all day and all nite and struck a small spring in the morning Cursing and Swareing 105 wagons together. 40 mi. **Samuel Parker Diary**

Upon leaving the dry camp on the bluffs, Eli Cooley goes into great detail in his diary entry regarding how they traveled the next day. He drew a diagram map representing their travel. Leaving the bluff, they descended into a valley, which today is named Sand Hollow. Sand Hollow has rimrock bluffs both to the east and west of the valley, forcing them to follow the valley in a northwesterly direction for about two miles. They pulled out onto a wide ridge top. At this point, they could again see in the distance a prominent landmark referred to as the second peak, which is Squaw Butte. They were able to see it when they were at Silver Creek.

---

[1]James Field mentions passing several graves made by emigrants on the Oregon Trail.

[2]Eli Cooley's "½ or 2 mile" means half a mile or two halves or in other words, he meant that they traveled half a mile to one mile and camped.

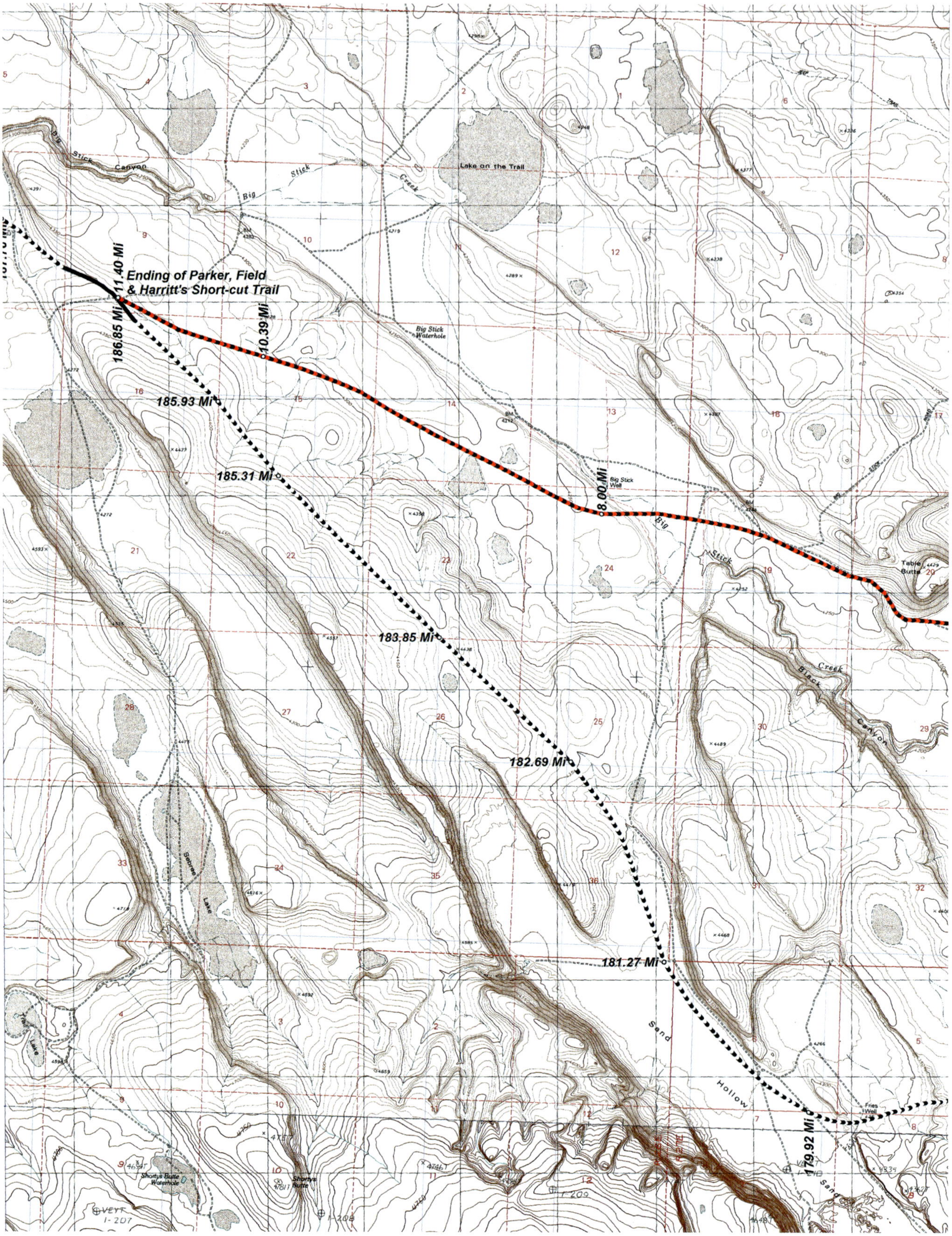

Lake on the Trail (Modified)

Circles: Picture Number and Its Location.
Solid Line: Traces of the Trail. Verified on the ground by these authors.
Dashed Line: Projected Trail Location. Verified on the ground by these authors.

They continued northwesterly another four miles to a location when they realized that the following companies the next day could make a short cut across the country to this location giving them a better road to travel. Word was sent back to these companies with instructions similar to those that Eli Cooley had drawn on his map of this area. (See map below).

Now they are approaching what is called Wilson Creek, passing near Big Stick Spring, though this spring is not mentioned. Crossing Wilson Creek, the trail passes along the southerly side of Alec Butte. The trail then crosses a low saddle on a ridge running westerly from Alec Butte. At this location and westerly of the trail, a few scattered junipers can be seen on the skyline as mentioned by Eli Cooley. From here, the trail turning westerly enters the second valley where it crosses present-day US Highway 395. Taking note at this time, there are two ridges between the trail's location and the prominent landmark Squaw Butte of which Cooley makes reference. From the highway, the trail continues westerly for a short distance, crossing present-day Egli Ridge. Today, Egli Ridge is covered with juniper. Then the trail parallels the western slope of Egli Ridge in a northwesterly direction for about four miles keeping the two ridges between the trail and the second peak, Squaw Butte. Here they turned southwesterly, or to the left as Cooley describes, keeping the second peak, Squaw Butte, to their back. They traveled about three quarters of a mile to spring. Cooley makes the statement, *"...for about ½ or 2 mile and camped to a first rate Spring."* These authors have interpreted his statement to mean one half or two halves (nearly a mile) to the spring.

Stephen Meek had now successfully guided the wagon train across uncharted country to a fine spring forming a small brook. This spring is called Egli Spring. Today, it is still considered a first rate spring. It was named after Anton Egli, a prominent homesteader and rancher that made the Wagontire Mountains his home.

The diarists' mileages vary considerably for this stretch of trail. The actual mileage for the stretch between Thorn Spring and Egli Spring is 26.85 miles. Field's mileage is 30 miles, and Samuel Parker's mileage of 40 miles is excessive. Cooley's mileage should have been referenced from their

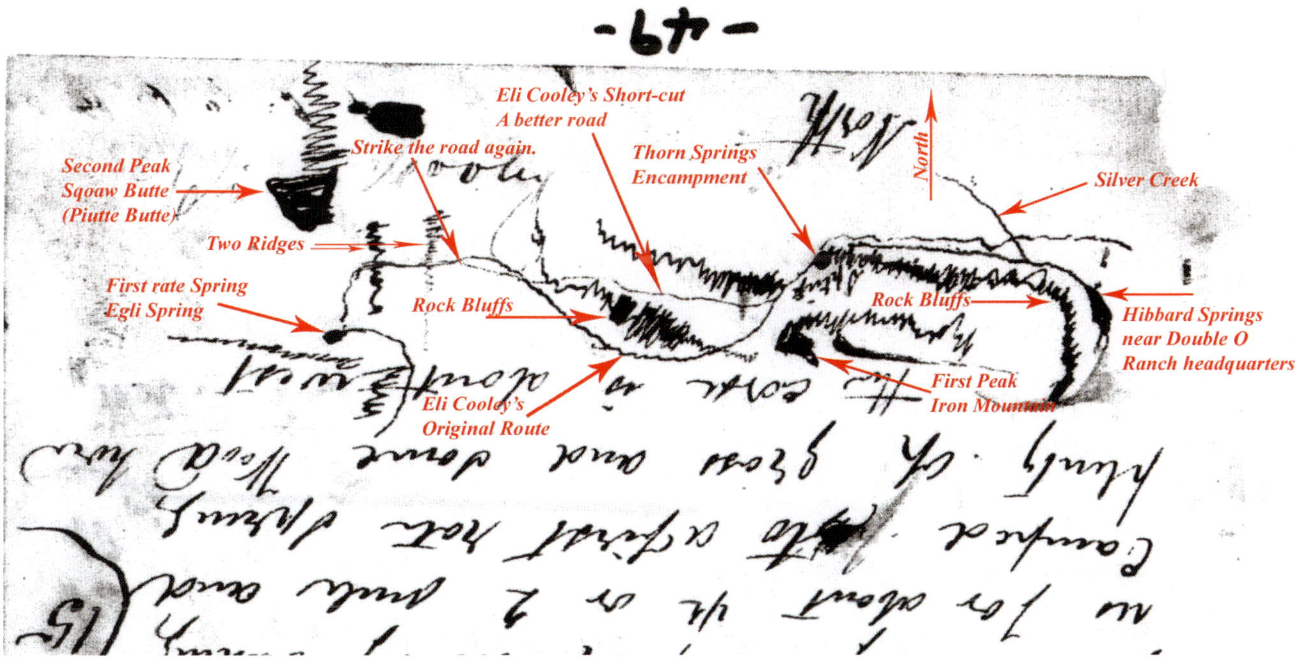

Eli Cooley's Map. At the bottom of Eli Cooley's page for the diary entry of September 9th (see page 81), he turned his diary upside down and drew a map to guide the companies in the rear to take a short cut, informing them that this would be a better road than the one they had just traveled. These authors' have interpreted and labeled Eli Cooley's drawing.

Picture 1 page 85, 43° 20' 5.520" N, 119° 43' 31.140" W.

Alec Butte

Circles: Picture Number and Its Location.
Solid Line: Traces of the Trail. Verified on the ground by these authors.
Dashed Line: Projected Trail Location. Verified on the ground by these authors.

campsite on the bluff to Egli Spring which was 23.03 miles. However, Eli Cooley's mileage of 15 miles is short, so perhaps Cooley only wrote the mileage they traveled from the point where the two routes came together and then on to Egli Spring. That distance is 13.75 miles. Whatever the reason for the variance, there is no doubt that they all ended up at the same location, Egli Spring.

Before leaving the encampment on September 10, 1845, James Field revisits the subject of salt. He writes in his diary, *"the ground about our encampment is encrusted with salt, which in some places may be scraped up with the hand in nearly pure state."* It must be pointed out that James Field had previously referred to a white substance resembling saleratus. In addition, previously he wrote in his diary that he had witnessed some of the emigrants collecting quantities of these salts to supplement their meager supplies. Visiting Thorn Spring today, it is possible to pick up quantities of this encrusted white salt, but the substance is nothing more than pure alkali salt, which is very dangerous to the human health when consumed in any large amount.

Sept Wen 10: The Company laid by to day weather fine yesterday Mr Wilborn started out to hunt Water and lost his horse and when he got in to camp was all most ded he was found in the road seting down resting and one of the men .....[torn corner] another company come here to nite from Spring gave him his horse and he got in to camp about 1 hour by Sun all so about 100 head of Cattle was let go off yesterday and was not got until the other Company got in several lost. **Eli Cooley Diary**

11th: Laid by all day to rest our teams. **Jesse Harritt Diary**

Thur Sept 11th: It being two o'clock this morning before we got to camp, we stuck to it the remainder of the day. Owensby's company left about noon for a camp six or seven miles ahead. His company are in as much confusion as any set of fellows I have yet seen on the road. Having lost confidence in Meek, many of them are trying to hunt a road for themselves. It seems there was misunderstanding between us and Meek when we left Snake River respecting the route he intended taking. We understood him that on leaving the Malheur river he intended striking over to the John Day river and down it to the old road. When we found ourselves on the branches of the Deschutes river it rather surprised us, and as we had a report in camp of a few days before that he was going to pilot Owensby across the Cascade Mtns. to the Willamette settlements, we supposed he was taking a straight shoot for them. It seems that he calls the Deschutes river the John Jay, which he says is the name by which it is known to the mountain traders, and the similarity in the sound of the two names made us mistake the one for the other. It was his intention to follow down Crooked river to the Deschutes and down it to the old road, but when he came to the marshy lake spoken of last Sunday, the company refused to follow him if he made the circuit necessary to get around it upon Crooked river again so he struck off in a westerly direction in order to get upon the main Deschutes River. He well knew that there was a scarcity of grass and water across here and so informed them, but it was nearer and they would have him go it, and now blame him for coming the route they obliged him to. **James Field Diary**

Since the companies had spent a large part of the night traveling, most of them rested the following day. Eli Cooley writes about Mr. Wilborn leaving to search for water. He probably rode off to look for water while the company was enroute to their encampment. He lost his horse and walked back to the trail. He would have died if one of the other companies had not come along and given him a horse. He made it to camp about an hour before dark.

Traces of the Trail West of Highway 395. *"...then over an other ridge with Sedar on it."* Eli Cooley. Trail leads toward the juniper ridge. Location 1 viewed westerly on Alec Butte map, p. 84.

Egli Spring Creek. Looking up Egli Creek. *"...camped to a first rate Spring."* Eli Cooley. Location 1 viewed southwesterly on Wagontire Mountain East (Modified) map, p. 86.

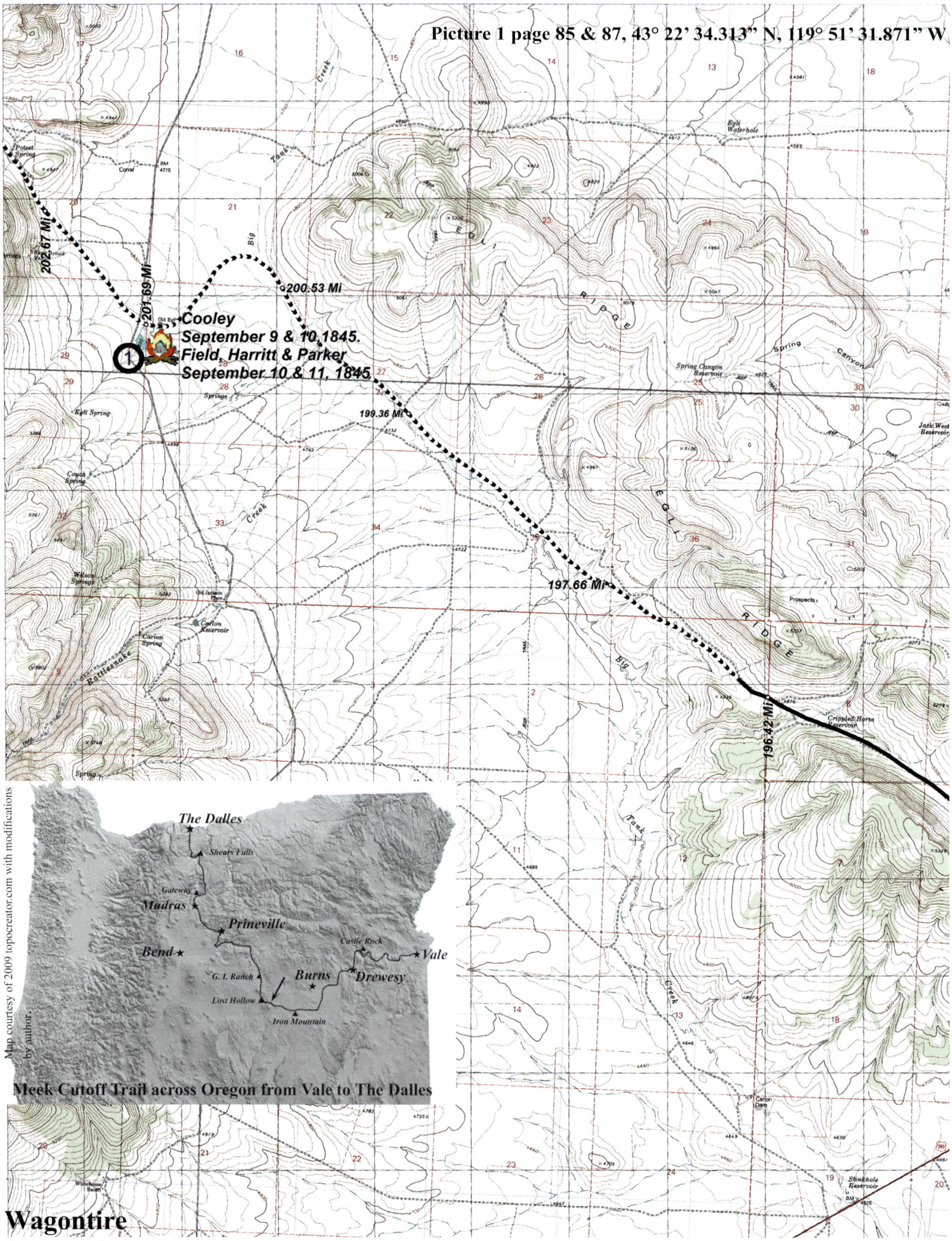

Wagontire Mountain East (Modified)

Circles: Picture Number and Its Location.
Solid Line: Traces of the Trail. Verified on the ground by these authors.
Dashed Line: Projected Trail Location. Verified on the ground by these authors.

PRESENT-DAY EGLI RESERVOIR. *"Still having the peak to the rite then Turned to the left leaving the peak nearly behind us for about ½ or 2 mile and camped to a first rate Spring."* Eli Cooley. Egli Spring now runs into this oasis in the desert called Egli Reservoir. On the horizon is the "second peak," Squaw Butte. Location 1 viewed northeasterly on Wagontire Mountain East (Modified) map p. 86.

At the Egli Springs encampment, Eli Cooley mentions a fight taking place on September 11th before his company left Egli Spring. James Field, also on September 11th, mentions considerable confusion among those present. They do not mention any names, but because of previous comments that the diarists have made, the fight was most likely between Nicholas Ownbey and Stephen Meek.

Reality was now beginning to sink into the emigrants' thoughts. The St. Joseph Company had not yet left the Egli Spring encampment when James Field remembers the heated argument that had taken place three days earlier and nearly 35 miles back along the trail at the Silver Creek encampment. In his diary, James Field writes very interesting words concerning how Stephen Meek had attempted to warn the emigrants regarding taking this route instead of the route on which he had intended to lead them. James Field writes on September 11, *"It was his intention to follow down Crooked River to the Deschutes and down it to the old road, but when he came to the marshy lake spoken of last Sunday, the company refused to follow him if he made the circuit necessary to get around it upon Crooked River again so he struck off in a westerly direction in order to get upon the main Deschutes River. He well knew that there was a scarcity of grass and water across here and so informed them, but it was nearer and they would have him go it, and now blame him for coming the route they obliged him to."*

Most of the emigrants were now realizing Stephen Meek had been right all along. They had crossed nearly 40 miles of this vast desolate wasteland and were observing the many prominent landmarks that dot this region, standing out like beacons guiding the way. Presently, these landmarks are named Iron Mountain, Squaw Butte, Wagontire Mountain, Round Top Mountain, Sheep Mountain, Big Glass Butte, Little Glass Butte, and Hampton Butte. The route the emigrants had insisted Stephen Meek take was a number of miles to the southwest of these landmarks.

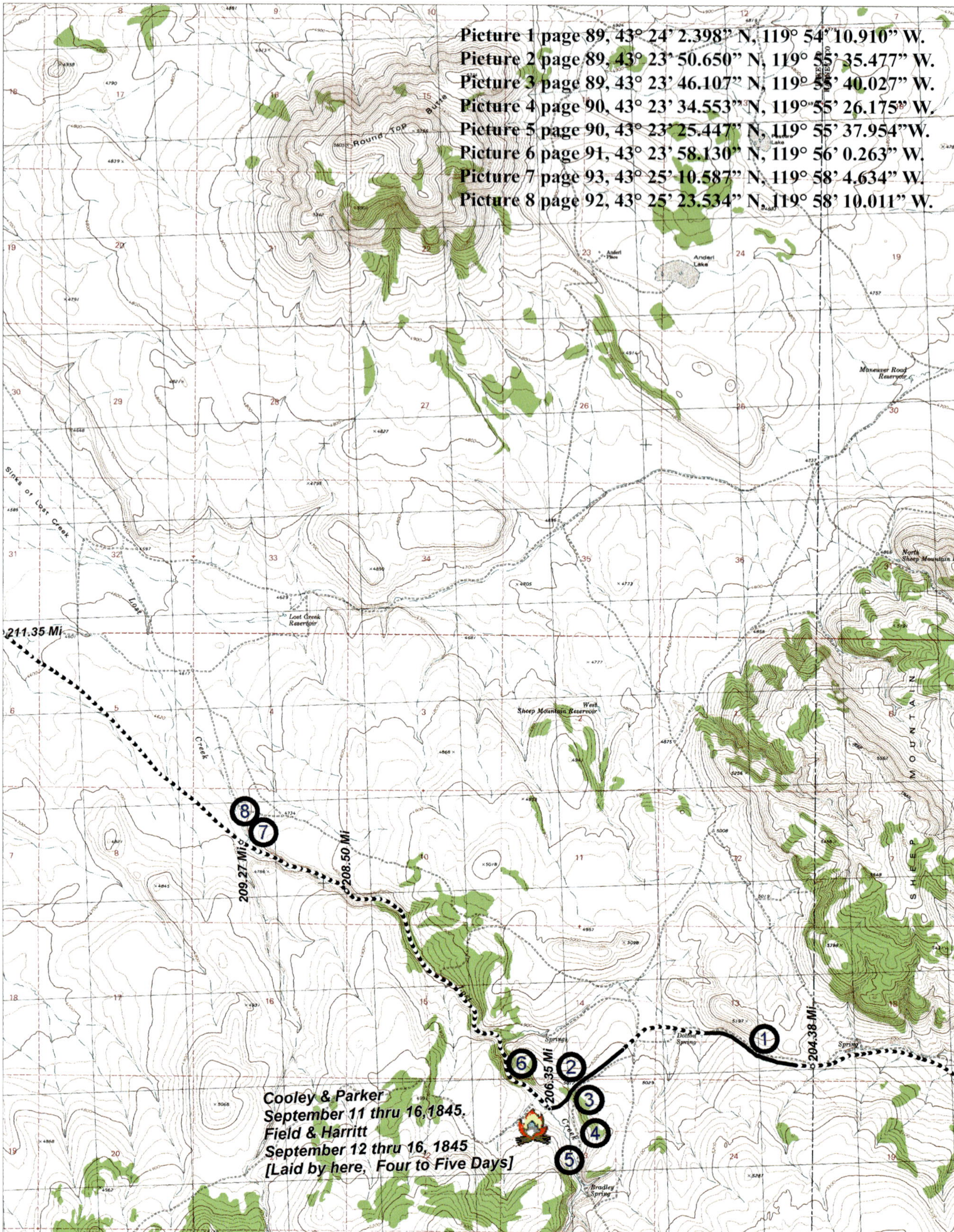

Round Top Butte

Circles: Picture Number and Its Location.
Solid Line: Traces of the Trail. Verified on the ground by these authors.
Dashed Line: Projected Trail Location. Verified on the ground by these authors.

After Leaving Egli Spring. Traces of the trail are visible as the wagons topped the summit of the low saddle from Egli Spring and began a gradual descent toward Lost Hollow. Photo is taken looking back on the trail.Location 1 viewed southeasterly on Round Top Butte map, p. 88.

Descending Into Lost Hollow on Lost Creek
Location 2 viewed southerly on Round Top Butte map, p. 88.

EGLI SPRING TO LOST HOLLOW IN THE BRADLEY SPRING AREA

Sept Thu 11: Weather fine today road Some what Broken and rockey the corse about west the Company started after Considerable confusion and 1 fite and come about 4 miles and Camped at a Spring plenty of grass and some Wood and Willow. 4 miles. **Eli Cooley Diary**

11: Went to another Spring laid heare 4 days and some 5 days Codent find no Water from 10 to 20 and 30 men out hunting water some come into camp and codent speak water found. 5 mi. **Samuel Parker Diary**

12th: made a small move of 5 ms and encamped on a small branch found tolerable grass and ceder timber in abundence. **Jesse Harritt Diary**

Fri Sept 12th: Went about 6 miles camping upon another little spring which running a short distance sinks again. The ravine looks as though a smart branch ran through it at some seasons of the year. The hills around are covered with cedars; with the exception of the plain to the westward that appears to be the case with all the country to the north and west of us as far as the eye can reach, and that appears to be the Cascade mtns. Found two thirds of Owensby's company still here, the remainder having gone on with the pilot and captain. A party of five men who left us last Tuesday morning to go back in search of the missing horses returned tonight bringing nine of them, which they had taken from a party of Indians near Crooked river. The Indians appeared loth to give them up but they charged upon them and took them, running the Indians off, who they say are a miserable set of wretches with no arms but bows and arrows. **James Field Diary**

The Trail Descending the Hill into the Hollow on Lost Creek
Location 3 viewed southwesterly on Round Top Butte map, p. 88.

Advancing nearly 5 miles, Nicholas Ownbey's Company, the lead company, and the Samuel Parker Company arrived September 11th, at what is now called Lost Hollow. After resting at Egli Spring on the 11th, the other companies began to arrive without any forward progress to be made for the next five days.

At Lost Hollow, there are two large springs named Lost Creek Spring and Bradley Spring, and several small springs and seeps, all of which feed Lost Creek. Lost Creek runs through Lost Hollow, down a canyon for about two miles, and out across the desert floor another two miles before disappearing into the Sinks of Lost Creek. Each of the large springs are about equal to Egli Spring in size.

These authors arrived at Lost Hollow for the first time 165 years and five days after the emigrants arrived at the same location in 1845. Upon our arrival, the sun was just beginning to set on the far distant western horizon. We spent the night camping under a full moon and experienced the bright moonlight of the night much like the emigrants of the wagon train of 1845. We enjoyed the natural beauty of the place, the quiet solitude, the howl of the distant coyote, the low hoot of the owl, and even the company of cattle coming in off the range to quench their thirst as they obtained a cool drink from Lost Creek. The landscape appears to have remained nearly the same other than the meadow may have been plowed at one time or another. This meadow probably consists of approximately 80 acres. Lost Hollow is located on private land consisting of several thousand acres of range land encompassing most, if not all of Wagontire Mountain. Longtime owner and rancher, Jack Peila, and his son Bill Peila, have grazed large numbers of cattle on this range land using it as their summer pasture and have done so for many years. In describing Lost Hollow, Jack Peila was proud to say, "As far as I am concerned, Lost Hollow is the most beautiful place on the entire ranch."

LAID BY AT LOST HOLLOW

Sept Fri 12: Weather fine to day a few of the Waggons started to day and Riggs Company come in here to day the pilott wanted the Company to lay by until he took a hunt for water but some of them would not do so. **Eli Cooley Diary**

Sept Sat 13: Weather fine to day the Balance of the Waggons started to day and also Mr Riggs Company but got word that they had not found no Water So we returned to the Spring again The men that first started had to Bring their oxen Back to the Spring for they had found no Water and took water Back to the Famileys to drink. **Eli Cooley Diary**

13th: made a start. Travleed 3 ms met the men who had accompanyed the pilot in serch of water found none we returned to our oald encampment and stoped for the night. **Jesse Harritt Diary**

Sat Sept 13th: Started this morning in expectation of a long drive across the plain before us, but when about four miles from camp met Meek's wife in company with a friend, returning with the news that they had found no water as yet and requesting all who were at the spring to remain there until he found a camp and returned or sent work back for them to come on. Nothing remained for us to do but drive back to the camp we had just left, where we found Tetherows company also, so if misery loves company here is enough of it, for this small camping spot is nearly eaten out by our own large stock of cattle and to add to all this there are some in the company nearly out of provisions. **James Field Diary**

Lost Hollow Encampment
Location 4 viewed northwesterly on Round Top Butte map, p. 88.

Lost Creek Fed by Bradley Spring and Lost Creek Spring
Location 5 viewed northerly on Round Top Butte map, p. 88.

Lost Creek Ravine. Upon leaving the meadow, the wagons entered the Lost Creek ravine and traveled about 2 ½ miles down to its mouth. On the horizon, in the upper right-hand corner of the photo, the high point seen is Glass Butte. Location 6 viewed northwesterly on Round Top Butte map, p. 88.

Sun Sept 14: Weather fine to day Mr Tetherow Companys got in here to day and the Waggons xcept Some 2 or 3 come Back to day Still found no Water and Mr Meek is Still Hunting for Water it is said that there is 4 Companys Back at the last Encampment. **Eli Cooley Diary**

Sun Sept 14th: Last evening the portion of Owensby's company which were out upon the plains returned with their cattle and water kegs, having left their wagons out upon the plain seven miles from here and no water had then been found within 30 miles of them. Today Meek ordered them to return to this place and sent an order for us to remain at this place until tomorrow morning, then to let 10 or 12 men accompany him with spades and dig for water at a place he thinks it can be found, in the dry bed of a creek. This evening Owensby returned with his wagons, teams, cattle and all, having enough of lying out upon the plain upon uncertainties. Meek came in after dark and said that from the tip of a mountain a short distance from here he had discovered a cut in the side of a mountain apparently 15 miles distant where from the bright green appearance of the willows and grass there could be no doubt of our finding water and requesting that some horsemen might accompany him to search the mountain sides still further; he thought there would be no danger in some wagons starting tomorrow. **James Field Diary**

14th: laid stil all day waiting the return of the pilot he returned late in the evening found no water. **Jesse Harritt Diary**

As Lost Hollow filled up with people, wagons, and cattle, frustration and anger must have grown day-by-day. Many were becoming extremely tired of the toilsome travel and inconvenience. They were anxious to get to their final destination and to have a little peace and quiet away from everyone else. First and foremost though, food supplies were running very low causing their already short tempers to get even shorter. For the emigrants of 1845, Lost Hollow became a place of gloom and despair.

A desperate search was being conducted by many of the men looking far and wide for water and a place for their next encampment. It appears the push to continue pressing westward to the Deschutes River and continuing on across the Cascade Mountains into the Willamette Valley was still very present. However, the success of finding any water to the west was short-lived. Beyond Lost Hollow to the west, lies vast desert plains as far as the eye can see. These desert plains are very dry and arid with no water to be found. The search area was gradually changing from a westerly course toward a northerly direction.

Some of the companies were in such a hurry to leave Lost Hollow that they took off without even knowing where they might find water. Then with no place to go, they had to return to Lost Hollow.

Sinks of Lost Creek and the Vast Desert Plains Beyond with the two Glass Buttes on the Right
Trail leads through the saddle between the two Buttes. Location 8 viewed northwesterly on Round Top Butte map, p. 88.

In the meantime, additional companies were arriving at Lost Hollow. One of the companies arriving on September 14th was Solomon Tetherow's Company. This was one of the larger companies which also had a large number of cattle. Solomon Tetherow was the original wagon master of the Savannah Oregon Emigrating Society. The breakup of this wagon train earlier along the Oregon Trail had left the larger part of the train of about 50 wagons loyal to Solomon Tetherow. They had been traveling about four days behind the advanced Nicholas Ownbey Company. Solomon Tetherow was a man of many talents; besides being wagon master of a large train, he had once been a mountain man and a riverboat captain.

On September 14th, Stephen Meek climbed to a high point believed to be Big Glass Butte, hoping to see evidence of water somewhere.[1] From this high point, it was possible to see all the prominent landmarks that dot this region. He had been keeping the landmarks they had passed in mind.[2] He had passed through this region in 1834 and had became familiar with them. Meek's intended route following the old Indian trail was actually paralleling these landmarks several miles to the northeast.[3] He could clearly see the vast reaches of the desert nearly 45 miles southeasterly toward Iron Mountain and the Silver Creek area near the vicinity of Harney Lake. Harney Lake is the same location where near mutiny had taken place on September 8th, when some members of the wagon train refused to follow his intended route along the old historic Indian trail.

From this high point, he was able to see evidence of greenery and willows growing in the distance some 15 miles or more in a northerly direction. This location was in the vicinity of present-day Buck Creek. Meek was now entertaining the prospect that there was water to be found nearly due north some 25 miles from their present encampment.

[1]These authors drove to the top of Big Glass Butte to see what Meek may have observed. It was like looking at the world from outer space. We could see all the prominent landmarks of that region. We could see evidence of water in the Buck Creek drainage. The water from the Buck Creek drainage sinks and seeps crossing the desert floor where it reappears at intervals. Prior to the Meek Wagon Train in 1845, there were no cattle grazing through this area to eat off the grass which grew up from the seeps. Therefore, this would make the presence of greenery at that distance even more visible.

[2]A true mountain man possessed an uncanny ability to read and understand the lay of the land. He relied on prominent landmarks, the distant horizon, and the celestial bodies to determine his direction of travel. He maintained his survival by living off the untamed land and coexisting with the Native Americans.

[3]These authors have became familiarized with the landmarks across this vast region and have personally utilized them in our quest to locate the actual trail as described by the diarists, especially Eli Cooley's account of their travels.

LOOKING FROM GLASS BUTTE ACROSS MISERY FLAT TO BUCK CREEK. *"Meek came in after dark and said that from the tip of a mountain a short distance from here he had discovered a cut in the side of a mountain apparently 15 miles distant..."* James Field Diary. The cut Stephen Meek referred to is Buck Creek located center right of the photo. Location 1 viewed northeasterly on Glass Butte map, p. 96.

LOST HOLLOW TO BUCK CREEK

Sept Mon 15: Weather fine to day Mr Tetherow and a part of his Company started to day late this Evening and also Some out of our Company and arrived at Camp next day. **Eli Cooley Diary**

Mon Sept 15th: This afternoon about three o'clock 21 of Tetherows together with 6 or 7 of Owensby's company made a start for a spot spoken of yesterday, which lies northeasterly from here, Meek accompanying them. A company of 8 or 10 wagons passed through the hollow we were encamped in, and started out into the plains by moonlight in the evening.[1] They were a company we had never seen before and they said they were the last to leave the states for Oregon this year, starting some two or three weeks behind us. Their loose stock were nearly all working steers, they having enough apparently to change teams every day. **James Field Diary**

15th: Dispatched a company of men with their packhorses loded with water and prision [provisions] in serch of water. **Jesse Harritt Diary**

Sept Tue 16: Weather fine to day all of our Waggons that had started out the other day got in to day, news come that thare was water and this Evening we started and got to Branch next Morning at Sun rise Traveled down the hollow out at the Mouth which is about 2 miles and along the way wee first started for about 3 miles further the corse this far is about South west then wee Turned to the rite and Traveled about a north corse for about 19 miles and camped on a Branch plenty of Grass and Some Willow and plenty of sage here for 5 miles the road is good then rocky and some what Broken for about 15 miles then good and level to the Branch.[2] 24 miles. **Eli Cooley Diary**

Tue Sept 16th: Capt. Riggs accompanied by the two Wilcoxes started yesterday to search for water at a place they had seen the day before, and which the description given by Meek of the spot he expected to find water at, applied to precisely. They returned this morning reporting it the same with plenty of water and grass. We made preparation for starting immediately, but could not get ready until late in the afternoon, as our cattle were so scattered. We had a clear, full moon to light us on our toilsome way, which lay across a mountain to the northward, and after traveling about 20 miles we reached the long sought spot at daybreak. **James Field Diary**

LOOKING UP LOST CREEK RAVINE. The wagons came out of Lost Hollow, down the Lost Creek ravine in this vicinity, and then headed out onto the plains. This photo is about 2 ½ miles from Lost Hollow. Location 7 viewed southeasterly on Round Top Butte map, p. 88.

[1]Who this company was or what happened to them was never known.

[2]At this point, Cooley wrote "South west" when it is obvious he meant northwest. Down the hollow (canyon) defines the direction.

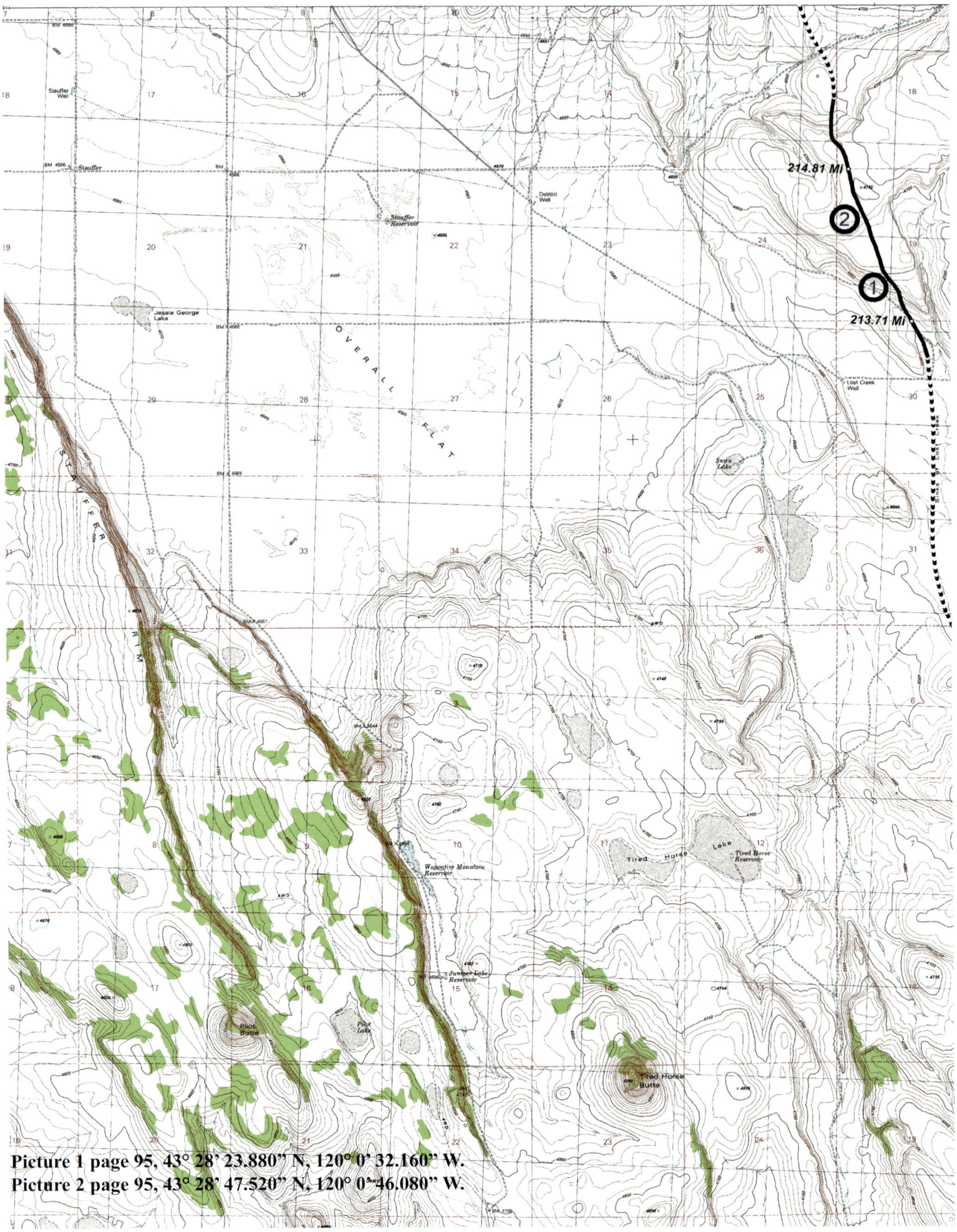

Picture 1 page 95, 43° 28' 23.880" N, 120° 0' 32.160" W.
Picture 2 page 95, 43° 28' 47.520" N, 120° 0' 46.080" W.

Tired Horse Butte

Circles: Picture Number and Its Location.
Solid Line: Traces of the Trail. Verified on the ground by these authors.
Dashed Line: Projected Trail Location. Verified on the ground by these authors.

Leaving the Sinks. *"...for 5 miles the road is good [across the Sinks of Lost Creek] then rocky and some what Broken..."* Eli Cooley Diary. Traces of the trail are visible where rocks are pushed to both sides of the trail. Location 1 viewed northwesterly on Tired Horse Butte map, p. 94.

Traces of the Wagon Swales. The trail as it heads toward the saddle between Glass Butte on the left and Little Glass Butte on the right. Location 2 viewed northerly on Tired Horse Butte map, p. 94.

16th: the hunters returned this morning at 9 oclock found water in 25 ms in a fiew minits the company were in parade for their oxen made a general collection of stock betwin 4 olock and sundown about 80 waggons left the branch for the next encampment travleed all night at day brake we reached the place of encampment at a small mountain stream winding its way through a level vally found no wood except sage which grew in abundance near its margin haveing come 25 ms we stoped to take some refreshment and rest our teams. **Jesse Harritt Diary**

16: Left at 3 pm about. Traveled all nite. come to water at sunrise.[1] missis But now Betor 198 wagons in Company. 2299 loose Cattle, oxen 811 head all these Cattle to git water and 1051 Soles also consume a heap of water. 30 mi. **Samuel Parker Diary**

When Stephen Meek returned to the encampment at Lost Hollow late on the evening of September 14th, he found that Solomon Tetherow's Company had now arrived. Solomon Tetherow had many of the same type of skills, experience, and knowledge as Meek. Therefore Meek was probably able to confide in Tetherow, something that had become impossible with members of the advanced company of Nicholas Ownbey. Solomon Tetherow had a chance to review the situation as Meek described it. Meek probably discussed the road he had intended to take following up the Silver Creek drainage where they would have had access to water most of the time before reaching the Crooked River, Deschutes River, and then on to The Dalles. He probably explained how Nicholas Ownbey's Company had refused to take this intended route, which was the reason they were now encamped and wasting time in Lost Hollow. No matter what, Stephen Meek requested that a group of men be sent to the place where he was confident that water could be found north of there. The horsemen left early the following morning of September 15 to confirm the presence of water.

Meek also thought that some of the wagons could start in that direction. So on the 15th, Solomon Tetherow exercised his authority and retook his rightful position as wagon master. They were so confident that water was to be found that by 3 o'clock that afternoon a group of Tetherow's company and part of Ownbey's Company, along with Meek, left for the place where he thought there was water.

In the meantime, the horsemen sent to confirm the location of water returned to the Lost Hollow encampment the morning of the 16th. They carried the good news that there was plenty of water and grass ahead. With great excitement, the remaining companies quickly prepared to make the move forward. However, the gathering of the cattle proved a chore so they were not able to leave until around 3 o'clock that afternoon. They traveled all night long, crossing the saddle between the Glass Buttes. and descended into a drainage of the headwaters of the Crooked River, passing Musser Reservoir. The trail parallels BLM Road #6540 for about five miles to where it crosses US Highway 20. After crossing the highway, it continues about ten miles out across Misery Flat, arriving at their new encampment on a small stream today called Buck Creek.

[1]Samuel Parker should have put the date "17th" for the rest of his entry and included the milage between Buck Creek and G I Ranch.

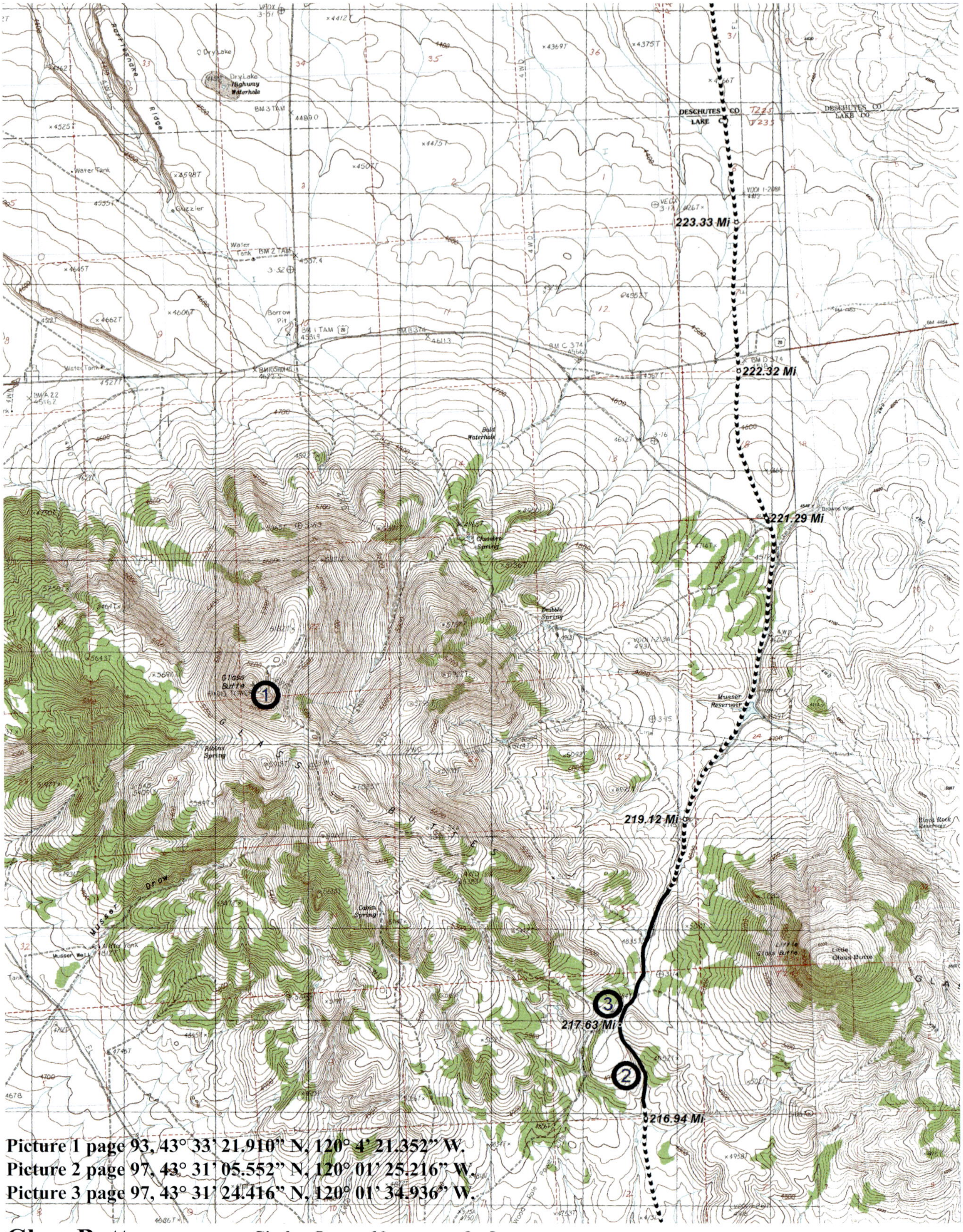

Picture 1 page 93, 43° 33' 21.910" N, 120° 4' 21.352" W.
Picture 2 page 97, 43° 31' 05.552" N, 120° 01' 25.216" W.
Picture 3 page 97, 43° 31' 24.416" N, 120° 01' 34.936" W.

Glass Butte (Modified)

Circles: Picture Number and Its Location.
Solid Line: Traces of the Trail. Verified on the ground by these authors.
Dashed Line: Projected Trail Location. Verified on the ground by these authors.

Traces of Wagon Swales. Through the center of the photo, traces are visible toward the author in the distance. Trail leading to the summit of the saddle between Glass Butte and Little Glass Butte. Location 2 viewed northwest on Glass Butte (Modified) map, p. 96.

Evidence of Wagon Swales Crossing the Summit of the Ridge This location is between Glass Butte and Little Glass Butte. Entering into the extreme headwaters of the Crooked River drainages. Location 3 viewed northeasterly on Glass Butte (Modified) map, p. 96.

BUCK CREEK TO THE G I RANCH AREA

Sept Wen 17: This Morning wee camped about sun rise and about 12 o clock started again and in about 6 miles struck a spring creek and camped near the head plenty of grass some Sage no Willow Mr Tetherow started this Morning and camped just Below us Weather fine. 6 miles. **Eli Cooley Diary**

17th: after takeing some refreshment we yoaked our teams at 2 oclock PM travleed 6 mi and encamped on sandy delightful stream running to the north west affording an abundence of fine grass no wood. **Jesse Harritt Diary**

[17 Should have read] Mssis But now betor. 198 wagons in company. 2299 loose cattle, oxen 811 head. All these cattle to get water and 1051 soles also consume a heap of water.*[missing the milage figure]* **Samuel Parker Diary**

Wed Sept 17th: We are now nearer or as near the spring from which we made the 30 mile stretch on the 10th inst. as at the camp after we had made it, and this too after lying in vexatious suspense, camped in a little, narrow, barren, rockey hollow among the mountains, with the dry plain some 40 or 50 miles in extent before us, with the delightful anticipation that we would be obliged to cross it before reaching water. Nor was this all; more than one family have shaken the last flour from their sack, and others could calculate to a certainty the day they would do likewise. Lay by today wishing to get a smaller company if possible, three large one being mixed together. **James Field Diary**

Thu Sept18th: Traveled about 11 miles in a northwesterly direction, striking a smart creek running in the same direction and camping upon it. This creek has no brush upon its banks, which was the reason for its being overlooked when they searched the country for water. It is evident that Meek's knowledge of the country has rather failed him here, since it is actually a shorter drive from the spring we left on the 10th inst. to the head of the branch we camped upon yesterday than it is from the 10th to the 11th, and apparently a better road. Had we taken that road we would be advanced now at least 80 miles on our journey, besides being saved the trying suspense of remaining in a miserable encampment several days, with no prospect of water ahead for 40 or 50 miles. **James Field Diary**

After resting for a few hours, the companies advanced about six miles farther, which brought them to some very large springs. These were the headwaters of the South Fork of the Crooked River.[1] Here was an abundant supply of water and a great deal of grass which made the ideal location to camp.

[1] This is exactly where Stephen Meek had intended to guide the wagon train in the first place when they were near the mouth of Silver Creek. On Thursday, September 11th, James Field writes, *"...when he came to the marshy lake spoken of last Sunday, the company refused to follow him if he made the circuit necessary to get around it upon Crooked river again so he struck off in a westerly direction in order to get upon the main Deschutes River."* Had they followed up Silver Creek, they would have been following an old historic Indian trail and would have had water for a large part of the way to the large springs.

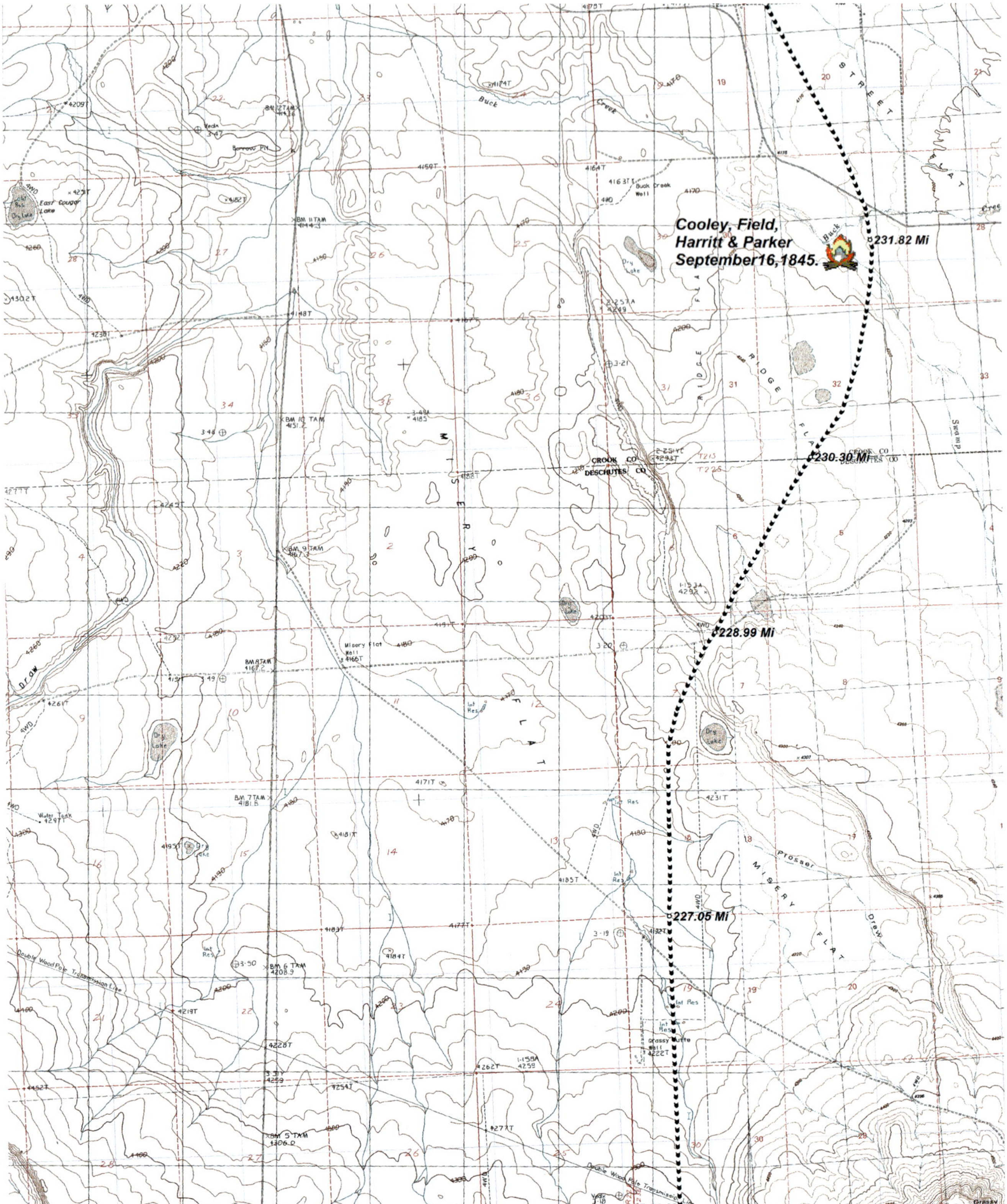

Misery Flat (Modified)

Circles: Picture Number and Its Location.
Solid Line: Traces of the Trail. Verified on the ground by these authors.
Dashed Line: Projected Trail Location. Verified on the ground by these authors.

G I Ranch Area. The desert plains that the wagon train traveled across to reach the large springs. The trail seen to the left of the traveled road is not the Meek Cutoff trail. Location 1 viewed northerly on G I Ranch (Modified) map, p. 100 and p. 104.

Headwaters of the South Fork of the Crooked River. Location 2 viewed northerly on G I Ranch (Modified) map, p. 100.

Samuel Parker's Company was one of those companies advancing to this large spring. Here Samuel Parker made an accounting of the entire wagon train. This accounting has been grossly misinterpreted by many *"...198 wagons in Company. 2299 loose Cattle, oxen 811 head all these Cattle to git water and 1051 Soles [people] also consume a heap of water."* Samuel Parker's accounting has now placed the entire wagon train congregating in the vicinity of the large springs, now referred to as the G I Ranch.

At this time, these authors discovered a discrepancy in the timeline of Samuel Parker's diary. After arriving at Lost Hollow on September 11th and noting it in his diary, he makes no further entries until September 16th upon leaving the Lost Hollow encampment. His diary entry on September 16th states that they traveled 30 miles from 3 o'clock in the afternoon to sunrise on the 17th. Then his diary entry for September 17th indicates that they traveled 11 miles for a total of 41 miles in the two days leaving no time for man or beast to rest or eat before reaching the next encampment. The only water source in that general area was Jaggi Spring. The actual distance measured is 48 miles. In any respect, such a claim would place Samuel Parker's Company traveling nonstop for a total of 48 miles in actually a little more than 24 hours considering they did not leave Lost Hollow until 3 pm on the 16th. If that actually occurred, it would place Samuel Parker's Company a minimum of 15 miles past Stephen Meek, Solomon Tetherow's Company, and the rest of the wagon train. Obviously, this is highly unlikely as Samuel Parker was a total stranger and unfamiliar with this country.

Samuel Parker's diary entry of September 16th brought his company to the Buck Creek encampment which is the same location the remaining diarists mention in their entries. After careful scrutiny of Samuel Parker's diary timeline between September 11th and September 26th, it became apparent to these authors that in Samuel Parker's entry on September 16th he writes the mileage for the day and then, beginning with a new line, he continues writing several other statements. It is after the mileage entry and at the beginning of the new line that Samuel Parker inadvertently left the date of September 17th out of the entry as his daily entries generally begin with a new line and most end with the mileage amount for that day. On September 17th his company does make the six mile advancement to the

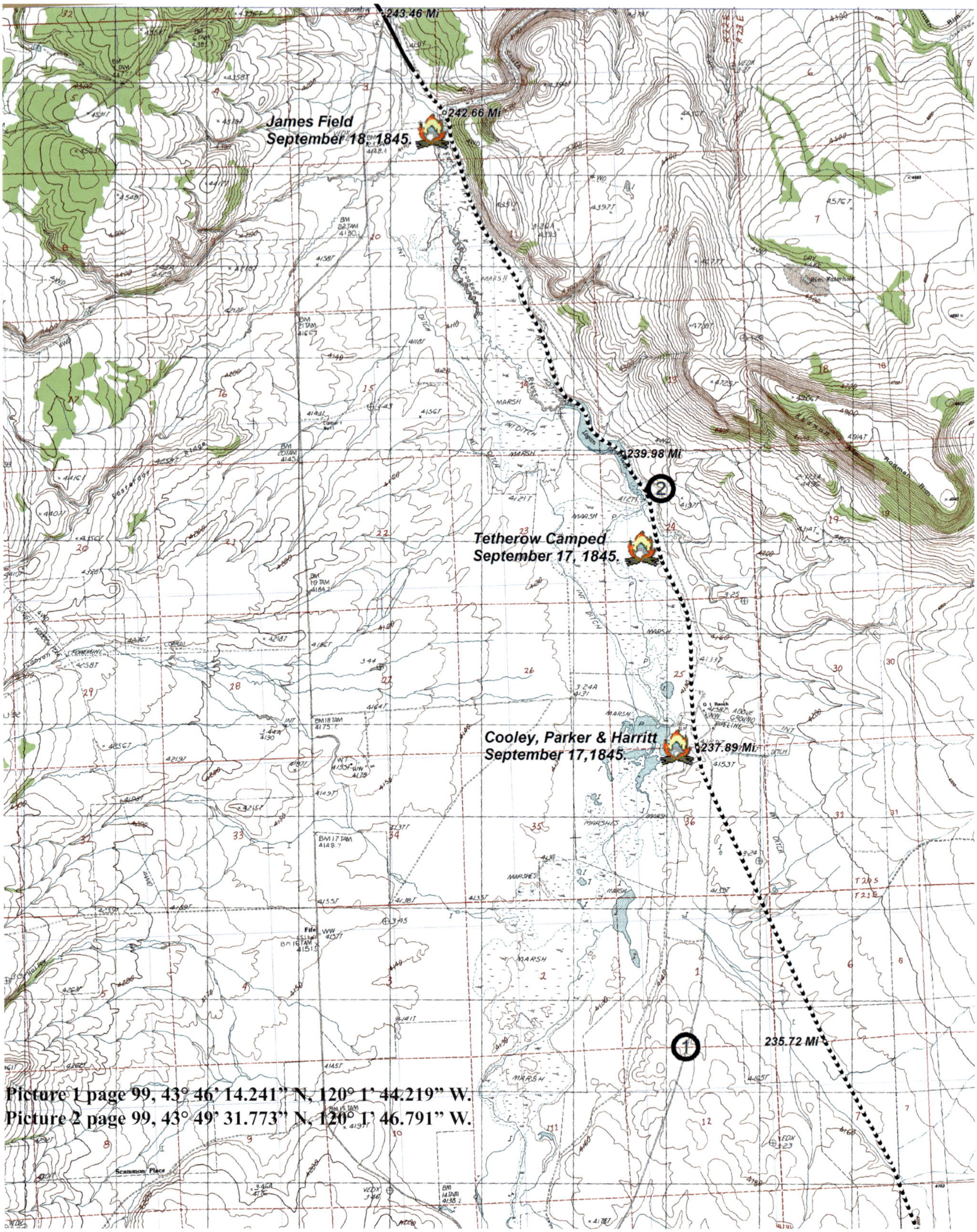

G I Ranch (Modified)

Circles: Picture Number and Its Location.
Solid Line: Traces of the Trail. Verified on the ground by these authors.
Dashed Line: Projected Trail Location. Verified on the ground by these authors.

large springs at the G I Ranch location as was mentioned by the other diarists. We must be reminded that it was Samuel Parker himself, who makes the important accounting of the entire wagon train now located at the large springs. He was only able to do so if on the 17th his company was with the others at the springs. Consequently, the following day September 18th, as the wagon train advanced to the next encampment at Jaggi Spring, Samuel Parker recorded it as September 17th. This now makes the date wrong for each additional day's diary entry until September 26th.

The realization of this date numbering mistake for his diary entries helps to clarify Samuel Parker's odd accounting of his travel timeline between September 24th and September 26th. In this time frame, it appears he may have discovered his previous date error but perhaps didn't know how far back the error originated. Therefore, by making extremely vague diary entries for September 24th and September 25th, he was attempting to make up the day he had previously lost. Please note, these authors have placed the correct day in brackets following his date for each given day between September 17th through September 25th.

Now recommencing at the springs, historically these large springs at the G I Ranch location have been a very prominent destination where old historic Indian trails converge from all across this region.[1] Stephen Meek had been in this area previously when he was with the Bonneville Expedition of 1834 while searching for beaver to trap and exploring the country as they progressed.[2] They had entered this region on one of the old Indian trails that came in from the northeast. (See map page 104).

The proper correlation of the diaries actually gives a clear picture of what transpired beyond the springs at the G I Ranch location. On September 15th, James Field writes that Stephen Meek left the Lost Hollow encampment with Solomon Tetherow and about 28 wagons. That puts Stephen Meek in the forefront at the head of the wagon train where the guide is supposed to be. Sadly, Samuel Hancock, who was a member of the wagon train of 1845, writes in 1860 in his reminiscences that he had hidden Stephen Meek in his wagon for the remainder of the journey. The problem with this claim is that Samuel Hancock evidently forgot what position he held on the wagon train. The "Organizational Journal" of the Savannah Oregon Emigrating Society lists Samuel Hancock, a single man, as a cattle drover. Consequently, Samuel Hancock having a wagon is quite questionable since his job was herding cattle and he would be riding a horse as opposed to guiding a wagon pulled by oxen.

Eli Cooley describes arriving at a spring creek (South Fork of the Crooked River), and camping near the head of it. At this time, he writes where Solomon Tetherow and his company are located. On the evening of September 17th, his diary entry contains this statement: *"Mr. Tetherow started this Morning and camped just Below us."* Though he does not say how far below them Tetherow is located, it certainly appears to be at least within sight. Two days later on September 19th, after they had traveled about 30 miles and reached the confluence of the North Fork of the Crooked River and the main stem of the Crooked River, Eli Cooley makes another important entry in his diary. His entry contains this statement, *"Tetherow just below on the creek."*[3] A published article written by Solomon Tetherow also shows that he was 30 miles north of the G I Ranch on the Crooked River.[4]

---

[1] Gale Ontko, *Thunder Over The Ochoco: The Gathering Storm Volume I* (Bend, Oregon:Maverick Publications, 1993), 44.

[2] The Bonneville Expedition left the South Fork of the John Day River, then most likely followed what is called Sunflower Creek in nearly a westerly direction to its headwaters. They crossed over a low summit into a stream now named Beaver Creek. This was a distance of about 10 miles. Once they arrived on Beaver Creek, they were in the headwaters of the Crooked River drainage. They continued trapping, following these streams in a southwesterly course. They were keeping to the old historic Indian trails as those were the highways of that time. Their advance eventually brought them to the large springs which was on the headwaters of the South Fork of the Crooked River. They had covered some 40 miles since leaving the South Fork of the John Day River. Upon leaving the springs, they again followed an old historic Indian trail toward the Silver Creek country. This was the section of trail that Stephen Meek had originally intended to guide the wagon train.

[3] Today, we call Crooked River a river. What Eli Cooley was accustomed to calling rivers had a size such as the Snake River. Crooked River was just a creek to Cooley, as well as to most of these emigrants. The diarists all called Crooked River a creek.

[4] Solomon Tetherow, *Oregon Spectator,* Thursday, March 18, 1847, p. 3 column 2+.

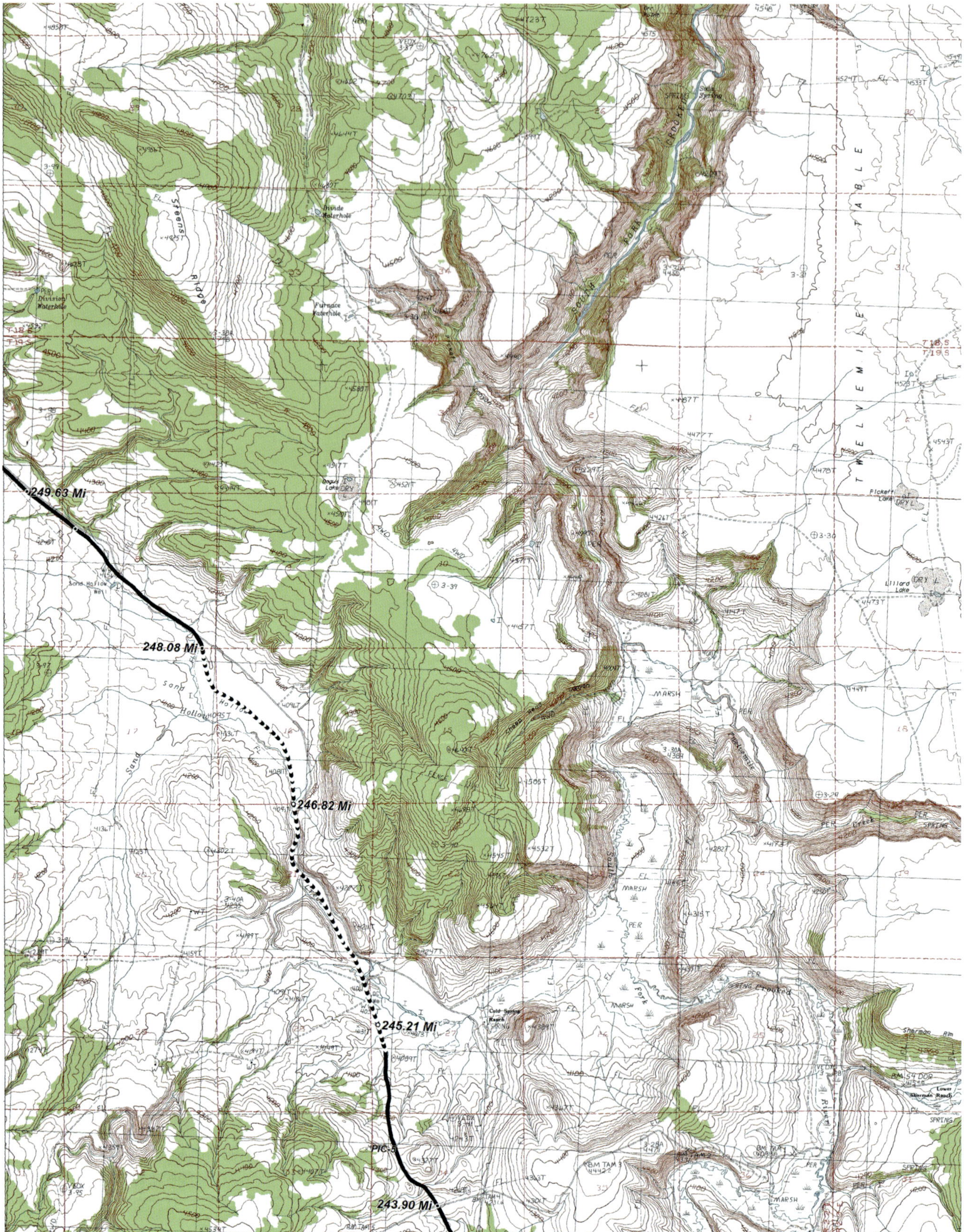

Sand Hollow

Circles: Picture Number and Its Location.
Solid Line: Traces of the Trail. Verified on the ground by these authors.
Dashed Line: Projected Trail Location. Verified on the ground by these authors.

The springs at the G I Ranch location are a site of confusion and misunderstanding that has plagued many writers as they interpret the story along the Meek Cutoff Wagon Trail. It has been purported in these interpretations that the wagon train split at this location. The writers of these interpretations believe that Solomon Tetherow left the springs at the G I Ranch location winding his way through the mountainous region west of the springs and crossing the desert waste lands before reaching the Deschutes River near the area of where Bend, Oregon, is located today. There he turned north crossing the deep gorge of the Crooked River and continued north across the Agency Plains arriving at a spring referred to as Sagebrush Springs. The actual spring where the wagon train congregated on September 26th is called Porter Springs and is located near the northern limits of Gateway, Oregon, not Sagebrush Springs as speculated by many writers and researchers. It indeed would have been a miracle for Tetherow to turn around and go back 30 miles in the direction he had just come from in order to get back to the G I Ranch to split off from the rest of the emigrants. His company would have had to cover 145 miles more, in the next nine days, averaging about 23 miles each day. This would have been over twice as fast as their daily travel had been for the past 1500 miles. They would then arrive and rejoin the rest of the wagon train on the exact same day at Porter Springs. These authors know that Tetherow was at this encampment at Porter Springs because of the accounting Jesse Harritt makes of the group at this location. His diary entry for September 26th includes this statement: *"...encamped at a good spring in company with about 200 wagons."* This is within two wagons of the accounting that Parker did of the wagons at the G I Ranch.

Therefore, based on the facts clearly presented in Eli Cooley's and Jesse Harritt's diaries and Tetherow's own published statements, these authors believe there was not a split in the Meek Wagon Train of 1845. This subject will be revisited in much more detail later in a separate chapter.

SOUTH FORK OF THE CROOKED RIVER. Looking down on the meandering marshy South Fork of the Crooked River as it continues to the north from the springs at the G I Ranch.

As the wagon train left the large springs and swampy ground, the emigrants followed the South Fork of the Crooked River northerly for nearly five miles to the river's only crossing where there was solid ground. At this point, the river turns to the northeast entering a winding crooked gorge or canyon. At this crossing, another historic Indian trail left the river in a northwesterly direction. It was at this crossing or very near here that Solomon Tetherow was referring to when he wrote the following response to a previous newspaper article, "New Roads to Oregon.-No.1" in the *Oregon Spectator* dated Thursday, March 18, 1847. The following is his letter exactly as it was printed, including parenthesis and italics:

For the Oregon Spectator

Polk County, Oregon, February 28, 1847.

Mr. Editor. In the second number of the Spectator, an article headed "New Roads to Oregon, No. 1, signed 'Oregonian,' attracted my attention. But it is not my intention

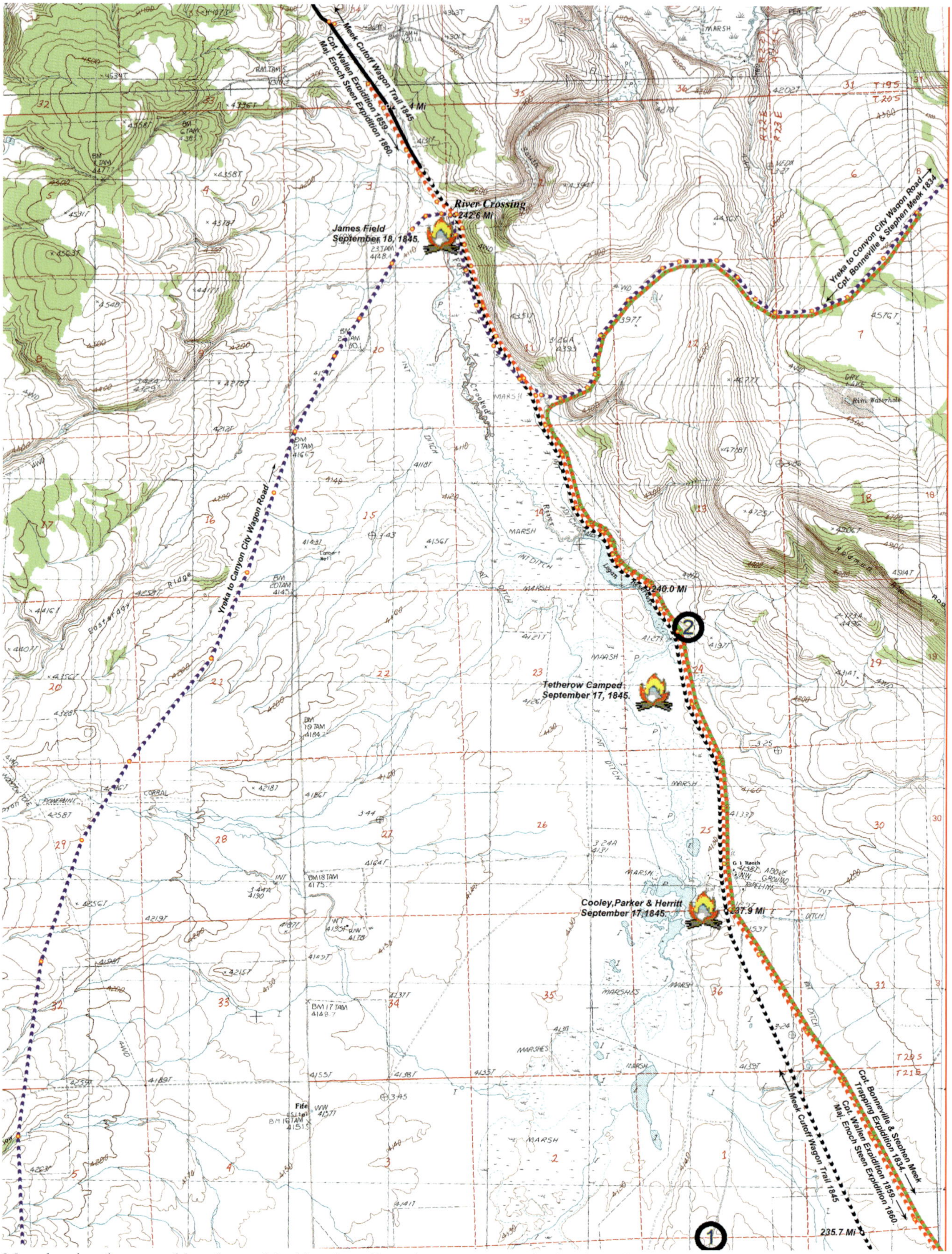

Map showing the general locations of the historic trails as they converge at the South Fork of Crooked River Crossing. Location 2 is the headwaters of the South Fork of the Crooked River as shown in the top right photo on page 99.

to enter into any review of the article in question, or a discussion of the subject of new roads, but to correct the writer in a mere matter of fact.

He states of the party piloted by Mr. Meek, that "After having progressed in a northerly course during the space of three or four days, they came in contact with some *friendly Indians*, who endeavored to dissuade them from the further prosecution of their northerly direction, and to persuade them to take a westerly course. These Indians assured them that it was only five days ride to *Mr. Lee's house,*" (Salem.) The truth is, four days after leaving a large rush marsh, which this writer pleases to designate "Silver Lake," and *two days* after taking a northerly direction, an *Indian* came to us, who pointed out the course to *Mr. Perkins's house,* (Dalles,) to which he said it was five days journey, and so far from refusing to follow the advice of the Indian, at my request he was employed by Mr. Meek to pilot us to Crooked River, which he did for a blanket. But of Mr. Lee's house, or Salem, the Indian said nothing and probably knew as little, as this writer appears to understand the subject on which he pretends to edify the public.

"The trail" seen by Mr. Meeks party led in a southwesterly direction, until it crossed the river DeChutes, where turned directly south, and probably leads by the Clamet Lake to California-- at least, I feel satisfied it does not lead to Salem or the Willamette Valley. This writer further says, "They (the Indians,) apparently manifested the strongest solicitude for the welfare of the company," etc. This, Mr. Editor, is really too bad. That a Digger, (for the "friendly Indians" were nothing else) would express or even feel solicitude for anything but to eat or to steal, could only be supposed by a man who would prefer the evidence of such beings to the statements of an intelligent officer of the U. S. Army.

I too, am in favor of bettering the road to Oregon, and have given better evidence of the fact, then by stringing together disjointed assertions and inapt quotations under one fictitious name, and answering them under another. Having traveled with Mr. Meek over the ground which this gentleman thinks will better the route to this country, I thought it my duty to set him right before the public.

Very respectfully,
Solomon Tetherow.[1]

Solomon Tetherow's letter contains several important facts which these authors would like to expound upon.

First, let us backtrack Solomon Tetherow's four-day journey from the crossing area on the South Fork of the Crooked River. Retracing two days would place Solomon Tetherow in Lost Hollow where the diary entries placed him on September 13th and 14th. Then backtracking an additional two days making the four days Solomon Tetherow was referring to, these authors are able to determine he was at the Silver Creek encampment on either September 10th or 11th. This site today is located near what is called the Double O Ranch headquarters. The location Solomon Tetherow referred to as the large rush marsh is the area where Silver Creek empties into Harney Lake. Solomon Tetherow called this area Silver Lake. The Silver Lake of today is actually up the Silver Creek drainage about 10 miles in a northwesterly direction.

Second, Solomon Tetherow states the fact that an Indian, not Indians, came to them describing a course toward The Dalles and Mr. Perkins' house indicating it was about a five-day journey.

Third, Solomon Tetherow requested Stephen Meek to employ the Indian to pilot them across the country to the Crooked River and paid for his services with a blanket.

[1]Solomon Tetherow, *Oregon Spectator,* Thursday, March 18, 1847, p. 3 column 2+.

Fourth, Solomon Tetherow confirmed the fact that both he and Stephen Meek were together when they arrived at the main stem of the Crooked River and paid the Indian his blanket.

Fifth, Solomon Tetherow says the Meek Wagon Train saw a prominent trail leading in a south-westerly direction. When the men were searching for water west of Lost Hollow, they no doubt crossed this trail as it made its way southwesterly. They may have even followed this trail for some distance as it crossed the desert about 10 to 12 miles due west of Lost Hollow. The Meek Wagon Train was fully aware of its location and the direction it was heading. This trail had been used by Indians and explorers for many years and continued to be used many years later. By 1875 this trail was being used as a stage line and was called the "Yreka to Canyon City Road" and intersected the Meek Cutoff Wagon Trail at the crossing of the South Fork of the Crooked River. From there, it continued northeasterly toward the South Fork of the John Day River, eventually making its way to Canyon City. Early survey field notes and maps of this area show the trail through the Hampton area to the location of Stauffer, which had became a stage stop and later a U.S. Post Office. The trail continues crossing the vast desert region heading toward Christmas Valley and on to Yreka, California.

Sixth, Solomon Tetherow was very much in favor of bettering the road to Oregon, but thoroughly disgusted with the inconsistencies writers had written in the *Oregon Spectator*.

Seventh, perhaps the most important fact was that Solomon Tetherow was confirming that he had personally accompanied Stephen Meek over the ground through this country and that Stephen Meek never abandoned the wagon train as other writers have written, nor was he hidden in anyone's wagon.

Rejoining the wagon train upon leaving the springs on September 18th, near the crossing of the South Fork of the Crooked River, they met an Indian along the trail who Solomon Tetherow speaks of in his letter. The Indian was hired to guide them by way of an alternate route. Using this trail would save many toilsome miles and be a more direct route, rather than following the winding course of the South Fork of the Crooked River to the main stem of the river. Stephen Meek and the entire wagon train, including Solomon Tetherow, turned to the northwest following the Indian guide across the country to the main stem of the Crooked River. The knowledge the Indian had pertaining to this new trail proved to be very valuable as most of it would make a good road.

In 1859 the U.S. Government issued an order to find a suitable wagon road through central Oregon. Henry D. Wallen, Captain of the 4th Infantry of the U.S. Calvary, was in command of this road location expedition. Captain Wallen's Expedition was basically retracing in reverse a great deal of the Meek Cutoff Wagon Trail through this vicinity. A map of his expedition shows quite clearly the path he took. Comparing the two routes, one can easily see the locations where they both coincide. Captain Wallen's Expedition began following this old historic Indian trail as it left the confluence of the North Fork of the Crooked River and the main stem of the Crooked River. The trail, heavily used by now, led directly to the large springs at the G I Ranch location on the South Fork of the Crooked River and was the same trail that Stephen Meek followed in 1845 as he left the springs at the G I Ranch location. Incidentally, Captain Wallen's Expedition, upon leaving this area, continued to follow the Indian trail that led southeasterly through the Silver Creek country passing by what he shows as being Pilot Butte, later named Squaw Butte. He continued on to Silver Lake, then to the mouth of Silver Creek at Harney Lake. This put Captain Wallen's Expedition back on the wagon ruts of the Meek Cutoff Trail. Capt. Wallen's Expedition had followed precisely the same trail Stephen Meek had previously described and had been planning to follow prior to the fight that eventually changed the course and pressured Meek into heading in a westerly direction.

Ascending the Slope Just Before Steens Lake. Traces of the trail are visible through the sagebrush growth. Trail runs from bottom left center up to the author. Location 1 viewed northwesterly on Gerry Mountain map, p. 108.

Dry Steens Lake Bed. Traces of the Meek Cutoff Wagon Trail through center of photo leaving the dry Steens Lake which is in the background. Trail crosses the lake near the center of the photo. Location 2 viewed southeasterly on Gerry Mountain map, p. 108.

G I RANCH TO JAGGI SPRING ON CAMP CREEK

Sept Thu 18: Weather fine to day road Tollerable good come down the creek north west about 3 miles and crossed it and in about 11 miles further struck a hollow and come Down about 1 mile further and camped at a Spring Plenty of grass and Some Wood on the Bluff here. 15 miles. **Eli Cooley Diary**

18th: 3 ms down we crassed over to the west side and after a travle of 12 ms we encamped at a good spring found good grass and some ceder timber. **Jesse Harritt Diary**

17 [18th]: Went to a Creek. 11 mi. **Samuel Parker Diary**

Upon leaving the South Fork of the Crooked River, the trail turns northwesterly, somewhat paralleling the "SE G I" County Road for about eight miles. Traces of wagon swales are visible today in many places throughout this area. In 1860, the U. S. Government commissioned Major Enoch Steen to make an expedition searching for a suitable route through central Oregon. This route was to be used as a military road, as well as a wagon road to haul freight. Major Enoch Steen's Expedition followed on the heels of Captain Wallen's Expedition through this immediate area. Both Major Steen and Captain Wallen traveled the same trail the Indian guide and Stephen Meek used in leading the 1845 wagon train. This historic Indian trail was now becoming a major highway of the day.

The trail traverses a portion of what is referred to as Steens Ridge and through a dry lake bed called Steens Lake, named after Major Enoch Steen. As it passes through the dry flat bottom of Steens Lake, it abruptly descends down a portion of the Steens Ridge into the drainage called Camp Creek. The Meek Wagon Train took quite a direct and steep course down the hill to the bottom and out into the valley floor of Camp Creek. Traces of these wagon swales are quite visible and have become a popular reference used by most writers regarding the Meek Cutoff Wagon Trail today. Careful study of this steep slope has revealed additional wagon swales a very short distance to the west of the main trail. These authors followed those swales traversing up a small finger ridge and across a side slope to the summit of the ridge, terminating at the

Descending Steens Ridge Into Camp Creek. Wagon swales are visible as the trail descends the steep hill. Location 3 viewed southeasterly on Gerry Mountain map, p. 108.

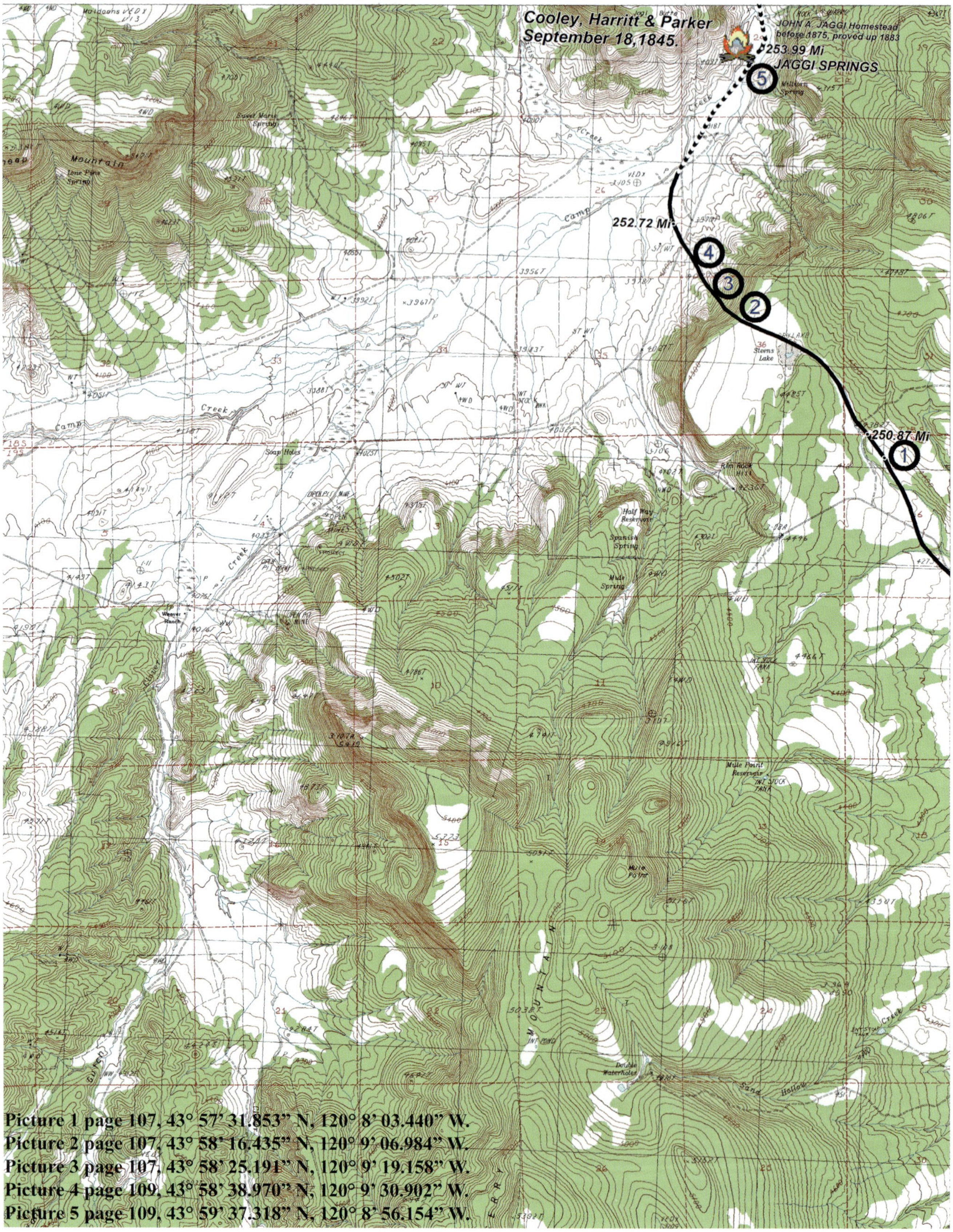

Circles: Picture Number and Its Location.
Solid Line: Traces of the Trail. Verified on the ground by these authors.
Dashed Line: Projected Trail Location. Verified on the ground by these authors.

Gerry Mountain

EVIDENCE OF WAGON SWALES ENTERING CAMP CREEK VALLEY FROM STEENS RIDGE. Vehicle parked on Camp Creek Road. Location 4 viewed northwesterly on Gerry Mountain map, p. 108.

Meek Cutoff Wagon Trail. Clearly the additional set of wagon swales are a product of graded construction. Both Major Steen and Captain Wallen's Expedition were travelling the Meek Cutoff in reverse. They each had wagons and equipment along. Therefore, it can only be assumed they improved this stretch of road to allow their wagons to be pulled up the steep hill to the top of the ridge and across Steens Lake.

Once the trail descends Steens Ridge on to the floor of the Camp Creek drainage, it leads about a mile down Camp Creek to a good spring where the companies camped. This spring was named Jaggi Spring after a homesteader, John Jaggi.

JAGGI SPRING TO CROOKED RIVER

Sept Fri 19: road Tallorable good today Weather fine Come down the Branch about 2 mile and Turned to the left up the hill and in about 5 mile struck the same creek wee crossed yesterday and Traveled Down it at about 3 mile and Camped plenty of grass and some Willow Tetherow just below on the creek the corse to the creek is about North west then down the creek this far about west Some Ind to see us to nite. 10 miles. **Eli Cooley Diary**

Fri Sept 19th: Went about 20 miles, road tolerably rough much of the way, camping upon a stream in a deep narrow glen resembling the Malheur much in character and which we believe to be Lohum's fork of the Deschutes or Falls River. **James Field Diary**

18 [19th]: Over hills and rock all day Came down a Steep hill got water. 15 mi. **Samuel Parker Diary**

19th: made an advance of 12 ms and encamped again on sandy found grass and a fiew small willows. **Jesse Harritt Diary**

JAGGI SPRING ON CAMP CREEK. Eli Cooley writes on Thursday, September 18th, *"...struck a hollow [Camp Creek Drainage] and come Down about 1 mile further and camped at a spring."* Jaggi Spring runs out of the slope in the lower right-hand corner of the meadow. Location 5 viewed northwesterly on Gerry Mountain map, p. 108.

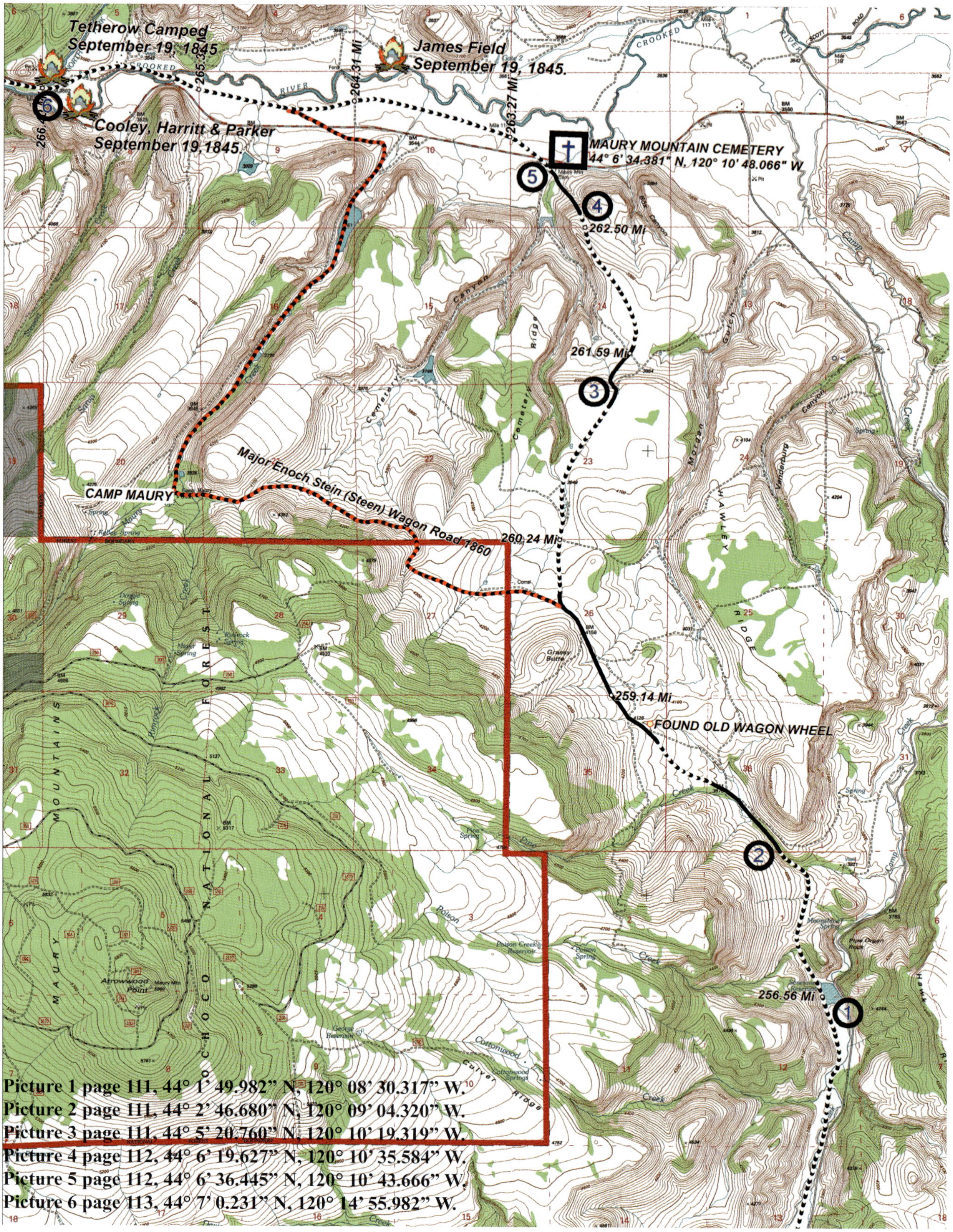

Arrowwood Point

Circles: Picture Number and Its Location.
Solid Line: Traces of the Trail. Verified on the ground by these authors.
Dashed Line: Projected Trail Location. Verified on the ground by these authors.

Mouth of Poison Creek. The trail leaves Camp Creek to the left making its way a short distance northwesterly up Poison Creek and through the low saddle depicted by the arrows. Location 1 viewed northwesterly on Arrowwood Point map, p. 110.

Heavily Eroded Portion of the Trail in the Pine Creek Drainage. Location 2 viewed northwesterly on Arrowwood Point map, p. 110.

The trail continued down Camp Creek for about 2½ miles to where it turned to the left, up Poison Creek a short distance before turning northerly, crossing a low saddle on a finger ridge, entering the Pine Creek drainage. Here the trail follows up the narrow bottom of the drainage for about 650 feet where it was necessary to cross the small meandering stream of Pine Creek several times. At this location, extensive erosion has taken place over the past 169 years. Water has eroded the wagon swales leaving a long straight gully 10 to 12 feet deep where the trail was once located.[1]

From the stream of Pine Creek, the traces of the trail lead in a northwesterly direction across gently rolling hills and bench land with only a small amount of rock. Just north of Grassy Butte, these authors found traces of a junction where another trail leads more westerly while the Meek Cutoff Wagon Trail goes north and leaves the bench.[2]

Descending the Bench. Traces of the wagon swales are visible with rocks thrown aside. Vehicle is located on a jeep road. Location 3 viewed easterly on Arrowwood Point map, p. 110.

[1]Later, Wallen's Expedition and Steens Military Road Expedition used this stretch of road. This would explain the excessive erosion.

[2]When Captain Henry D. Wallen in 1859, and Major Enoch Steen in 1860, came to the Crooked River from the north on their military road expeditions and left Crooked River heading south, they deviated from the Meek Cutoff Wagon Trail to develop a better graded route more conducive to the uphill pull on their wagons. Leaving Crooked River, they followed up what is now called Maury Creek, until they reached a spring of good water near the edge of timbered mountainous country. Here at this location, a camp was established and later was called Camp Maury. From the camp site, the expedition route skirted the timbered region in an easterly direction to where it joined the Meek Cutoff Wagon Trail at Grassy Butte.

Wagon Swales are Visible Descending into Crooked River
The Maury Mountain Cemetery is visible just left of top center in the photo. Location 4 viewed northwesterly on Arrowwood Point map, p. 110.

Remains of an Old Wagon Wheel. This wheel is probably from some homesteader. These authors found this a short distance from the trail between Pine Creek and Grassy Butte.

Descending the last bench before arriving in the valley, traces of the wagon ruts can clearly be seen from the present Crook County Highway 380. On the photo below, the trail leads from the top left to the right down the slope. Notice the fence line that cattle have followed which runs from the top right down to the left. Both lines create an X. Once the trail reached the valley floor, it passed the Maury Mountain Cemetery which was established around 1885. The companies camped between the location of the present-day Cemetery and the confluence of the North Fork of the Crooked River and the main stem of the Crooked River.

Evening Sunlight Highlights the Wagon Swales and a Cattle Trail
Location 5 viewed southeasterly on Arrowwood Point map, p. 110.

DOWN CROOKED RIVER

Sept Sat 20: Bad road to day Weather fine Traveled down the creek to day and Generally in the Bottoms of it some scattering seder and pine Timber on the hills they is plenty of grass and Willow to camp any whare on the creek Camped on the creek plenty of grass and wood here. 12 miles. **Eli Cooley Diary** *[Camped near Horse Heaven Creek on Crooked River.]*

Sat Sept 20th: Went about 8 miles, encamping upon the same stream mentioned yesterday, down which we followed all day, frequently crossing it, and at one narrow pass we were obliged to follow the bed of the river for nearly a fourth of a mile. **James Field Diary** *[Camped on Crooked River.]*

19 [20th]: Down the Creek some times in and some times out. 7 mi. **Samuel Parker Diary** *[Camped near Horse Heaven Creek on Crooked River.]*

20th: continued down the creek passed through several narrow evenus where the mountains closed in on both sides where we ware compelled to follow down the channel of the for several hundred yards in water up to our waggon beds continued to follow its meanders crassing its channel a number of times after an advance of 13 ms we encamped found grass and willows. **Jesse Harritt Diary** *[Camped near Horse Heaven Creek on Crooked River.]*

Sept Sun 21: Still Bad road Weather fine Traveled down the creek to day and have crossed it several times to day and have Camped on it plenty of grass and Willow here and all along the creek still Seder and pine on the hills West 12 miles. **Eli Cooley Diary** *[Camped at Mouth of Bear Creek on Crooked River.]*

Sun Sept 21st: Went about 16 miles today, still keeping down the river, occasionally cutting across the lowest points of the bluffs and camping upon it again. The hills along the stream on either hand are in many places covered with tall pines. **James Field Diary** *[Camped near the mouth of Sanford Creek on Crooked River.]*

20 [21st]: Down same creek in and out. 10 mi. **Samuel Parker Diary** *[Camped at Mouth of Bear Creek on Crooked River.]*

21st: down the creek 10 ms had bad road we encamped found grass willow and ceder timber in abundence. **Jesse Harritt Diary** *[Camped at Mouth of Bear Creek on Crooked River.]*

Mon Sept 22nd: Went about 7 miles, keeping still down along the river, which has to be crossed every mile or two and sometimes two or three times to the mile. Camped at the foot of a tremendous hill which it is necessary to ascend, and which when we first came in sight of appeared to be strung with wagons from the bottom to the top, several companies being engaged in the ascent at the same time. **James Field Diary**

It is common knowledge that there was a great deal of Indian activity along the Crooked River, so it is only fair to assume that the trail the Indian guided the wagon train over from the G I Ranch vicinity to the main stem of the Crooked River continued on down along the river. While this foot trail used by the Indians would have been considered a good road to them, it certainly would not have been conducive to wagon travel.

Leaving this encampment the following day, all the diarists tell of entering a narrow gorge and traveling down the middle of the river for several hundred yards. This is actually the Narrows on Crooked River about one mile west of the Les Schwab Ranch headquarters in Crook County. Obviously, as the diarists indicate, as they continued on they had to cross the river on many occasions.

Crooked River Entering the Narrows of the Canyon. This is just west of the confluence of the North Fork of the Crooked River and the Main Stem of the Crooked River. Location 6 viewed westerly on Arrowwood Point map, p. 110.

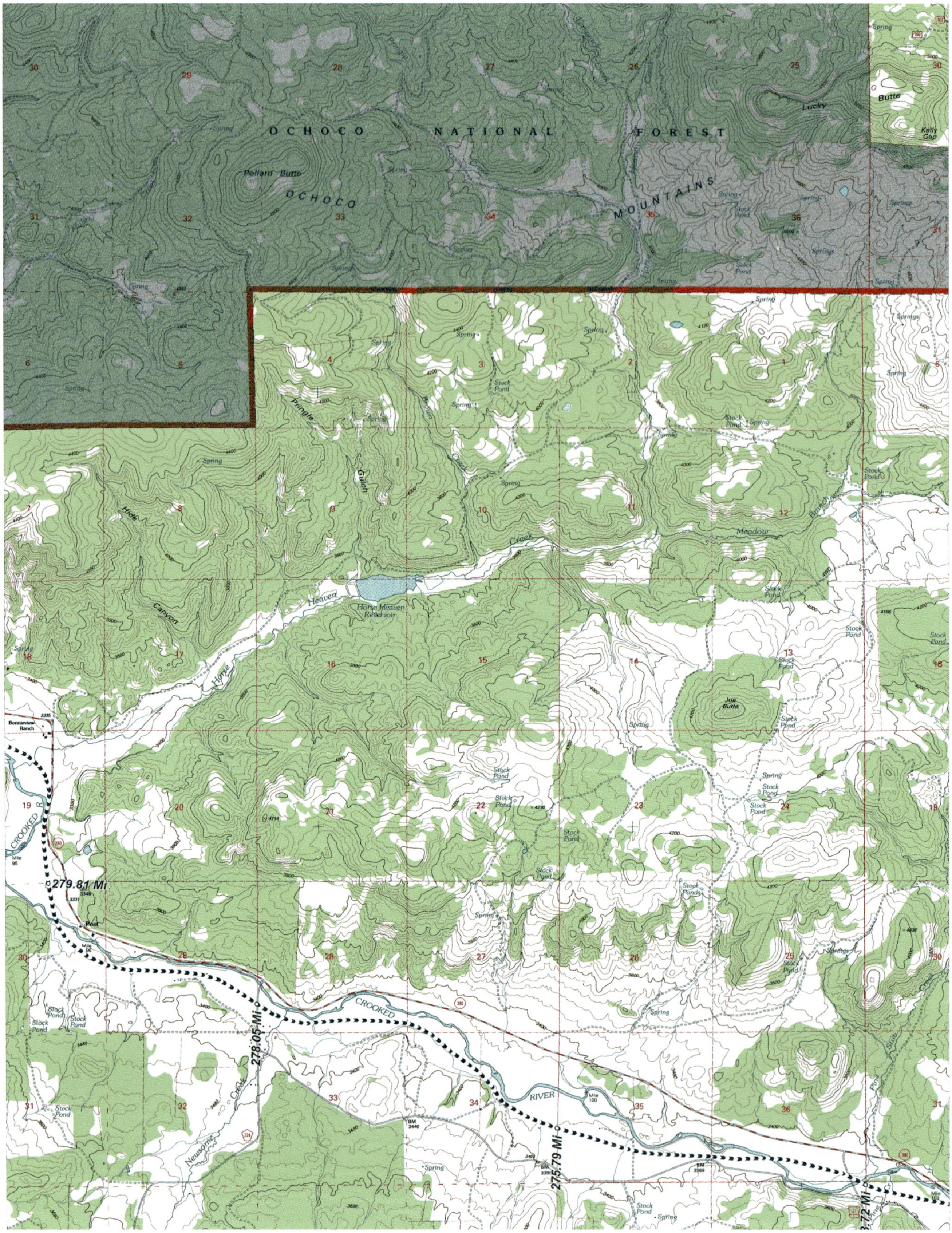

Circles: Picture Number and Its Location.
Solid Line: Traces of the Trail. Verified on the ground by these authors.
Dashed Line: Projected Trail Location. Verified on the ground by these authors.

Post

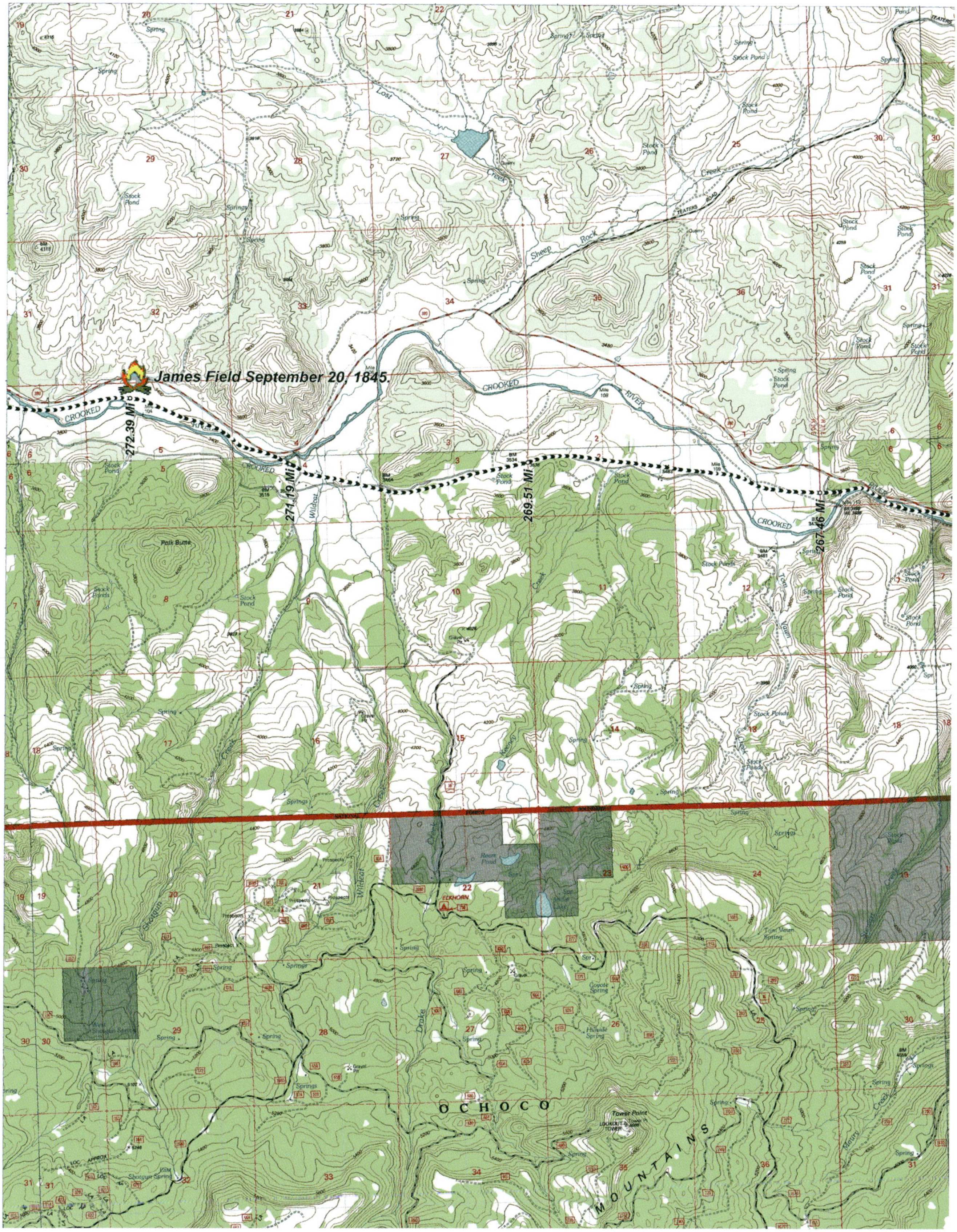

Circles: Picture Number and Its Location.
Solid Line: Traces of the Trail. Verified on the ground by these authors.
Dashed Line: Projected Trail Location. Verified on the ground by these authors.

Drake Butte (Modified)

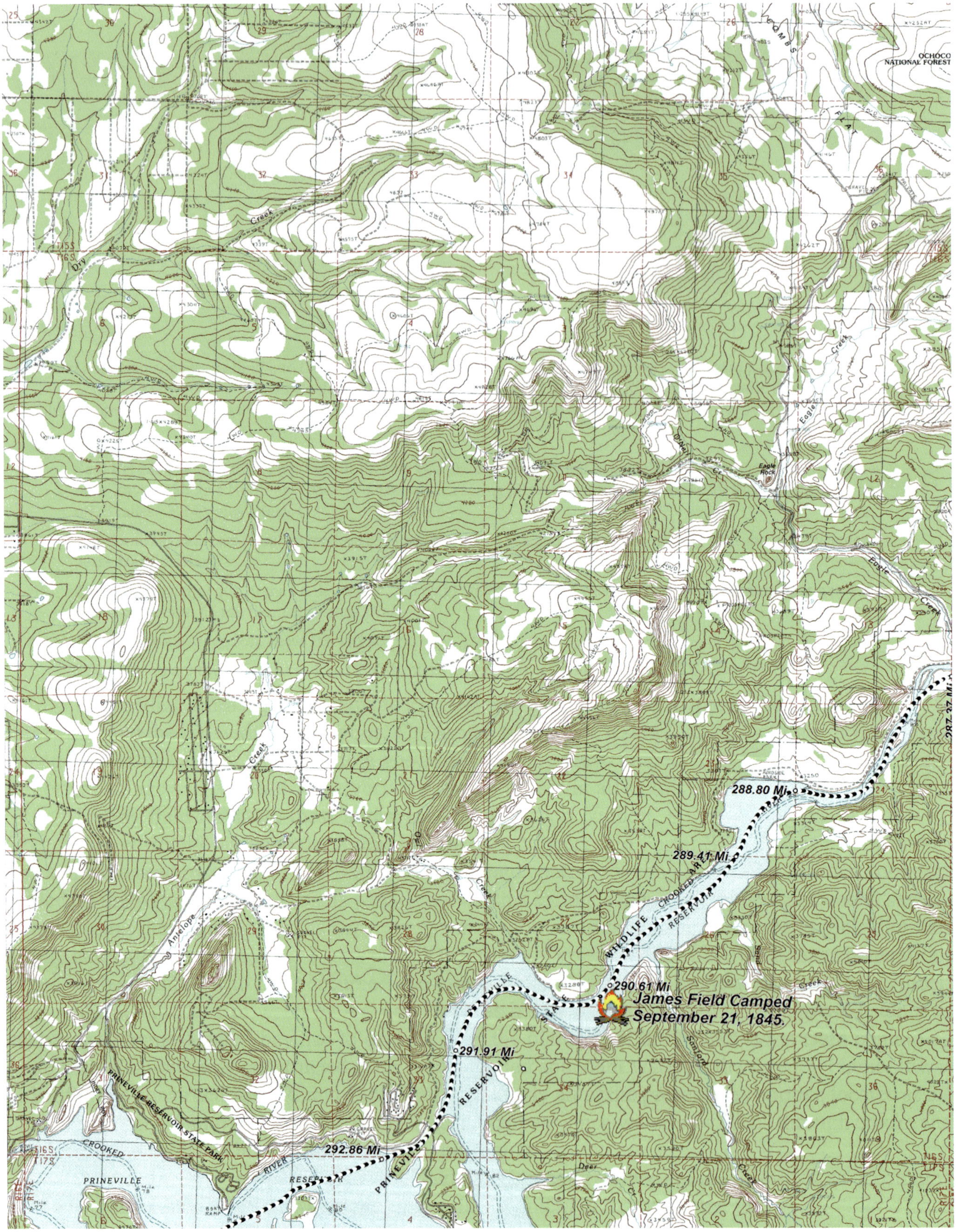

Circles: Picture Number and Its Location.
Solid Line: Traces of the Trail. Verified on the ground by these authors.
Dashed Line: Projected Trail Location. Verified on the ground by these authors.

Eagle Rock

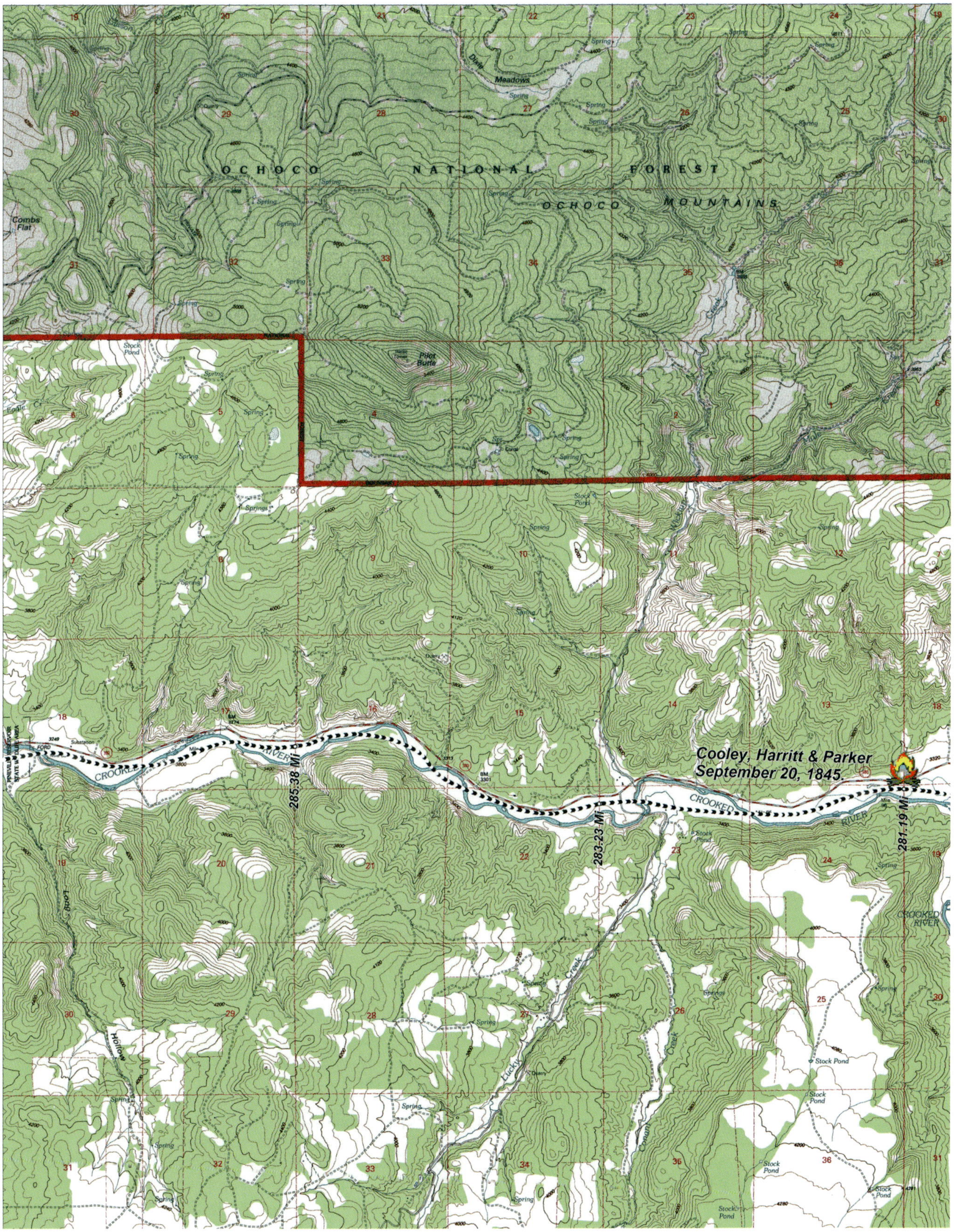

Circles: Picture Number and Its Location.
Solid Line: Traces of the Trail. Verified on the ground by these authors.
Dashed Line: Projected Trail Location. Verified on the ground by these authors.

Pilot Butte

There are no identifiable traces of the trail as it makes its way down the Crooked River, somewhat following the Paulina County Highway for about 23 miles. The bottom land along the river has been farmed and homesteaded, erasing all traces of wagon ruts. Following the diary accounts and the estimated mileage they traveled each day, coupled with the brief description of their surroundings, these authors have attempted to determine the general location of campsites they might have used along the river. They passed major creeks coming in from the north: Horse Heaven Creek, Wickiup Creek, Eagle Creek, Antelope Creek, and then Bear Creek, which was the only one coming in from the south.

The emigrants have now traveled about 1600 miles since they began their journey. They have been traveling at an average rate of about 2 ½ miles per hour. There are inconsistencies in the distance each diarist listed traveling down the river, yet they were all referring to the same locations. They started following the river at the confluence of the main stem of the Crooked River and the North Fork of the Crooked River, and they left the river climbing a long steep ridge going to the north which is about two miles below the mouth of Bear Creek. Bear Creek was the encampment of several of the companies. On September 22 after leaving their encampment on the river, Eli Cooley writes, *"... down the creek about 2 miles and then Turned to the rite and left it [Crooked River] after crossing it 3 times Here wee had a very steep hill..."* This was also the location where the long steep ridge was visible where Fields said he could see wagons ahead of them climbing from the bottom to the top. The actual measured distance is 32.2 miles. James Fields' mileage of 31 miles for this distance appears to be the most accurate. All of the other diaries indicate a much shorter distance.

There are several theories insinuated by other writers and researchers about where the Meek Wagon Train left the Crooked River. The first theory is that the Meek party left the Crooked River following Wickiup Creek to its headwaters, passing to the east side of Pilot Butte, then crossing the summit into the headwaters of Lawson Creek near Dixie Meadows, and then continuing down Lawson Creek to Ochoco Creek, and eventually on into the Prineville area.[1] While there is mention of pine trees being seen on the slopes in the diaries, this route would lead into a heavily forest-covered mountainous region with no possible correlation whatsoever to the diarists' mileages or geographic descriptions. Furthermore, after the diarists mention the pine trees, they still describe following the channel of the river.

The second theory is that the Meek party turned northerly up Eagle Creek, then out across Combs Flat, and eventually into the Prineville area.[2] Again, there is no possible correlation between the terrain of this location, the mileage, or geographic details the diarists mention.

The third theory some researchers entertain is the possibility that the Meek Wagon Train may have left Crooked River and went northerly up a creek called Antelope Creek, making their way over the summit and into Ochoco Creek near where Prineville is located today. The mileage along this route would come closer to fitting the diarists' accounts, however this route is completely devoid of a combination of details in the diaries such as coming into view of a very steep hill with wagons strung from the bottom to the top, and reaching the summit where they could immediately see the Cascade Mountains in the distance. Again, this route has no correlation between the physical features of the area and the diary accounts.

---

[1]Major Steens Military Expedition in 1860 came into this area from the north near the vicinity of the headwaters of the Ochoco Reservoir and Steins Pillar, on what is called Mill Creek today, continuing up Ochoco Creek to the mouth of Lawson Creek. There the expedition turned in a southerly direction up Lawson Creek, to a point about a half mile below what is called Gravy Creek, taking the gentler slopes in a southerly direction, crossing the eastern reaches of Combs Flat, over a low summit, and into Eagle Creek. There following Eagle Creek, the expedition passed near Eagle Rock and on to the Crooked River.

[2]In 1859, Captain H. D. Wallen was ordered to explore and ascertain if a wagon road could be made from Ft. Dalles to the Great Salt Lake Valley. When he arrived in the present-day Prineville location, he traveled close to the location of today's Crook County Highway 380, crossing the length of Combs Flat and descending down Eagle Creek, passing Eagle Rock, and on to the Crooked River striking the Meek Cutoff Wagon Trail of which he began to follow up the Crooked River to the large spring at the G I Ranch Location.

CROOKED RIVER TO PRINEVILLE

Sept. 22. Mon: Bad road today Weather fine come down the creek about 2 miles and then Turned to the rite and left it after crossing it 3 times Here wee had a very steep hill to pull up and about 8 miles further struck a creek and camped in the forks the creek wee camped on is to our rite some cedar on the hills the corse to whare wee left the creek is about west then about North to here. 10 miles. **Eli Cooley Diary** *[Camped at the confluence of Ochoco Creek and Crooked River.]*

22nd: 3 ms braught us to the foot of a huge mountain where we commenced ascending through thick ceder timber at 2 oclock P.M. we gained the top the seen of the country became butiful and levle passed through several groves of pine and ceder timber at 11 oclock we came to a stream affording an abundence of water grass and timber where we encamped haveing come 14 ms. **Jesse Harritt Diary** *[Camped at the confluence of Ochoco Creek and Crooked River.]*

21 [22nd]: left the Creek 2 miles up the same some of the company didn't git up till after dark Went 4 miles to a small spring Swaring without end Comeing in all nite. 6 mi. **Samuel Parker Diary** *[Camped at Dry Creek.]*

Tue Sept 23rd: Went about 20 miles, striking away from the river and camping upon a small branch of it. Had a long hard pull in the morning to ascend the mountain spoken of yesterday, but once up we felt amply repaid the trouble of climbing by the prospect which lay before us. There were the Cascade mountains stretching along the western horizon, apparently not more than 40 miles distant, forming a dark outline varied by an occasional snow peak, which would rise lofty and spire like, as if it were a monument to departed greatness. **James Field Diary**

22 [23rd]: To a Creek. 19 mi. **Samuel Parker Diary** *[Camped at the confluence of Ochoco Creek and Crooked River.]*

After doing in-depth research, these authors are firmly convinced the Meek party continued their course down the Crooked River to just below the Bowman Dam which contains the Prineville Reservoir. Therefore, the last ten miles of their journey down the river is covered by the waters of the reservoir. Here, just below the dam, at the point of a hogback ridge, the trail left the river and follows an old historic trail northeasterly, climbing a narrow hogback ridge out of the canyon and onto bench lands. The difficulties the river presented beyond this point were not conducive to wagon travel, forcing the emigrants to take this old historic trail. During the construction of the Bowman Dam in 1960, a Spanish sword artifact was unearthed.[1] This helped confirm that this trail had been used for centuries by both Indians and Spaniards traveling northerly into Ochoco Creek where Prineville, Oregon, is now located.

LONG STEEP HILL JUST BEYOND BOWMAN DAM. *"...tremendous hill which is necessary to ascend, and which when we first came in sight of appeared to be strung with wagons from the bottom to the top..."* James Field. Today, the Prineville Reservoir occupies the location where James Field first saw a tremendous hill. Location 1 viewed northwesterly on Bowman Dam (Modified) map, p. 120.

[1]"History - Or Wishful Thinking?" Sorraia Mustang, accessed June 2, 2014, http://www.spanish-mustang.org/SorraiaMustang/History.html.

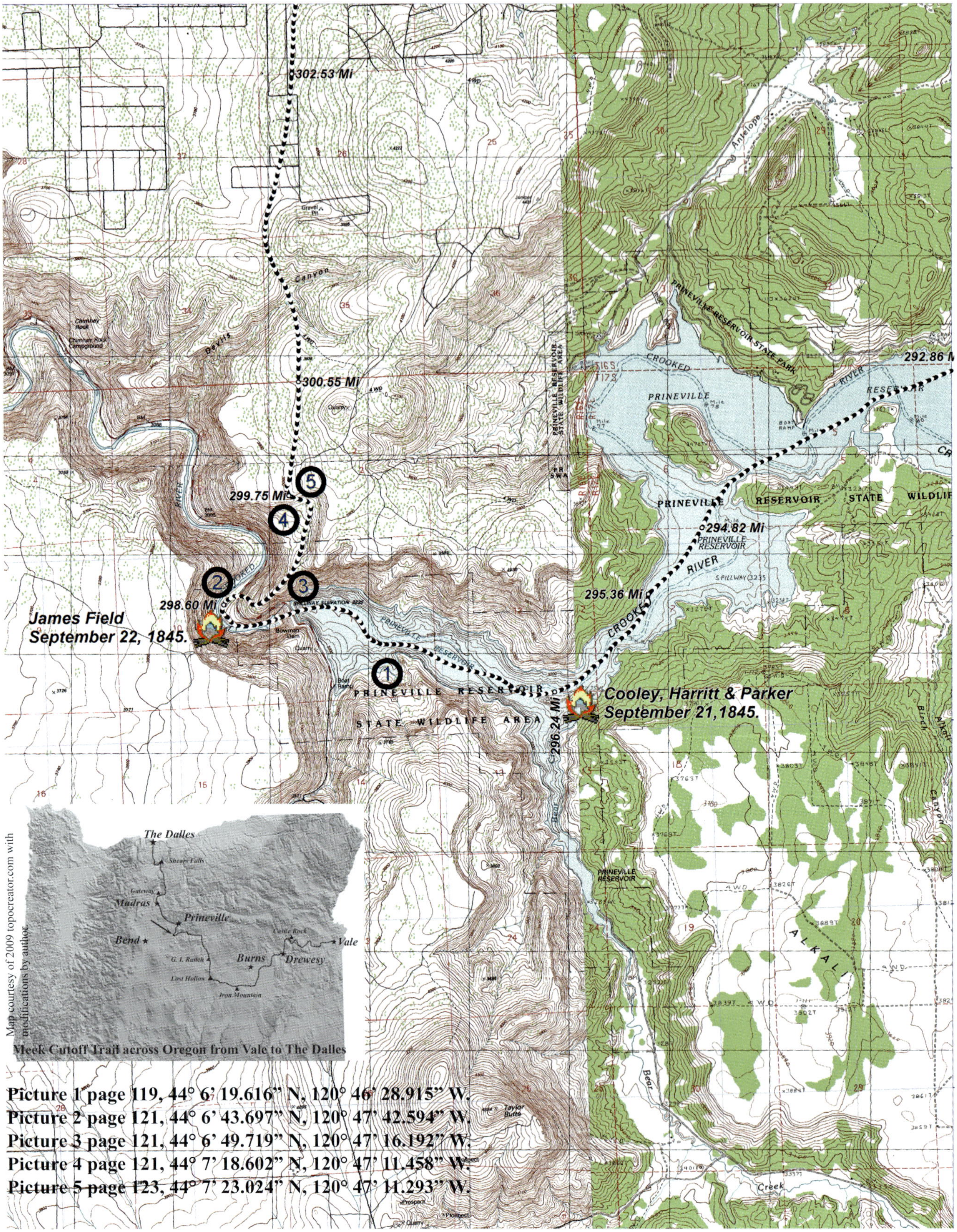

Bowman Dam (Modified)

Circles: Picture Number and Its Location.
Solid Line: Traces of the Trail. Verified on the ground by these authors.
Dashed Line: Projected Trail Location. Verified on the ground by these authors.

Campsite Below Bowman Dam. The Bureau of Land Management has developed a campground on County Highway 27 in the vicinity where James Field camped on the 22nd of September. Looking up the long, steep hill that the trail ascended. Location 2 viewed easterly. on Bowman Dam (Modified) map, p. 120.

Looking Up the Steep Hill From the Crooked River. *"Here wee had a very steep hill to pull up..."* Eli Cooley. Traces of the original trail have been destroyed by four-wheel vehicles. Location 3 viewed northeasterly on Bowman Dam (Modified) map, p. 120.

James Field describes the amazing scene they witnessed as they came into view of this hogback ridge. He writes in his diary on September 22nd, *"...appeared to be strung with wagons from the bottom to the top...."* There was a straight stretch in the river with no obstruction, so it would have been possible to observe such a scene two miles up the river. Today, the backwater of the reservoir covers this area.

As the wagons began their ascent up this ridge, crossing County Highway 27, the first 1000 feet of the ridge would definitely have been a hard and difficult climb as they were climbing about a 38% slope. The rest of the trail up the ridge would have been a hard pull but less difficult. The total length of the climb to the top of the bench was nearly one mile.

Looking Down on the Long Steep Ridge Out of Crooked River. *"Had a long hard pull..."* James Field. The shadow in the center of the photo highlights the ridge top of the tremendous hill. Once they had made the long, hard pull, they came across the basin and climbed out of the canyon at the location where these authors are standing taking this photo. Location 4 viewed southerly on Bowman Dam (Modified) map, p. 120.

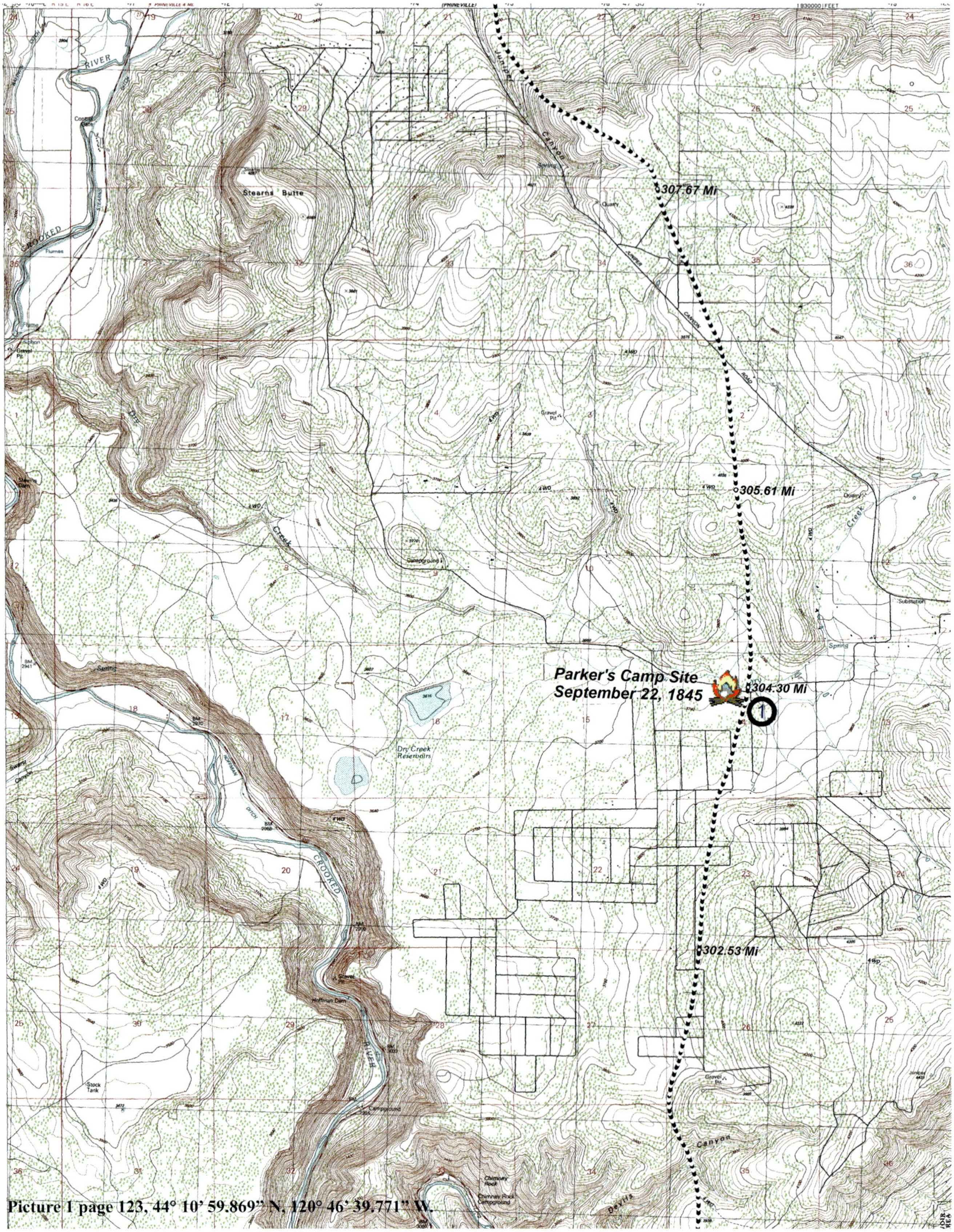

Circles: Picture Number and Its Location.
Solid Line: Traces of the Trail. Verified on the ground by these authors.
Dashed Line: Projected Trail Location. Verified on the ground by these authors.

Stearns Butte

CASCADE MOUNTAINS. *"...once up we felt amply repaid the trouble of climbing...There were the Cascade mountains stretching along the western horizon apparently not more than 40 miles distant..."* James Field. This location is the first time the Cascade Mountains could be seen along the trail. Location 5 viewed westerly on Bowman Dam (Modified) map, p. 120.

At the top of this difficult climb, the emigrants were awestruck by the splendor of the western view. Those elusive Cascade Mountains were actually looming up on the horizon some 40 or 50 miles in the distance. They had now traveled some 200 miles from the location where they had seen the Steen Mountains and incorrectly identified them as the Cascade Mountains.

The Savannah Oregon Emigrating Society Wagon Train with Eli Cooley made the steep ascent without difficulty. They traveled in a northerly direction for about six miles across gently rolling slopes above the rimrock gorge of the Crooked River. Near the six mile location, the trail crosses the present-day Juniper Canyon Highway following the ridge top down into the valley leading into Prineville, Oregon, and camped at the confluence of Ochoco Creek and Crooked River. They traveled about sixteen miles for the day.

Samuel Parker's Company had difficulty making the climb and only traveled four miles to a spring and camped. Some of his company did not arrive until after dark. This spring is near the headwaters of Dry Creek.

"...some of the company didn't git up till after dark Went 4 miles to a small spring Swaring without end Comeing in all nite." Samuel Parker. The general location of the small spring located on Dry Creek. Photo taken near intersection of Hagen Way and Davis Loop Road in the Three Peaks Subdivision. Location 1 viewed northerly. on Stearns Butte map, p. 122.

The St. Joseph Company, with James Field traveling with the Riggs' family, were trailing the other companies by one day. Therefore, on September 22nd, they camped at the base of the big hill. Ascending the hogback ridge on September 23rd, the St. Joseph Company, James Field and the Riggs' family continues until they reach the confluence of the Ochoco Creek and the Crooked River, and camps with Parker's Company.

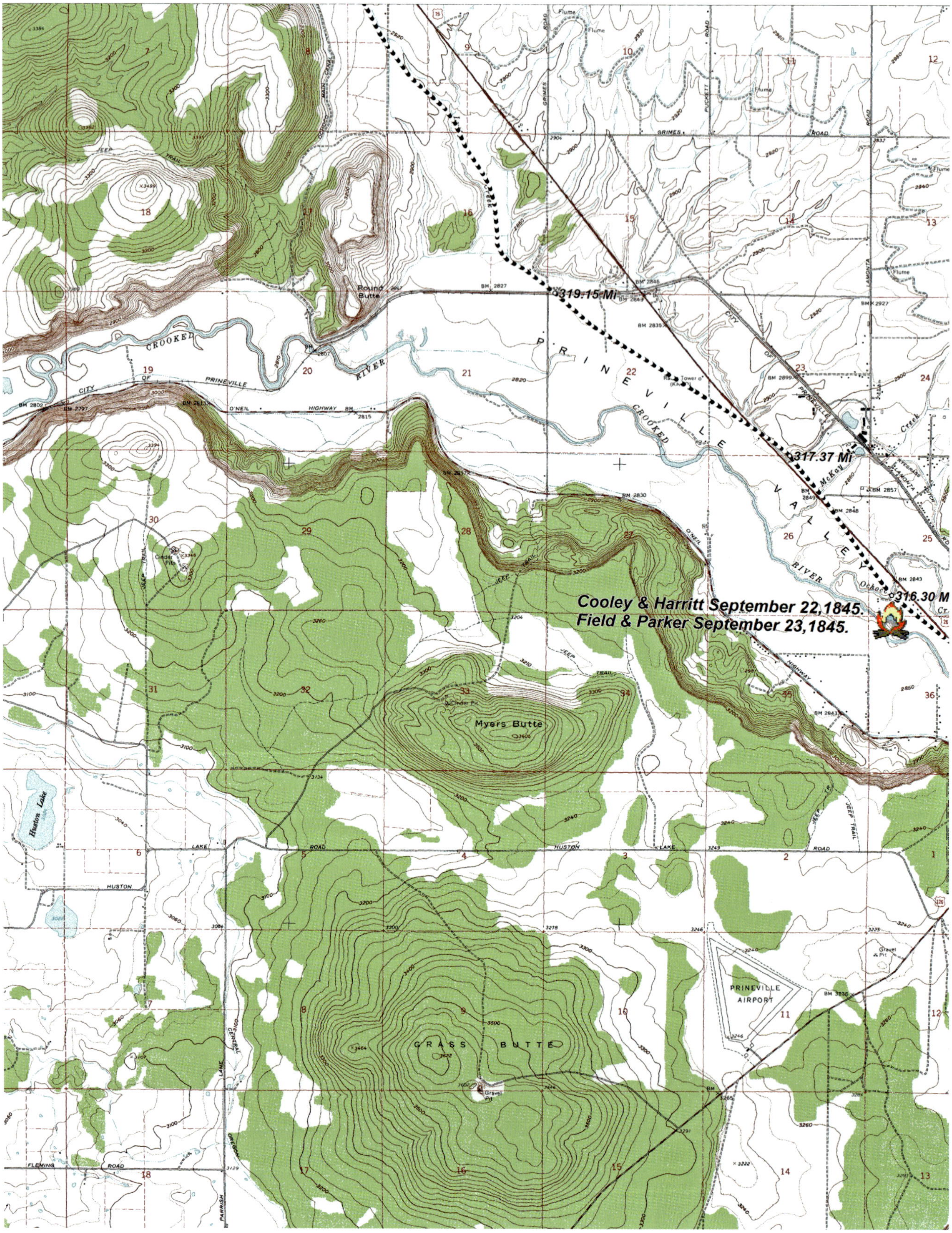

Circles: Picture Number and Its Location.
Solid Line: Traces of the Trail. Verified on the ground by these authors.
Dashed Line: Projected Trail Location. Verified on the ground by these authors.

Huston Lake

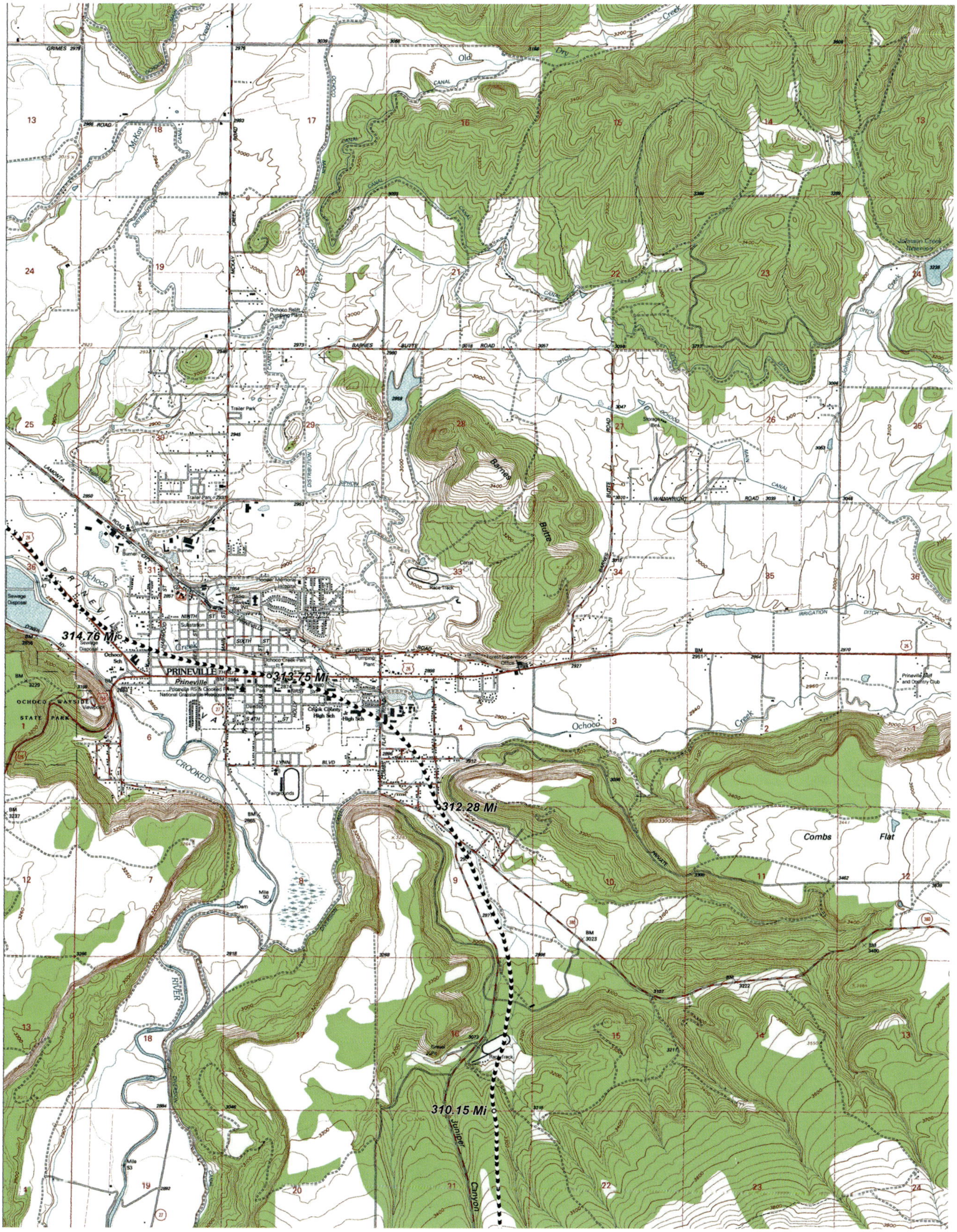

Circles: Picture Number and Its Location.
Solid Line: Traces of the Trail. Verified on the ground by these authors.
Dashed Line: Projected Trail Location. Verified on the ground by these authors.

Prineville

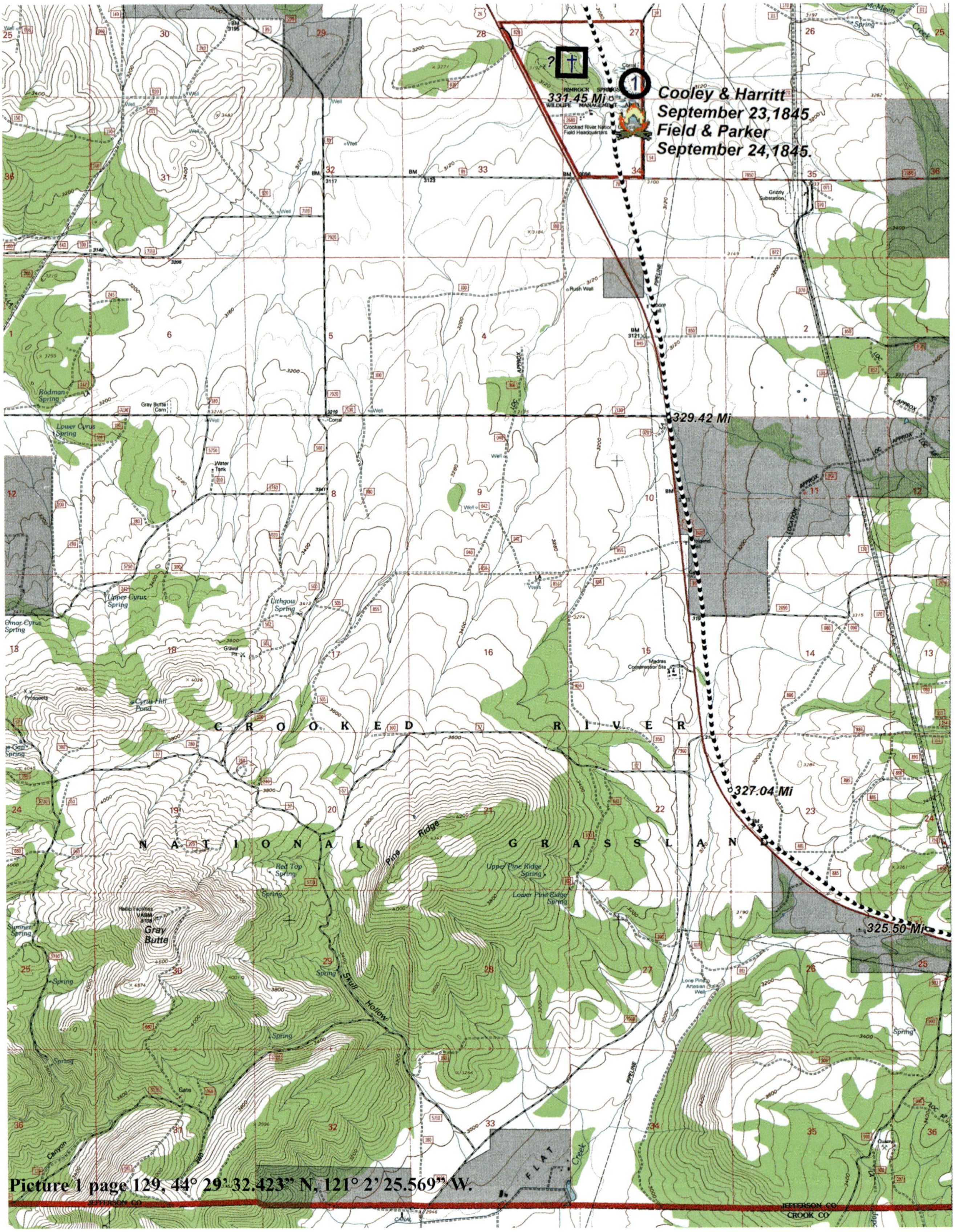

Circles: Picture Number and Its Location.
Solid Line: Traces of the Trail. Verified on the ground by these authors.
Dashed Line: Projected Trail Location. Verified on the ground by these authors.

Gray Butte

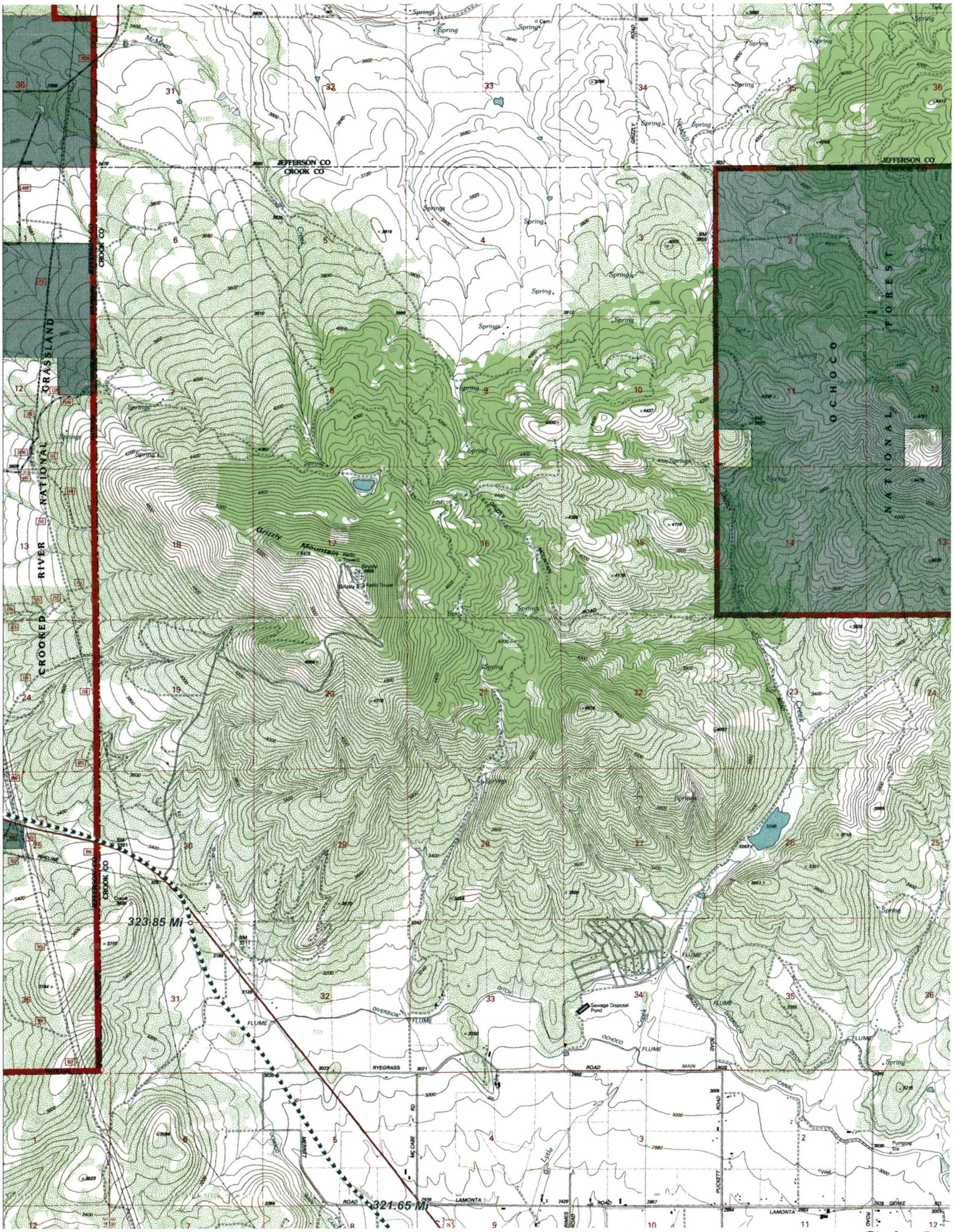

Circles: Picture Number and Its Location.
Solid Line: Traces of the Trail. Verified on the ground by these authors.
Dashed Line: Projected Trail Location. Verified on the ground by these authors.

Grizzly Mountain

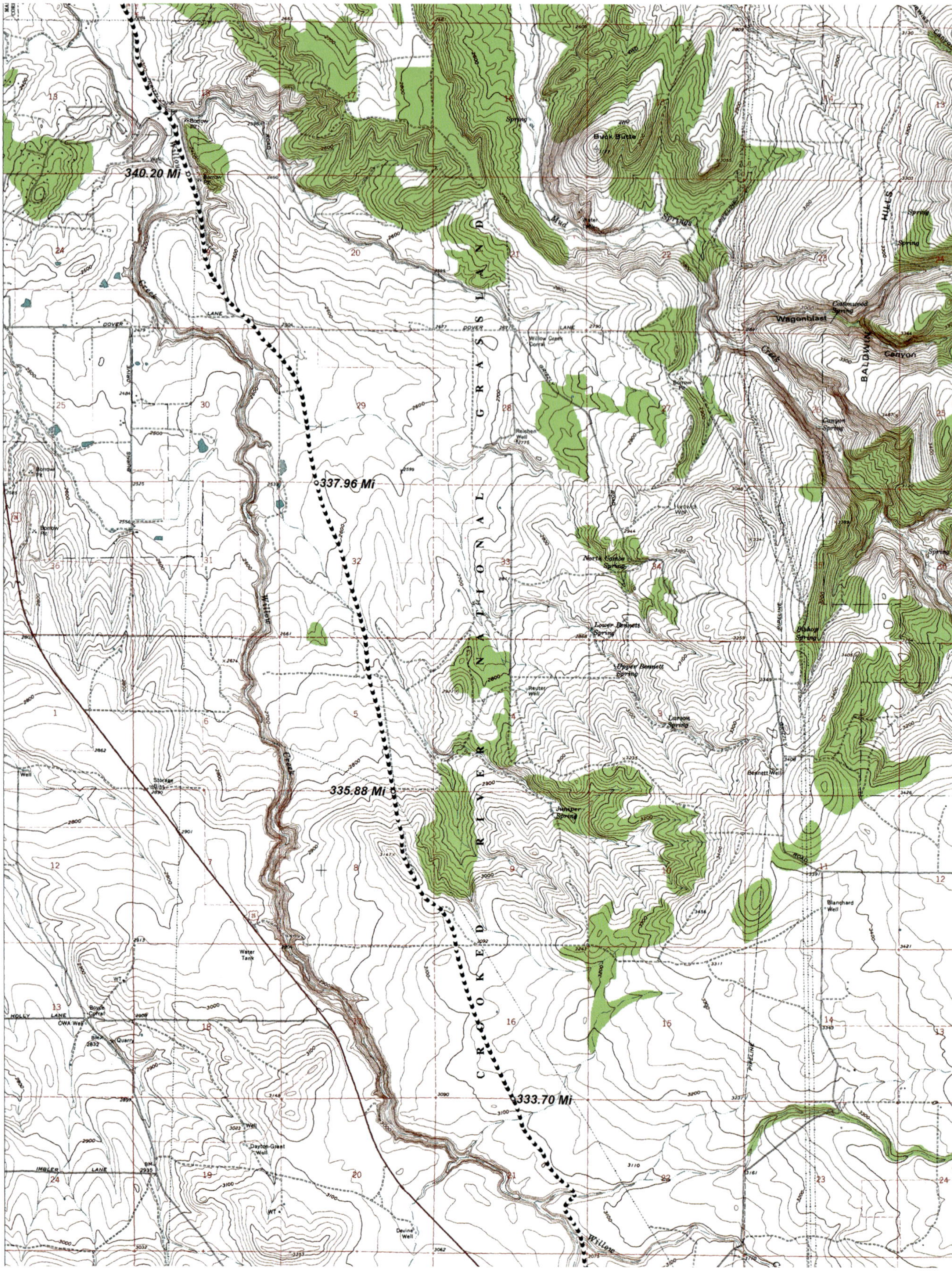

Circles: Picture Number and Its Location.
Solid Line: Traces of the Trail. Verified on the ground by these authors.
Dashed Line: Projected Trail Location. Verified on the ground by these authors.

Buck Butte

PRINEVILLE TO RIMROCK SPRINGS

Sept Tue 23: The road to day has been Tollerable good Weather fine Crossed the Creek this Morning near its Mouth whare it runs into the same creek wee have been traveling Down and come about 3 miles down the creek here leaving it to our left and have Traveled about a South West corse about 3 miles from whare wee left the creek is a Spring plenty of grass and Some few Willow Camped about 8 miles further at a Branch or spring plenty of grass and some seder Wood on the hills to the left about ¼ mile. 12 miles.[1] **Eli Cooley Diary**

23rd: started late had good road travleed 12 ms stoped at 9 oclock at a spring found good grass no wood except a little sage. **Jesse Harritt Diary**

Wed Sept 24th: went about 15 miles, camping at a spring in the midst of the plains without a single landmark to tell its situation. **James Field Diary**

23 [24th]: To a spring. Beried 4 persons heare. 18 mi. **Samuel Parker Diary**

Leaving the confluence of Ochoco Creek and the Crooked River, the emigrants traveled a calculated distance of 15 miles in a northwesterly direction over a good road. US Highway 26 pretty much follows the trail location throughout this area.

By September 23rd, a very serious situation was beginning to unfold as the companies advanced in tandem, making their way to a spring located in the middle of the plains. This spring is called Rimrock Springs and is located in the Rimrock Springs Wildlife Management Area. James Field's last diary entry was at this spring as he took ill and was unable to maintain a diary from then on.[2]

Severe sickness had now taken over Samuel Parker's Company. It is not clear how many were actually sick. What is clear though, is that disaster struck with a vengeance as four members of Samuel Parker's Company died and were buried at this location. This was just 15 days after September 8th near Harney Lake where James Field's diary entry indicates that some of the women were experimenting with a substance resembling saleratus and were using it in their cooking. On September 10th James Field again mentions the subject of the soil, "*The ground about our encampment is encrusted with salt, which in some places may be scraped up with the hand in nearly pure state.*" It is not known for sure, but apparently a large quantity of this substance had been collected by the Riggs' Company of which James Field was a member, and most likely also by the members of the Samuel Parker Company, as this company was extremely short of provisions. Both companies were camped together at that time. What quantity of alkali salt was collected or how many emigrants indulged in such a practice, no one will ever know. However, it is obvious that within 15 days after the first mention of experimenting with alkali salts, people were becoming ill and dying. This could also explain James Field's illness, which he described as "camp fever."

Rimrock Springs Area Between Prineville, Oregon, and Madras, Oregon. "*...camping at a spring in the midst of the plains without a single landmark to tell its situation.*" James Field. Location 1 viewed westerly on Gray Butte map, p. 126.

[1]At this point, Eli Cooley wrote "South west" when it is obvious he meant "North west." Had he turned southwest, it would have taken him back to the Crooked River and the rimrock bluffs.

[2]See letter written by James Field in 1879, on p. 181 of this book.

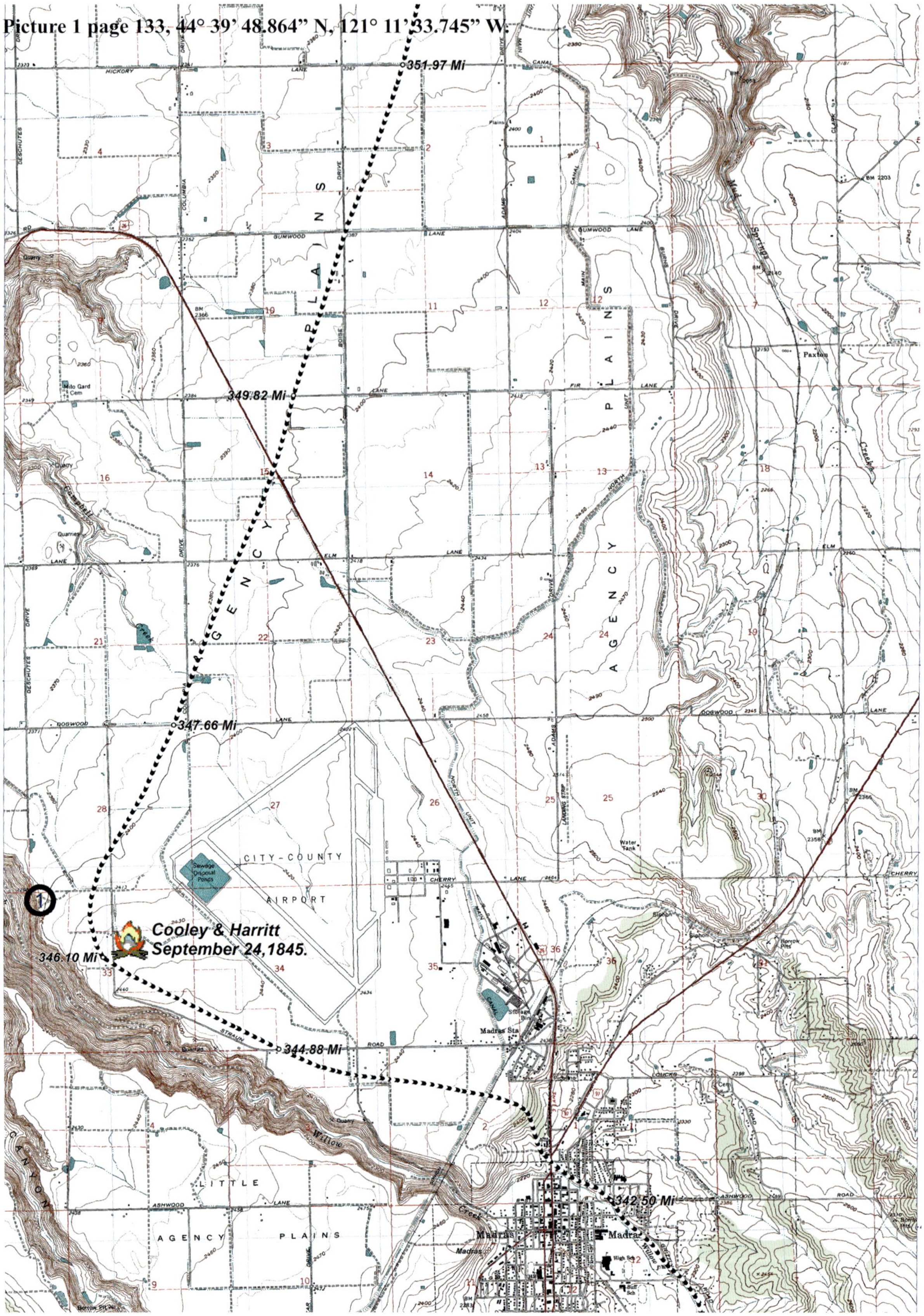

Madras (Modified)

Circles: Picture Number and Its Location.
Solid Line: Traces of the Trail. Verified on the ground by these authors.
Dashed Line: Projected Trail Location. Verified on the ground by these authors.

It has been alleged by other writers that the cause of the deaths was attributed to cholera, which was a common disease associated with bad water. If there was any disease that was associated with the water, the following question comes to mind: why wouldn't all of the companies be affected in the same way? All of the companies were camping and using the same water sources. Yet Samuel Parker is the only diarist to mention these deaths, and he was the diarist who used the least amount of words in his diary entries. All of the other diarists wrote with more detail. Therefore, these authors believe that they would have recorded the death of any member of their company.

Samuel Parker makes an interesting comment upon arriving at the The Dalles Mission on October 7th. He not only said that some of his company had gone without bread for the last 15 days, which would have been September 23rd when they were encamped at the confluence of the Ochoco Creek and Crooked River, but he also states all that they had to eat was "pore" beef. This beef was very possibly cured or seasoned with the alkali salts they had previously collected. If this was the case, the poison was continuing to accumulate in their systems. From September 23rd sickness seemed to prevail and ultimately followed with several deaths.

These authors do not have chemistry or medical backgrounds, but we have done some research on alkali salt. Consequently, it is merely our own opinion pertaining to the dangers of alkali salt. These emigrants were somewhat familiar with a substance called saleratus which had been recognized as a leavening agent, similar to what we know as baking soda. Prior to 1853, physicians in New Brunswick, Canada, had determined that more than half of the number of children dying were killed by the use of saleratus. A newspaper article written n 1853 makes the statement, "How much salts of lye and carbonic acid can a human stomach bear and remain healthy, is a question for the Saleratus eaters."[1] Thus, the safety of ingesting saleratus was questioned even at that time. The emigrants of these companies were indulging in the use of a similar substance about which they knew nothing. What impurities or toxins did this alkali substance contain? Their thinking may have been that alkali salts are similar to saleratus so it would be all right to use. This may have been a dangerous conclusion and the very reason why the emigrants were getting sick. While every person's system is different, consuming undetermined quantities of alkali salt could cause a number of medical problems. Some of the symptoms are extreme stomach cramps, intense dehydration, nausea, vomiting and diarrhea, stiffness of muscles and joints, and weakness and fatigue. These symptoms are much harder on the small bodies of children, although adults are not exempt from them either. A combination of these symptoms can ultimately result in death. The journey along the trail was stretching the upper limits of human endurance. The human body can only stand so much abuse; it is no wonder some people died.

RIMROCK SPRINGS TO PORTER SPRINGS

Sept Wen 24: The road to day has been Tallerable good Weather fine Traveled about a North west corse for about 10 mile then Turned about west with the Expectation of Striking the river But did not Strike it and stopped without any water. 12 miles. **Eli Cooley Diary**

24th: the roade good travleed 14 mi through the levle plain and stoped for the night without wood or water. **Jesse Harritt Diary**

24 [25th]: Traveled all day and that nite **Samuel Parker Diary**

Sept Thu 25: The road to day has been Tollerable good Except Some few rockey places Weather fine this Morning wee Started Early and Traveled nearly North for about 8 mile and Camped on the hill about 1½ mile from Shoots or Falls River and drove our cattle down a hollow to water Some seder wood here and some grass the rite hand road is some nearest as the Company biching made a cutoff on us. 8 miles. **Eli Cooley Diary**

25th: made an erly start travleed 6 ms and encamped on Shouts or fall river this river is the most singula in its carrecter of any we have seen it washes the eastern margin of the Cascade mountains and flows with a rapid current

[1] *"The Adams Sentinel and General Advertiser,"* Gettysburg, Pennsylvania. August 15, 1853, p. 5.

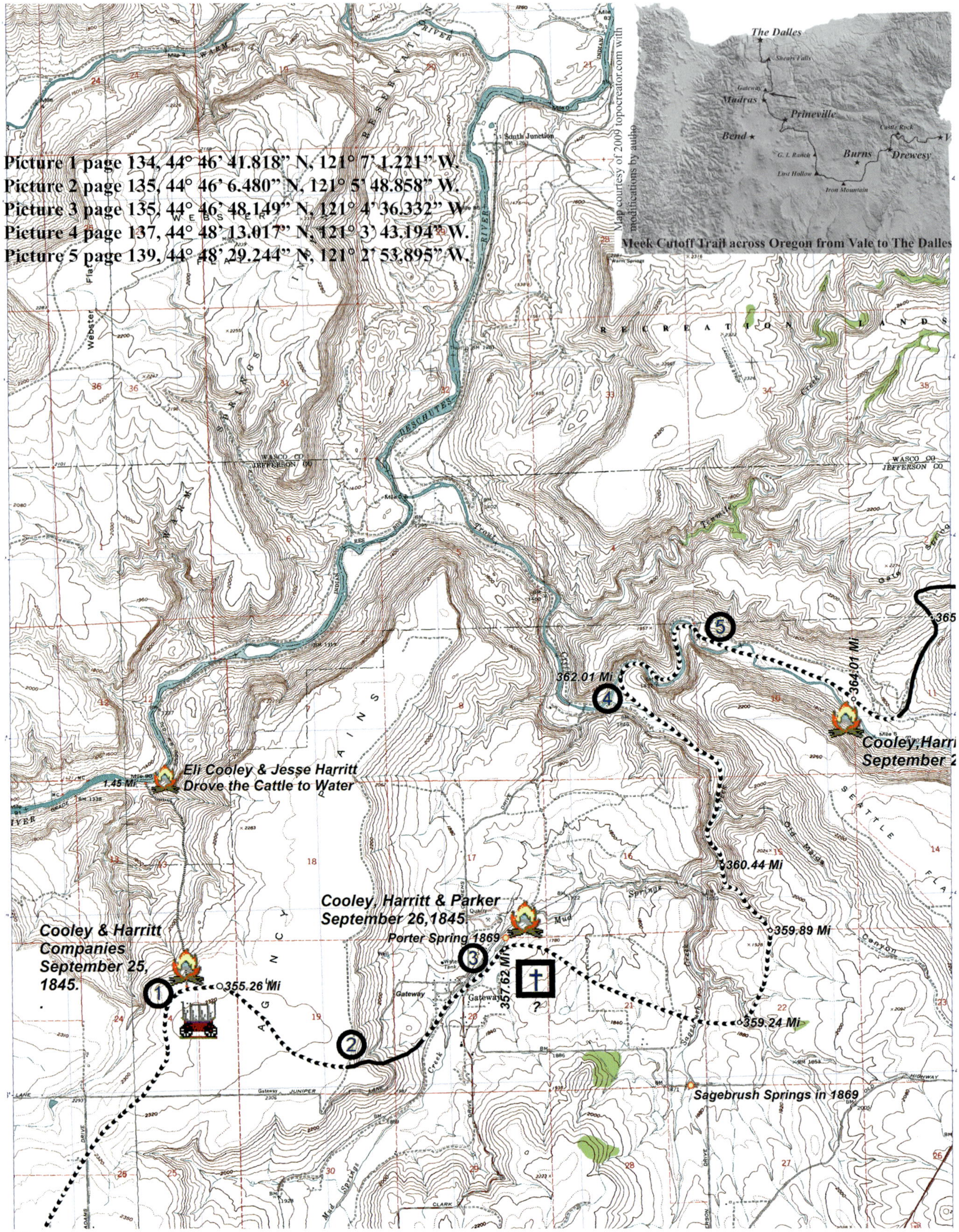

Gateway (Modified)

Circles: Picture Number and Its Location.
Solid Line: Traces of the Trail. Verified on the ground by these authors.
Dashed Line: Projected Trail Location. Verified on the ground by these authors.

Looking in a Westerly Direction into the Willow Creek Canyon Toward the Deschutes River. Photo is taken on the rim near the location of Cooley's campsite on Agency Plains on September 24. This is the view they would have seen. Location 1 viewed westerly on Madras (Modified) map, p. 130.

through a deep cavern of rock haveing a channel from 20 to 30 yards wide and is from 3 to 4 hundred feet below the levle plain.[1] **Jesse Harritt Diary**

From Rimrock Springs, the Savannah Oregon Emigrating Society and the St. Joseph Company continued northerly to the northern reaches of the plains. Today, this area is called the Agency Plains. US Highway 26 somewhat parallels the trail location for the next 18 miles passing through the town of Madras, Oregon. Both Cooley and Harritt described the trail as a good road. However, there was no water available at either of their encampments on September 24th or 25th. On September 25th, it appears both of these companies camped very closely to one another. Here, the decision was made to drive the livestock down through a basin to the Deschutes River in order to get water, knowing they would have to drive them back up the next morning. There is only one location in this vicinity where such an effort would have been possible. The distance to the river was about 1½ miles. Once reaching the river, Jesse Harritt gave a detailed description of how it flowed through the canyon. He writes on September 25, *"...this river is the most singula in its carrecter of any we have seen it washes the eastern margin of the Cascade mountains and flows with a rapid current through a deep cavern of rock haveing a channel from 20 to 30 yards wide and is from 3 to 4 hundred feet below the levle plain."*

On the following three days, September 24th, 25th, and 26th, Eli Cooley and Jesse Harritt wrote they had traveled a total distance of 23 miles mostly over level plains. The actual distance measured from Rimrock Springs to Porter Springs at Gateway, Oregon, is 25 miles, just two miles farther than Cooley and Harritt claimed.

Agency Plains. *"... Camped on the hill about 1½ mile from Shoots or Falls River..."* Eli Cooley. General vicinity of the wagon trains' dry camp on Sept. 25th on Agency Plains. Location 1 viewed southwesterly on Gateway (Modified) map, p. 132.

[1]Jesse Harritt is a cattle drover so he camped on the river that night with the cattle.

Basin and Drainage Descending into the Deschutes River. *"... and drove our cattle down a hollow to water..."* Eli Cooley on Sept. 25th. The only location where Cooley and Harritt could access the Deschutes River with the cattle through the rimrock bluffs from the northerly area of the Agency Plains. Location 1 viewed northerly on Gateway (Modified) map, p. 132.

Sept Fri 26: The road to day has been Tollerable good Except one Big hill to come Down which is Rockey. Weather fine. Traveled about a North East corse and camped at a spring plenty of grass here some seder Wood Some Distance off. 3 miles. **Eli Cooley Diary**

26th: turned a north east direction travleed 3 ms and encamped at a good spring in company with about 200 waggons. **Jesse Harritt Diary**

26: Struck water about 10 the 26 day many Codent to water and water was taken to them 32 in number heare we beried 6 Persons. 65 mi. **Samuel Parker Diary**

27th: laid by all day to rest. **Jesse Harritt Diary**

27: laid by heare my wife tuck sick and Child missis But not expected to live. **Samuel Parker Diary**

Descending from Agency Plains to a spring, the emigrants had to widen the old Indian trail to safely descend the hill with their wagons. The wagon train made a short advance of three miles, crossing Juniper Lane County Highway, to a good spring where they camped. This spring is known today as Porter Springs and was one of the very few water sources in all of this area.[1]

During field research, these authors met Mr. Herbert Vibbert, a farmer residing in Gateway, Oregon. He currently farms on the Agency Plains. Mr. Vibbert said Porter Springs was a very important campsite used by Indians for possibly centuries and continued many years after his own ancestors settled on the Agency Plains. Indians would come to this spring, set up their teepees and spend several weeks during the summer months harvesting camas root, an important food source in their diet. His family had settled on the Agency Plains in the early 1900s. Currently, there have been seven generations of the Vibbert family who have occupied and grown up on the original homestead lands. Mr. Vibbert also confirmed the lack of water on Agency Plains as his family had to haul water a great distance to supply their homesteads. They had to dryland farm the plains until the Round Butte Dam containing Lake Billy Chinook was constructed. This then supplied abundant water to the Agency Plains. It was only after the construction of Round Butte Dam that nearly all of the present-day springs located at the base of the rimrock bluffs around the plains began to appear since water now seeps through cracks and crevices in the layers of lava rock throughout this region.

As the remaining members of Samuel Parker's Company arrived at Porter Springs, an accounting of the wagons at this location was made. Jesse Harritt enters in his diary that they were *"...at a good spring in company with about 200 waggons."* This number was within two wagons of the number

[1]Porter Springs was named after a homesteader, Oliver Porter, who obtained a patent on 160 acres on March 21, 1881, surrounding this spring. This is the same general area where Gateway, Oregon, is located.

Trail Descending Hill Into Present-Day Gateway, Oregon. Both photos show sections of the trail at the top of the "Big hill" that Eli Cooley mentions in his diary. Rocks have been laid aside in the construction of the trail for a short distance around the side slope. Location 2 viewed northeasterly on Gateway (Modified) map, p. 132.

Samuel Parker had spoken of at the G I Ranch spring location about 120 miles back along the trail, and therefore, it is quite apparent that Solomon Tetherow's Company was also at Porter Springs since his company was in the count at the G I Ranch.

Instead of resting on September 27th, the Savannah Oregon Emigrating Society left this encampment, putting it one day ahead of the rest of the wagon train. However, Jesse Harritt and the St. Joseph Company chose to rest, in addition to Samuel Parker's Company. By this time, ten members of Samuel Parker's Company had died, six of them were buried somewhere in the area surrounding Porter Springs. Parker also writes that his wife and one of his children has become ill, as well as Mrs. Butts, who was a close friend of the Parker's and having been sick for many days, was not expected to live.

Other writers and researchers have claimed that the Meek Wagon Train camped at the location that is called Sagebrush Springs. From Sagebrush Springs, they turned nearly due east traveling about 2½ miles before passing through an area called Lyle Gap, where US Highway 97 is located today. Then continuing in the same general course that the highway takes into the Trout Creek drainage, the wagon

Continuing Down the "Big" Hill Toward Present-Day Gateway, Oregon

Porter Springs Along Mud Springs Creek Near Gateway, Oregon. *"...encamped at a good spring in company with about 200 waggons."* Jesse Harritt. Location 3 viewed southwesterly on Gateway (Modified) map, p. 132.

train supposedly somehow followed through the extremely rough defile called Cow Canyon, reaching the summit of the canyon near Shaniko Junction.

Another theory has been expressed that the trail climbed through the steep and rough terrain north of Trout Creek, out onto the main ridge that leads directly toward Shaniko Junction. There it is theorized, the wagon train turned northeasterly, crossing through the headwaters of Bakeoven Creek and eventually followed the top of the main ridge dividing Bakeoven Canyon and Buck Hollow Creek. They continued to follow the top of the ridge to a point where the wagon train would descend the bluffs into the Deschutes River, finally crossing the river somewhere near Sherars Falls. This has been the general line of thinking by people for many years. However, neither of these routes actually existed. Eli Cooley's diary helps to paint a clear picture of where the trail is actually located as they left Porter Springs and on to the Deschutes River crossing.

PORTER SPRINGS TO TROUT CREEK NEAR BAKER CANYON

Sept Sat 27: Some rock in the road to day Weather fine Traveled about a North East corse Come about 2½ mile and struck a hollow and Turned to the left and in about ½ mile is a spring. plenty of grass no Wood and in about 1 mile further struck a small creek and Traveled about 2 mile up it and Camped Plenty of grass and Wood on the creek Saw a few Indians this Morning. 6 miles. **Eli Cooley Diary**

28th: travleed 8 ms and encamped on a small branch found good grass and wood. **Jesse Harritt Diary**

28: Went ten miles. 10 mi. **Samuel Parker Diary**

Upon leaving Porter Springs, the trail went in a southeasterly direction for about 1½ miles to Sagebrush Creek, where they turned left to the north. At this point, Sagebrush Springs is about ½ mile south of the trail.[1] After turning to the left and making their way down the hollow or canyon, they

MOUTH OF SAGEBRUSH CREEK WHERE IT JOINS TROUT CREEK. *"...struck a hollow and Turned to the left and in about ½ mile is a spring.... and in about 1 mile further struck a small creek..."* Eli Cooley. Looking up the hollow/canyon the way the wagon train came down. Location 4 viewed southerly on Gateway map, p. 132.

[1]Jno [sic] H. McClung, Deputy Surveyor under Contract Number 127 dated March 2, 1869, commenced surveying in this general area on May 18, 1869. During the course of his survey, his field notes reveal the true location of two particular springs, although he did not name the springs. Today, those springs are named Porter Springs and Sagebrush Springs. This clearly shows that the two water sources were present in 1869.

Looking Up Trout Creek From Near the Mouth of Sagebrush Creek. Location 4 viewed easterly on Gateway (Modified) map, p. 132.

Trout Creek Gorge. As they progressed up Trout Creek, they had to pull out upon the bench near where the present-day road is located in order to avoid the rimrock bluffs that defined the Trout Creek gorge and the rocky creek bottom.

traveled about ½ mile where Eli Cooley mentions coming to a spring which was present in the bottom of the hollow. They then traveled one mile farther to where they struck a creek called Trout Creek. They traveled up the creek for approximately two miles where Cooley writes they camped. This is where the old Trout Creek Ranch headquarters were located. Eli Cooley makes the comment that they traveled about a northeast course of six miles for the day. At the location where they camped, they would have actually traveled 6.4 miles from Porter Springs and were located almost directly northeast of Porter Springs. The following day Harritt and Parker write somewhat longer mileages while traveling to the same campsite on Trout Creek.

Looking up Trout Creek With the Trout Creek Ranch in the Distance The old ranch headquarters is located in the general vicinity where Eli Cooley says they camped on Saturday, September 27. Location 5 viewed southeasterly on Gateway (Modified) map, p. 132.

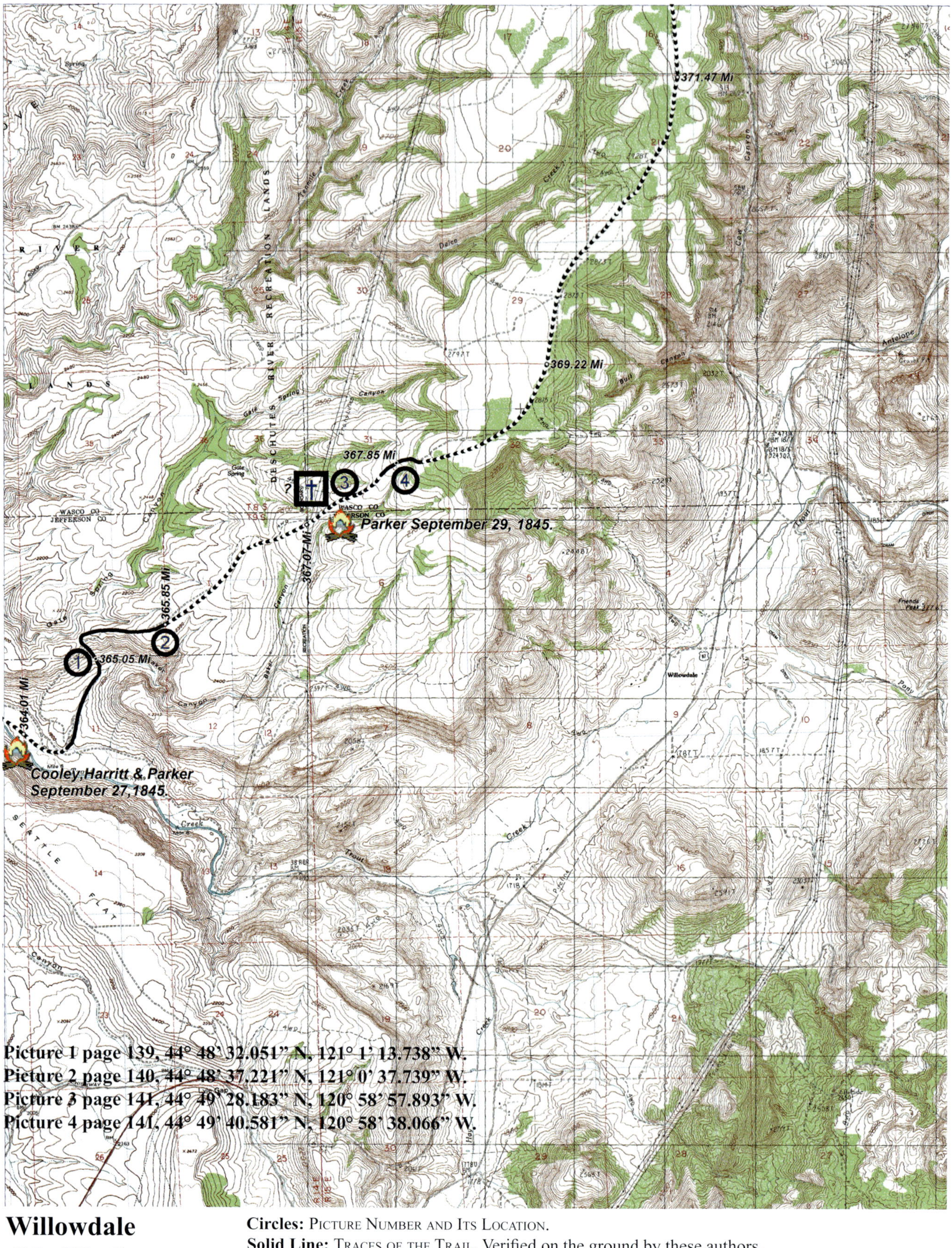

Willowdale (Modified)

Circles: Picture Number and Its Location.
Solid Line: Traces of the Trail. Verified on the ground by these authors.
Dashed Line: Projected Trail Location. Verified on the ground by these authors.

Ascending the Slope Out Of Baker Canyon. Jesse Harritt mentions that in order to ascend the huge mountain, they had to double their teams. Location 1 viewed northerly on Willowdale (Modified) map, p. 138.

Looking Down the Trail into Baker Canyon. View from the same location as the photo above but looking the opposite direction.Traces of the wagon swales are just to the left of center in the photo. Location 1 viewed southerly on Willowdale (Modified) map, p. 138.

TROUT CREEK TO SHANIKO JUNCTION

Sun Sept 28: The road today has been verry Rockey Weather fine Come up the creek a short Distance to a dry fork and Turned to the left up a verry steep hill then the road is level but Rocky Camped at a Spring in a hollow plenty of grass here Wood Scarce Saw a few Indians here. 8 miles. **Eli Cooley Diary**

29th: this morning we ascended a huge mountain ware compelled to double our teams gained the top at 12 oclock we continued our journey over the levle plain until 8 oclock when we encamped on the margin of a bluff down which we descended 200 feet and found a small stream of water shaded by a butiful grove of pine trees distance 10 ms. **Jesse Harritt Diary**

29: all day gitting up hill laid without water beried 3 heare. 3 mi. **Samuel Parker Diary**

On September 28th, Eli Cooley writes they came up from the Trout Creek encampment a short distance and then turned to the left or northerly. This places them in Baker Canyon where a very steep hill had to be climbed. About one mile from the Trout Creek Ranch headquarters and up Baker Canyon, one can clearly see traces of the wagon road.[1] The trail the Meek Wagon Train traveled up this steep slope was used for many years afterwards. Clearly, rock had to be moved aside in order to make the road passable for the wagons. It might be noted that this slope is approximately a 36% slope, somewhat similar to the first 1000 feet of the climb out of Crooked River, although this slope has more rock.

Stephen Meek was remaining in the lead with Solomon Tetherow of the Savannah Oregon Emigrating Society. Eli Cooley's diary shows his company ahead of the others by one day. Apparently, this

[1]The Trout Creek Ranch was homesteaded by two brothers, John and Otto Jasili in 1892. Their homestead patents totaled 320 acres. After living at this location for several years, they sold the property to Albert Kampfer around 1900. Albert Kampfer was the great-grandfather of Jennie Ward who presently resides in Madras, Oregon. She said her great-grandfather Albert Kampfer was a sheep rancher, raising large numbers of sheep in and around Trout Creek. In the spring, after the sheep had been sheared, Mr. Kampfer would take his wool by wagon to Shaniko, Oregon, the wool capital at that time, over an already established wagon trail. The route he followed was the same trail used by Stephen Meek and the Meek Wagon Train. Mr. Kampfer used this route for several years, after which time he hired local Indians to help him construct a graded road to the top of the main ridge, thus bypassing this very steep slope. Traces of this additional road are also visible today located just a short distance below another existing improved dirt road.

THE TRAIL ASCENDING OUT OF BAKER CANYON. Traces of the trail are clearly visible from a viewpoint on the ridge. Rocks had to be moved to both sides of the trail as they climbed the steep hill out of Baker Canyon. Location 2 viewed westerly on Willowdale (Modified) map, p. 138.

company had little difficulty ascending the steep hill, as they traveled on to a spring which is located in the headwaters of Tenmile Creek, an actual distance of 10.3 miles, although Eli Cooley thought it to be only 8 miles. After the steep climb, the trail followed the summit of the main ridge in a north-easterly direction with the Tenmile Creek drainages to the left of the ridge and Trout Creek drainages to the right.

The following day, the St. Joseph Company had some degree of difficulty in making the climb. Jesse Harritt writes that it was necessary to double their teams to pull the wagons up the steep slope. However, they completed the climb by approximately 12:00 noon. They continued to travel in a northerly direction until 8 o'clock. At this location, the St. Joseph Company found water some distance down from the trail over what they termed as a bluff, with a little stream located in a grove of pine trees. These authors were able to locate this particular water source in a small basin 200 feet below the summit of the ridge. The distance to the basin that was covered with pine timber agrees with Jesse Harritt's description. Most of the larger pines have been logged. (See photo at the top left on page 143). They actually traveled 14.4 miles, although Jesse Harritt indicated it was only 10 miles. There are no other water sources or pine trees near the trail in this general vicinity.

Samuel Parker's Company was the last to make it up the hill and only traveled three miles where they made a dry camp. Here Parker writes, "*...beried 3 heare.*"

Top of Ridge Out of Baker Canyon. *"all day gitting up hill laid without water beried 3 heare."* Samuel Parker. This photo shows the landscape in the general vicinity of Parker's dry camp on September 29. Location 3 viewed southwesterly on Willowdale (Modified) map, p. 138.

Traces of the Trail. Notice the trail is just a short distance to the left of a present-day road. The trail follows the long, gentle ridge in a northeasterly direction for about 8 miles to where Shaniko Junction is located today. Location 4 viewed northeasterly on Willowdale (Modified) map, p. 138.

SHANIKO JUNCTION TO JONES SPRINGS ON TRAIL HOLLOW

Sept Mon 29: Through Mistake left out a day which I put in here the Road Is Rocky and Broken Weather fine. 8 miles. **Eli Cooley Diary** *[Eli Cooley added this day in his diary between Oct. 4 and 5.]*

30: traveled all day un till in the nite and came to water Coming in all nite 5 beried heare. 35 mi. **Samuel Parker Diary** *[Samuel Parker's milage is apparently off here.]*

30th: traveled 10 ms and encamped on a small branch found a fiew willows. **Jesse Harritt Diary**

Eli Cooley neglected to make a diary entry for September 29th. He did not discover his error until October 4th, at which time he apparently attempted to recall enough of the day's journey by inserting the missing day of September 29th between the days of October 4th and October 5th, where he states he had made a mistake. His memory must have failed him concerning the missing day, because the actual mileage they traveled that day was 15.9 miles, instead of eight miles as he claimed.

When they left their camp site the morning of the 29th, they traveled in a northerly direction. Their trail closely parallels US Highway 197 from Shaniko Junction, crossing the Criterion Summit, continuing about four miles farther, and passing near the present Criterion Ranch headquarters.[1] They continued northerly into Trail Hollow Canyon where they arrived at a good spring which was later named Jones Springs.[2] This is the only source of water present anywhere near the trail in this vicinity. Later, the portion of the Meek Wagon Trail between Shaniko Junction and Jones Springs was renamed as a part of the historic Maupin Trail, which ended at the town site of Maupin, Oregon.[3]

The St. Joseph Company arrived at this spring on September 30th. Jesse Harritt confirmed the spring's location and the mileage when he claimed to have traveled 10 miles. The distance from his last encampment, which was a well-defined location, was actually 11.8 miles.

Samuel Parker's Company left their dry camp on the ridge and traveled without water until they passed the spring at the location where Eli Cooley mentions that their company camped the previous evening. Samuel Parker does not mention stopping for water. It is hard to believe that he did

[1]Criterion Summit is at the top of the summit on US Highway 197, The Dalles-California Highway. It is a view point where one can see the snow-capped mountains in all directions.

[2]The area around Jones Springs was homesteaded by Horatio W. Wells. He received his patent for 160 acres, on June 25, 1892. His homestead later changed hands to a family named Jones in the early 1900s, thus the spring was named Jones Springs.

[3]The Maupin trail ran in a southeasterly direction from the town of Maupin, Oregon. It went past Jones Springs, up Trail Hollow Creek, crossing the Criterion Summit. Then near the present Criterion Ranch headquarters, it continued in a southeasterly direction into the Maupin Trail Canyon. There the trail went across Deep Creek, up Shoestring Creek (formerly Pole Creek), before making its way into the Shaniko area and beyond.

Shaniko Junction

Circles: Picture Number and Its Location.
Solid Line: Traces of the Trail. Verified on the ground by these authors.
Dashed Line: Projected Trail Location. Verified on the ground by these authors.

Pine Grove and Spring

"...we encamped on the margin of a bluff down which we descended 200 feet and found a small stream of water shaded by a butiful grove of pine trees...." Jesse Harritt's diary on the 29th. Location 1 viewed easterly on Shaniko Junction map, p. 142.

Three Sisters

Taken from Criterion Summit Viewpoint. Location 2 viewed south southwesterly on Shaniko Junction map, p. 142.

Mt. Jefferson

Taken from Criterion Summit Viewpoint. Picture viewed southwesterly.

Mt. Hood

Taken from Criterion Summit Viewpoint. Picture viewed northwesterly.

Mt. Adams

Taken from Criterion Summit Viewpoint. Picture viewed north northwesterly.

not stop when water sources are so few and far between in this dry region. They must have at least paused to become somewhat refreshed. They had probably arrived at this water source early in the forenoon and then continued to push on forward the rest of the day and into the night before reaching the Jones Springs encampment. Much of Samuel Parker's Company continued straggling in the rest of the night. Parker claims they had traveled 35 miles. However, the maximum actual mileage they could have covered was only 22.4 miles and only that if Parker covered the three miles he claimed on the day they climbed the very steep hill. Again, this is showing Samuel Parker's mileage estimates to be very unreliable. His company's health was continuing to drastically deteriorate. More people were becoming sick and dying. Here again, Parker writes, *"...5 beried heare."* The number of deaths from his company has now reached 18 souls meeting their maker. Still, there is no mention of any deaths from the other diarists of the other companies.

Jones Springs, located in Trail Hollow Creek, was historically a good water source. Indians used this spring many years before trappers, explorers and settlers passed through this region. This spring was somewhat at a crossroads. The Indian trail which the Meek Wagon Train was following ran in a northerly direction and later the Maupin Trail came into the spring in a southeasterly direction.

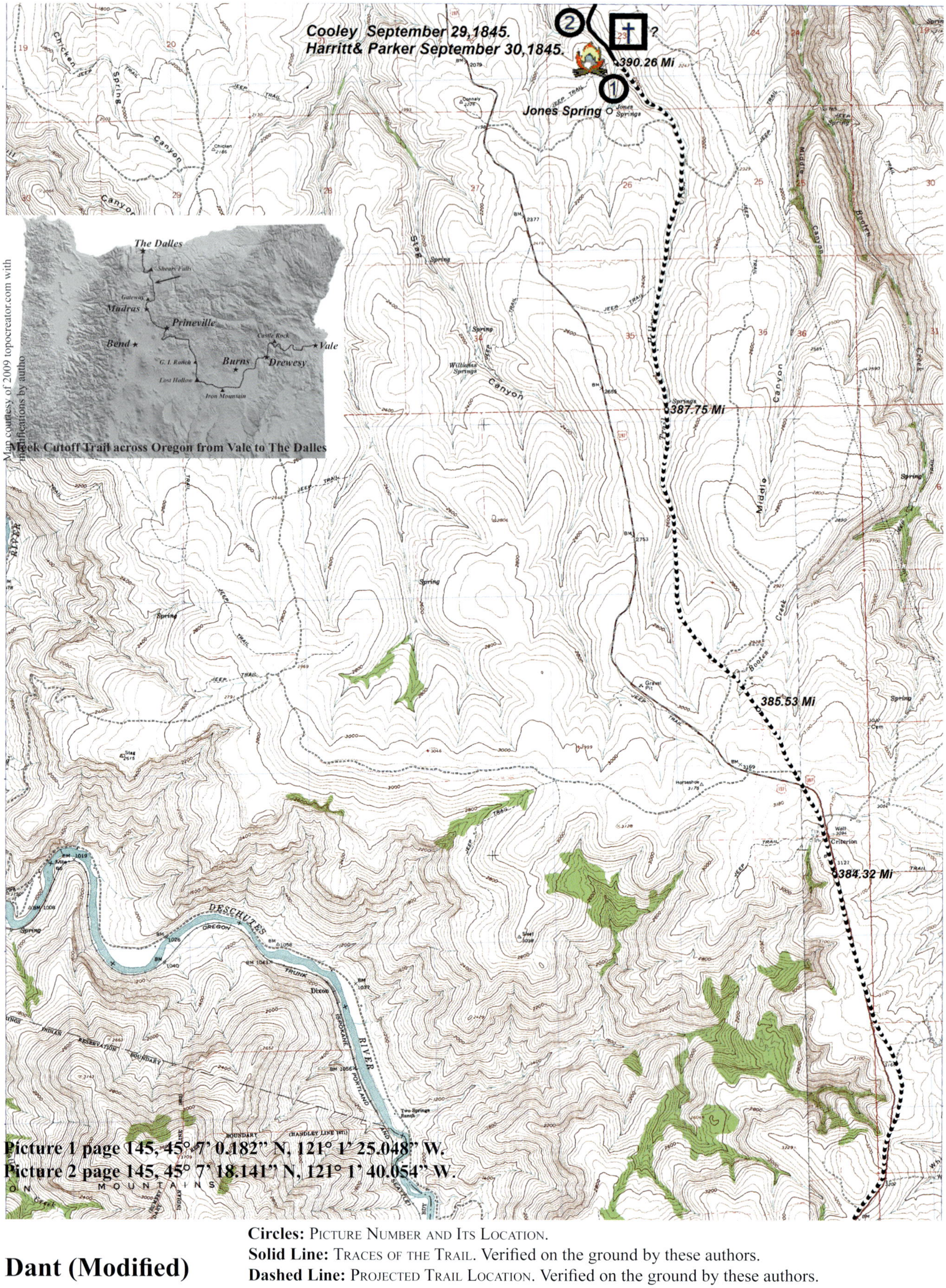

Circles: Picture Number and Its Location.
Solid Line: Traces of the Trail. Verified on the ground by these authors.
Dashed Line: Projected Trail Location. Verified on the ground by these authors.

Dant (Modified)

JONES SPRINGS TO NYE SPRING

Sept Tue 30: The road to day has been quite Rocky Weather fine had a verry steep hill to pull up to day and also to come down Camped at a spring Some Wood and grass here a short Distance Back is an other Spring. 6 miles. **Eli Cooley Diary**

Oct. 1st: had bad roade travleed 6 ms and encamped at a good spring found a fiew willows. **Jesse Harritt Diary**

October 1: Went 9 mi. **Samuel Parker Diary**

Staying on the Indian trail, the Meek Wagon Train left Trail Hollow Creek about a half mile below Jones Springs, turning to the right, northeasterly, up a side draw. Traces of the trail are visible up this side draw and out upon the main ridge. Crossing the bench lands in a northerly direction, the trail then descends in a northwesterly direction down the point of the main ridge between Trail Hollow Creek and Bakeoven Creek, crossing at the confluence of the two creeks. The trail then turns northeasterly up Bakeoven Creek for approximately a quarter of a mile before turning left, again in a northerly direction, ascending a steep slope of nearly a 30% grade, for a distance of about 250 yards. Eli Cooley was reflecting back on the day's travel and best described this stretch of the trail by writing, *"...had a verry steep hill to pull up to day and also to come down..."* Then the trail follows bench lands into Nye Creek arriving at a good spring called Nye Spring where they camped. Nye Spring is the only source of water anywhere near this vicinity. The actual distance from Jones Springs to Nye Spring is 5.7 miles. Both Eli Cooley and Jesse Harritt claim the mileage to be 6 miles, which is very close to the actual mileage. Samuel Parker claims the distance to be 9 miles.

Jones Springs in What is Known as Trail Hollow Creek *"...encamped on a small branch found a fiew willows."* Jesse Harritt's diary on September 30th. Location 1 viewed northerly on Dant (Modified) map, p. 144.

Traces of the Trail Leaving Trail Hollow Creek. The wagons turned to the right leaving Trail Hollow Creek and went up a small swale and on toward Bakeoven Canyon. Location 2 viewed northeasterly on Dant (Modified) map, p. 144.

Nye Spring is a very good spring having a strong flow of water, possibly 60 to 70 gallons per minute, which made this location a very refreshing and popular campsite used by the Indians, the Meek Wagon Train, and later by Capt. Charles Hilton and his sheep.[1] Surprisingly, the area around this spring was not homesteaded until John M. Davis acquired a patent, April 10, 1899, for 40 acres encompassing the spring. Today, this is a very important spring. Water is pumped nearly two miles supplying water to the headquarters of this ranch.

[1]Capt. Charles Hilton was a very industrious sheep rancher, settling on the John Day River near Clarno, Oregon, in about 1873. During the following years, he trailed his bands of sheep to the closest market which was The Dalles, Oregon, following the general route of The Dalles Military Road to where Shaniko, Oregon, is located today. From there he went in a northwesterly direction crossing the Criterion Summit. At this location, the trail coincides with the old Indian trail that the Meek Wagon Train followed. Hilton established cabins and corrals at strategic locations with good springs along this trail. One cabin and corral site was located at Nye Spring in the headwaters of Nye Creek. By 1880, this trail had became known as the Hilton Trail. The field survey notes of Alonzo Gesner, US Deputy Surveyor, under contract number 347, dated January 8, 1880, shows the Hilton Trail coinciding and/or running parallel to an old Indian trail.

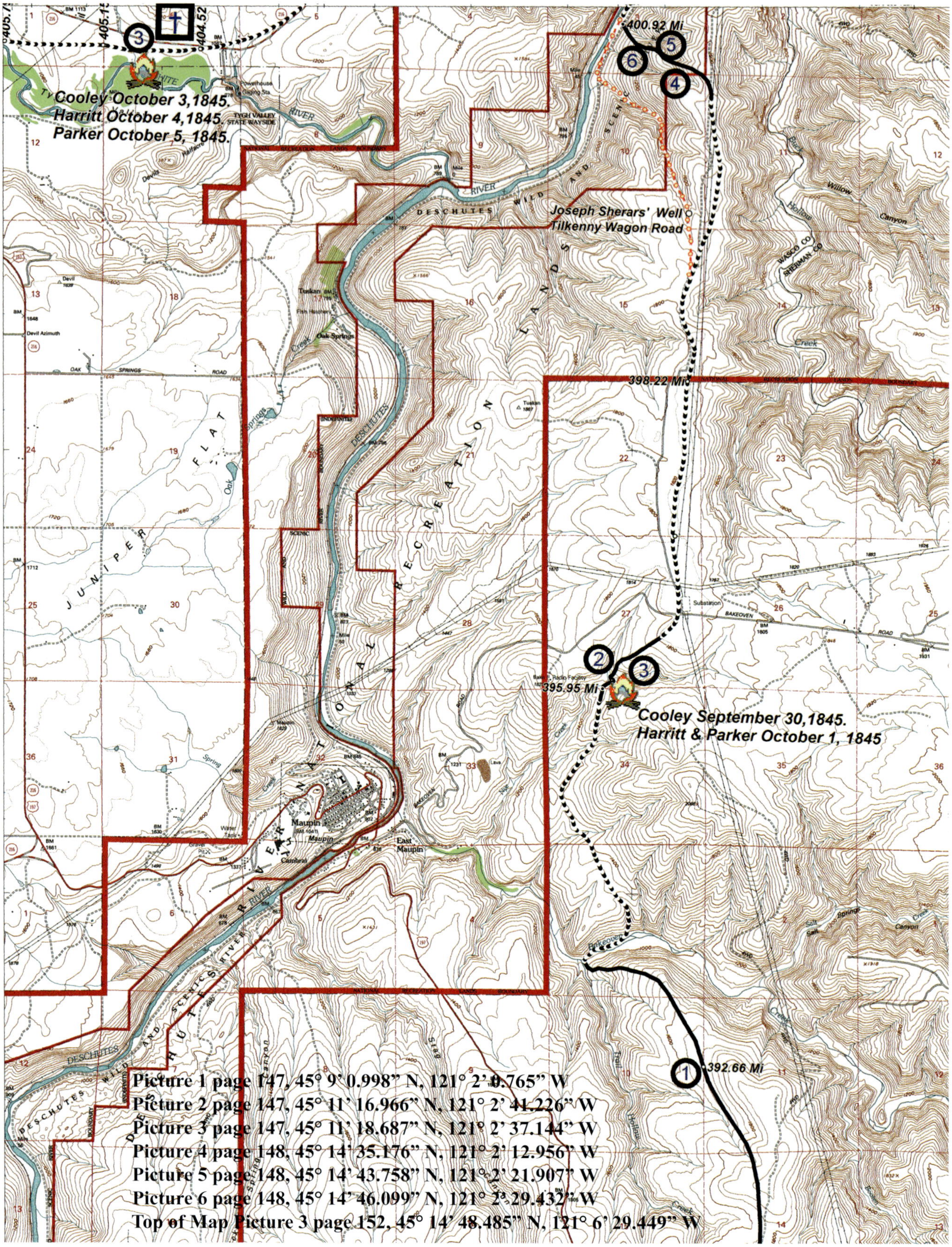

Circles: Picture Number and Its Location.
Solid Line: Traces of the Trail. Verified on the ground by these authors.
Dashed Line: Projected Trail Location. Verified on the ground by these authors.

Maupin

Traces of the Trail. Headed toward Bakeoven Canyon. Alonzo Gesner, in his GLO survey notes of 1880, described this location as being an old Indian trail. Location 1 viewed northwesterly on Maupin map, p. 146.

Nye Spring. *"...encamped at a good spring..."* Jesse Harritt. Location 2 viewed southerly on Maupin map, p. 146.

NYE SPRING TO DESCHUTES RIVER JUST ABOVE SHERARS FALLS

Wen Oct 1: The Road Way is still Rocky and Broken Weather fine Come about 4 miles and struck Falls river after coming down a long steep hill. Seviril Indians here Falls just below here whare we crossed. 4 miles. **Eli Cooley Diary**

2nd: road continues bad travled 4 ms and encamped on Shouts or fall R. **Jesse Harritt Diary**

2: Got to the deshutes river missis But Dyed this day my wife and child and Suane daughter all sick. 9 mi. **Samuel Parker Diary**

Upon leaving Nye Spring, the Meek Wagon Train follows the old Indian trail up a short finger ridge toward the summit of the main ridge.[1] Traces of the wagon swales can be seen and followed today going up this slope to where the main ridge begins to flatten out. The trail, going in a northerly direction, crosses present-day Bakeoven County Road near the Substation. After about a mile and a half, the main ridge becomes long and narrow, still running northerly between the Deschutes River on the left and Buck Hollow Creek on the right. About 3½ miles from the Bakeoven County Road, the Meek Wagon Train left the main ridge northwesterly. They descended a long steep ridge, crossing the Deschutes River County Road, to the banks of the Deschutes River. On October 1st, the Savannah Oregon Emigrating Society arrived

Leaving Nye Spring. Traces of the trail can be seen as they ascended the ridge. At this photo's location, they are just over 4 miles before they reach *"...Shouts or fall R."* Jesse Harritt. Location 3 viewed northeasterly on Maupin map, p. 146.

[1]The field survey notes of Alonzo Gesner, US Deputy Surveyor, under contract number 347, dated January 8, 1880, shows this old historic Indian trail. This is the same trail the Meek Wagon Train followed in 1845.

Long Steep Hill Into Deschutes River. *"...Come about 4 miles and struck Falls river after coming down a long steep hill."* Eli Cooley. From these authors' vantage point on a ridge across the draw, traces of the trail can be seen as they traveled down to the Deschutes River. Location 4 viewed northeasterly on Maupin map, p. 146, and on Sherars Bridge (Modified) map, p. 150.

at this location and camped, while Eli Cooley and the rest of the drovers drove the cattle across the river about a quarter of a mile above Sherars Falls. The rest of the company began making preparations to cross the river.

Traces of the trail are visible and can be followed for the length of the slope, which is about 3200 feet from top to the bottom. This trail averages approximately a 30% grade. One section of the trail is on a cross slope where nearly 600 feet of the trail had to be constructed wide enough for the wagons to travel. Soil on this side slope has very little rock. It is mostly sandy topsoil, so it would have been quite easy to construct a road for the wagons to pass over. Abandonment and lack of use of this portion of the trail has caused it to erode and slough to such a degree that only faint traces of the graded trail exist today.

Looking Down the Long Steep Hill Into the Deschutes River. Traces of the trail can be followed around the steep cross slope. Some construction had to be done for a short distance, bypassing a steep rocky point. Location 5 viewed westerly on Maupin map, p. 146, and Sherars Bridge (Modified) map, p. 150.

Descending Into the Deschutes River. Time has nearly erased evidence of the trail. Only dim traces can be seen as you look back up the slope. The trail here is about 1000 feet from the Deschutes River. Location 6 viewed easterly on Maupin map, p. 146, and Sherars Bridge (Modified) map, p. 150.

CROSSING DESCHUTES RIVER

Oct. 2 Thurs: Weather fine today, we got over the River to day by the assistance of the Indians here wee had to take Waggons over by ropes and some used Waggons Beds The corse to here is about or Nearly North. **Eli Cooley Diary**

3rd: Spent the day in crassing the river had no timber to make boats ware compelled to make boats of our waggon beds to crass our families and goods. **Jesse Harritt Diary**

3: Crossed the deschutes river in a wagon box and tuck the wagons apart and I tuck a wheale at a time by ropes this day my 2 smalles boys tuck sick Gideon and George and Susan my forth girl 6 of my family sick at one time **Samuel Parker Diary**

Over the course of their 1680 mile journey to this point, they had crossed several large rivers and apparently saw the Deschutes River as just another river. Solomon Tetherow was an experienced riverboat captain and he clearly understood the current of a river. Other members of the company had experience and knowledge and devised a good system to cross the river. Preparations were put into place to cross at a location just above Sherars Falls where the river is the narrowest, being only about 80 feet wide and running through a deep crevasse in the lava rock. Because of the depth of the river channel, the current at this location runs quite slowly. Crossing the Deschutes River was challenging to say the least, though apparently the task was not overwhelming. A prompt crossing of the river was made with the assistance of some Indians.

On October 2nd, Eli Cooley writes that they got all the wagons over by using ropes and floating their wagon beds with the assistance of the Indians. Jesse Harritt and Samuel Parker both write that their companies got down to the river and camped. Samuel Parker also comments that Mrs. Butts died, and his own wife and two of his children are sick.[1]

Deschutes River. *"Falls just below here whare we crossed."* Eli Cooley. Arrow depicts location where they crossed the Deschutes River. Sherars Falls can be seen in the right side of the photo. Location 1 viewed southwesterly on Sherars Bridge (Modified) map p. 150..

[1]A descendant of Mrs. Butts lived in Baker City, Oregon. This relative stated that she died from a wagon rollover as they went down the hill to the Deschutes River.

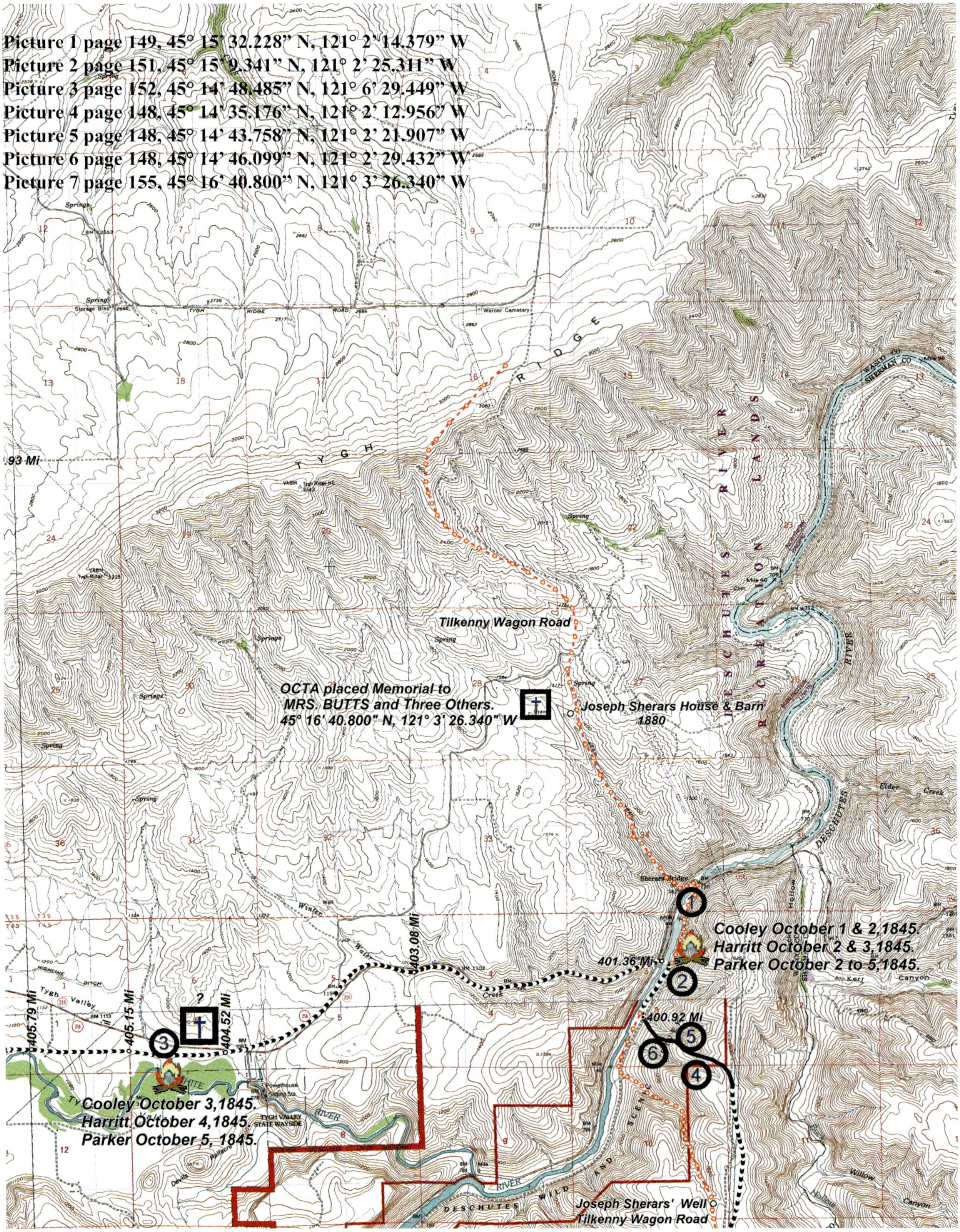

Sherars Bridge (Modified)

Circles: Picture Number and Its Location.
Solid Line: Traces of the Trail. Verified on the ground by these authors.
Dashed Line: Projected Trail Location. Verified on the ground by these authors.

On October 3rd, Jesse Harritt states that the St. Joseph Company completed their crossing using their wagon beds as boats to cross their families.

Samuel Parker's Company spent the 3rd and 4th preparing and crossing the river. Also Samuel Parker says that he "*Crossed the deschutes river in a wagon box and tuck the wagons apart and I tuck a wheale at a time by ropes....*" To make matters worse, two more of Samuel Parker's children became sick, making six in his family ill. October 5th, Samuel Parker writes in his diary, *"day I got all over..."* The entire 200 wagons made the crossing of the river within four days. It appears it only took 15 to 30 minutes for each wagon to safely cross.

The rest of the Meek Wagon Train left Samuel Parker's Company behind by one day. This itself shows there was little camaraderie between the companies. It was necessary for each company to fend for themselves; far different than the popular present-day belief that a wagon train of this size with this many people must have been a great big happy family. It was fortunate there were Indians in the area. They probably assisted this company in crossing the river just as they helped the Savannah Oregon Emigrating Society.

DESCHUTES RIVER TO WHITE RIVER

Oct 3 Fri: Weather fine to day wee got about to days crosin up out oxen today and come about 3 miles and struck a Creek and Camped plenty of Wood here and some grass from the River wee come up a Big hollow Some rock then to the creek the road is good to here no Wood at the River Except a few Willows on this side West corse today. 3 miles. **Eli Cooley Diary**

4th: rigd our waggons loaded up and travleed 3 ms to a delight stream shaded by a fiew cottonwood trees where we encamped for the night. **Jesse Harritt Diary**

5: day I got all over and went 3 miles to a small Creek heare we beried missis but and 3 more. **Samuel Parker Diary**

DESCHUTES RIVER CROSSING. *"... we got over the River to day by the assistance of the Indians here wee had to take Waggons over by ropes and some used Waggons Beds..."* Eli Cooley. The river here is between 60 and 80 feet wide, running smooth and deep. Location 2 viewed westerly on Sherars Bridge (Modified) map, p. 150.

White River. *"rigd our waggons loaded up and travleed 3 ms to a delight stream shaded by a fiew cottonwood trees where we encamped for the night."* Jesse Harritt Diary. *"... I got all over and went 3 miles to a small Creek heare we beried missis but and 3 more."* Samuel Parker Diary. The stream they mentioned is White River running through Tygh Valley with cottonwoods along its banks. Location 3 viewed southerly on Maupin map, p. 146 and Sherars Bridge (Modified) map, p. 150.

Once the river crossing was complete, the wagon train turned nearly a westerly course, following the Indian trail that was now becoming a better "road." The Indians in this area were quite friendly and familiar with seeing white people. The trail, leaving the Deschutes River and Sherars Falls, turned up a hollow or canyon for about two miles. This is the same canyon Oregon State Highway 216 follows today. The terrain in this narrow canyon pretty much dictates where the original trail might have been: right up the bottom. The trail goes through a low saddle following the state highway. Approximately one mile farther is White River.

The original trail the Meek Wagon Train followed from the Deschutes River to White River has long since been destroyed by road improvements over the years, leaving the paved two-lane highway of today. Both Eli Cooley and Samuel Parker simply write that they traveled three miles from the river and came to a creek and camped in the eastern end of Tygh Valley. Knowing the distance they traveled from the Deschutes River, coupled with Jesse Harritt's description of a delightful stream with cottonwood trees on its banks, there is no doubt the stream was White River. There are no other streams in the vicinity that would come remotely close to this description.

At this time, these authors would like to point out and bring to light the comments Joel Palmer made in his journal published in 1847.[1] This is where some of the first flagrantly false writings, misconceptions, and rumors were actually spawned and perpetuated about the Meek Wagon Train.

Joel Palmer, young writer and politician, originally joined the Independence Group near the beginning of the 1845 emigration to Oregon. A short time later, he left this group and joined a group of 30 wagons and quickly became the captain. This group was a part of the original 450 to 500 wagons that Stephen Meek began guiding along the Oregon Trail. Joel Palmer and his company arrived at Fort Boise ten days after the Meek Wagon Train had taken the Cutoff. They chose not to follow the Meek Cutoff Wagon Trail, but remained on the old road, the Oregon Trail. After arriving at The Dalles on the 29th of September, Palmer left The Dalles on October 1st, following Samuel Barlow, who had also been a member of the Independence Group. They were in quest of what later became the Barlow Trail.

Palmer writes on September 30, *"We succeeded in persuading fifteen families to accompany us in our trip over the mountains, and immediately made preparations for our march. On the afternoon of the fourth of October, our preparations were announced as complete, and we took up our line of*

[1]Joel Palmer, *Journal of Travels* (Cincinnati:J.A. & U.P. James, 1847, 55-57, Digitized by Google.

march;...But before preceeding with a description of this route, I will enter into a detail of the difficulties undergone by the company of two hundred wagons, which had separated from us at Malheur creek, under the pilotage of Mr. Meek....They [the Meek Wagon Train] *at length arrived at a marshy lake, which they attempted to cross, but found it impracticable; and as the marsh appeared to bear south,and many of them were nearly out of provisions, they came to a determination to pursue a northern course, and strike the Columbia. Meek, however, wished to go south of the lake,but they would not follow him. They turned north and after a few days' travel arrived at Deschutes or Falls River. They traveled up and down this river, endeavoring to find a passage, but as it ran through rocky kanyins, it was impossible to cross. ...at length Meek informed them that they were not more than two days' ride from the Dalles. Ten men started on horseback for the Methodist stations, with the view of procuring provisions; they took with them a scanty supply of provisions, intended for the two days' journey. After riding faithfully for ten days, they at last arrived at the Dalles. ...they were so exhausted in strength, and the rigidity of their limbs, from riding, was so great, as to render them unable to dismount without assistance. They reached the Dalles the day previous to our arrival. [September 28] ....Black Harris, ...with several others, started in search of the lost company, whom they found...They succeeded in finding a place where their cattle could be driven down to the river, and made to swim across; after crossing, the bluff had to be ascended. Great dificulty arose in the attempt to effect a passage with the wagons....A large rope was swung across the stream and attached to the rocks on either side; a light wagon bed was suspended from this rope with pulleys, to which ropes were attached; this bed served to convey the families and loading in safety across; the wagons were then drawn over the bed of the river by ropes. The passage of this river occupied some two weeks. The distance was thirty-five miles to the Dalles, at which place they arrived about the 13th, or 14th of October. The statements I have given are as corrct as I could arrive at..."*

Then Palmer writes, *"October 1. At four o'clock, P.M. everything was ready for our departure... Our camp was pitched on a small spring branch. October 2. This day we made about ten miles...October 3. This morning I started on horseback in advance of the company,...After a travel of fourteen miles,.... in the bottom are seen several small enclosures, [Tygh Indian Village] where Indians have cultivated the soil; a few Indians huts may be seen along the stream [White River]. Meek's company crossed Deschute's River near the mouth of this stream which is five miles distant. After ascending, we turned to the right...for some five miles or more...October 4. This morning myself and companion, with a scanty supply of provisions for a two days' journey, started on a westerly course into the mountains..."*

There seems to be some blatantly inaccurate information contained within Joel Palmer's journal. First, he said that he had succeeded in persuading fifteen families to accompany them in an attempt to cross the mountains to Oregon City. He said that their preparations to start this journey were completed on the 4th of October. However, he contradicts himself when he writes that on the 1st of October they left The Dalles, continuing their journey on the 2nd of October, traveling about 10 miles. On October 3rd, he is passing through Tygh Valley, and on the 4th he is continuing his travel around the south face of Mt. Hood.

The second inaccurate detail that Palmer relates in his journal is that the emigrants were at the Deschutes River on the 18th of September. He claimed that ten men were sent to procure provisions for the emigrants stranded at the Deschutes River and that they had been riding for ten days when they supposedly arrived at The Dalles on September 28th. In reality, the emigrants were at the North Fork of the Crooked River on September 18th, and the diarists make no mention of any men being sent to procure provisions.

Thirdly, while placing the emigrants at the Deschutes River, Palmer makes the erroneous statement that the emigrants had to search up and down the river for a place to cross. However, the emigrants did not need to search for a place to cross, as the rocky banks along the river and the current of the river would not allow any deviation in the crossing. There was only one place to cross and that was obvious, just above the falls, and they did not cross in the manner that he stated.

The fourth piece of inaccurate information propagated by Joel Palmer was that it took a two week time period to cross the river. However, the diarists of the Savannah Oregon Emigrating Society and the St. Joseph Company both claim they spent the better part of two days crossing the river and advancing to the next encampment. Samuel Parker wrote that it took his company two days and a portion of the third day. Then they proceeded to the next encampment.

When continuing to analyze Joel Palmer's journal, several very perplexing questions come to mind: If supplies, provisions, and manpower were brought to rescue this wagon train, then why didn't the diarists make mention of such a heroic event taking place? And, if such rumors were true, why was Samuel Parker's Company so brutally shunned? This was the company that needed provisions in the worst way, and yet, Parker writes on October 7th, that they had no food for the day upon arriving in The Dalles in the evening. In addition, Palmer writes that the Meek Wagon Train had crossed the Deschutes River on the 3rd of October, yet he has already stated that the emigrants did not arrive at The Dalles until October 13th or 14th. Why did he think it was going to take them ten days to travel the thirty-five miles to The Dalles over a well-traveled road?

Many of the writings up to now have been seriously clouded by erroneous information and the discrepancies recorded in Joel Palmer's journal. The dissemination and embellishment of such information was probably where the story of the Lost Meek Wagon Train originated. These authors cannot help but think of the damage that has been inflicted upon the character and credibility of Stephen Meek due to this blatantly inaccurate journal.

Returning to the Meek Cutoff Wagon Trail, Samuel Parker's Company is following the other companies as they leave the Deschutes River crossing location. When he arrives at White River, he simply writes, *"...went 3 miles to a small Creek heare we beried missis but and 3 more."* This makes a total of 22 people dying from his company alone. Samuel Parker rather minimizes White River as just a small creek, but one has to realize the interchange of such words as creek and river depends upon what these emigrants were accustomed to and can vary a great deal across the country. Is there a possibility that he went a different route than the other companies ahead of him? The answer is emphatically "No." The other companies have cleared the road ahead of him; he has six of his immediate family extremely ill, not to mention how many others in the company are also deathly sick. Mrs. Butts and three others have passed away, and he needs to find a place away from the river to bury them. With these things on his mind, there is no doubt that he followed the other companies. Mrs. Catherine Butts and three unnamed souls were laid to rest near this encampment on White River. During the course of our research these authors have attempted to be as accurate as possible, using the diaries first and foremost. Any additional evidence or previously determined locations have been carefully analyzed before accepting anything as legitimate information pertaining to the Meek Cutoff Wagon Trail. This is specifically one of those sites.

In 1987, members of the Oregon-California Trails Association (OCTA) placed a marker memorializing the death and burial of Mrs. Catherine Butts and the three other unnamed persons at a mound of stones located on private land. This is about 3½ miles in a northeasterly direction from the White River encampment with limited access. The location where the marker was placed, has had a considerable amount of activity immediately adjacent to the mound of stone. As early as 1862, freight was being transported by pack mule to settlers and miners in Eastern Oregon. There was a rough pack trail

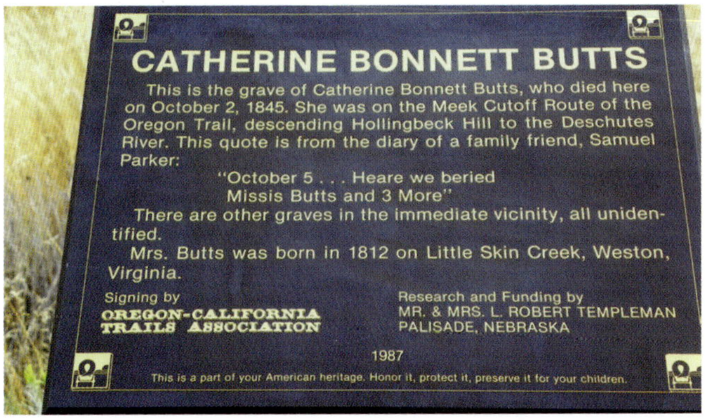

CATHERINE BONNETT BUTTS GRAVEMARKER. Marker set by Oregon-California Trails Association in 1987 at the NE 1/4 of SE 1/4 of Section 28, T 3 S R 14 E, W.M. in Wasco County, Oregon. OCTA memorial marker viewed east on Sherars Bridge (Modified) map, p. 150.

about 1300 feet east of this marker's location. This pack trail became known as the Tilkenny Road.[1] It had been developed as a more direct route from The Dalles to a toll bridge crossing the Deschutes River. In about 1867, the route referred to as The Dalles to Fort Boise Military Wagon Road followed the same route passing by Joseph Sherar's house and barn before crossing the Deschutes River at the toll bridge. In 1864, Joseph Sherar settled in the Tygh Valley vicinity. He built a house and barn at a spring location adjacent to the Tilkenny Road and about one mile northwesterly up the very narrow ravine from the Falls. This was his residence until 1871 when he purchased the toll bridge at Sherars Falls. Joseph Sherar's house and barn were located southeasterly about 1200 feet from the mound of stone and the OCTA gravemarker. The marker is on top of a bluff overlooking Joseph Sherar's house and barn location of which only traces exist today.

Another interesting fact pertaining to this particular mound of stone and the OCTA marker, is that it is located nearly in the center of a forty acre parcel which is a part of the 360 acre homestead tract settled by Ina and William Head. They farmed much of this area in the early 1900s. There is a possibility that this mound could have been just a pile of rocks removed from their field during the course of their farming operations as there is evidence of many other small mounds of stones similar to the one in question.

It is most likely however, that this particular mound of stone lying on the bluff overlooking the homesites is the gravesite of a loved one belonging to some early settler of the area or a passing traveler on the Tilkenny Wagon Road later called The Dalles to Fort Boise Military Wagon Road. These authors do not believe it has anything to do with Samuel Parker's Company. They would have had to travel out of their way on a very difficult six mile round-trip journey to bury their loved ones in such an obscure location, only then to resume following the trail behind the rest of the wagon train.

Concerning the claim on OCTA's marker that Catherine Butts died while descending Hollingbeck Hill to the Deschutes River while on the Meek Cutoff, research has revealed that Edward W. Hollenbeck received a 320 acre homestead entry-stock raising patent dated September 2, 1921. Mr. Hollenbeck's property encompassed Hollenbeck/Hollingbeck Hill. This hill is located to the east of Buck Hollow Creek and was a part of the Oregon Trail Cutoff to the Barlow Road. This road bypassed The Dalles and the dangerous Columbia River rapids. The earliest record of this wagon trail was its inception in 1847, after the Barlow Road had been established in 1846. Hollingbeck Hill did not have anything to do with the Meek Cutoff Trail of 1845.

[1]"Mr. Sherar had incorporated his toll road under the title of the Till Kinny Toll Road, Inc." Wm. H. McNeal, *History of Wasco County, Oregon*, 237. Also Alonzo Gesner, US Deputy Surveyor, under contract number 347, dated January 8, 1880, shows in his field survey notes the specific location of this trail, which by 1880 was now improved, making the road conducive to freight wagon travel and was now called the Tilkenny Wagon Road.

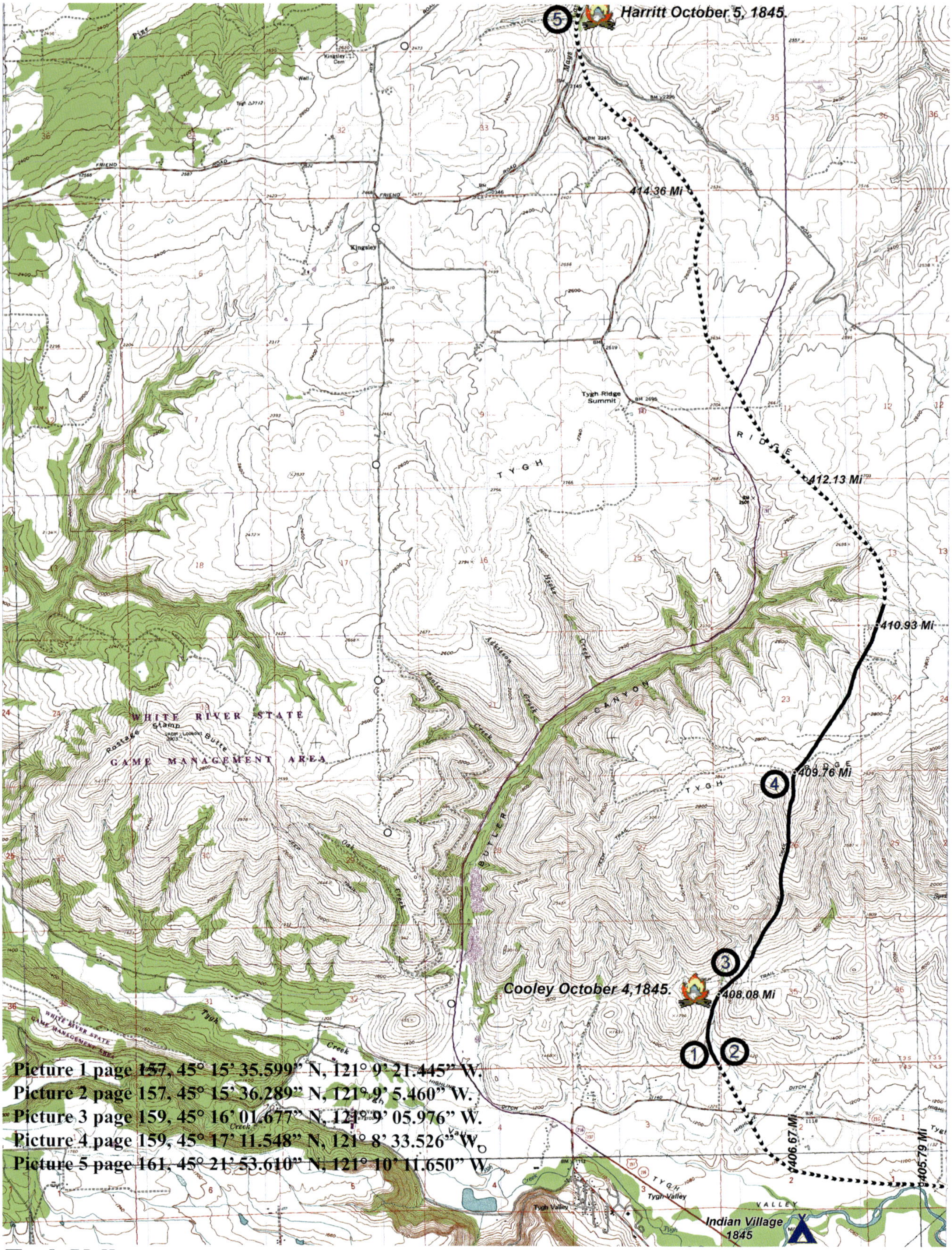

Tygh Valley (Modified)

Circles: Picture Number and Its Location.
Solid Line: Traces of the Trail. Verified on the ground by these authors.
Dashed Line: Projected Trail Location. Verified on the ground by these authors.

WHITE RIVER TO THE DALLES

October 4 Sat: The road to day has been Tollerable good Weather fine Come up the Creek about 3 miles to an Indian Village then Turned to the rite up a hollow and Went about 1 mile further and Camped at a Spring grass and Wood plenty. here is Some Oak Timber Some waggons has gon on wee are now at the foot of a Big hill which the road runs up this Morning on the Bank of the Creek the ground was froze the Indians here raises peas and Some little corn. 4 miles. **Eli Cooley Diary** *[Camped approximately one mile north of Indian Village at Tygh Valley.]*

5th: Travleed 12 ms and encamped in a butiful white oak grove found no water. **Jesse Harritt Diary**

Oct Sun 5: Broken road to day Weather fine come about 12 miles and struck a creek and Camped plenty of Wood and grass here. 12 miles. **Eli Cooley Diary** *[Camped at Pine Creek.]*

6th: made an erly start travleed 5 ms to a branch where we stoped to take brakefast rested 2 hours and started again 5 ms further braught us to another stream where we encamped for the night. **Jesse Harritt Diary** *[Camped at Eightmile Creek.]*

6: the wagons started on and I went back for a horse and ox and Cow got the horse but never got the ox nor cow my family sick I codent stay over tuck the wagons about midnight all my family very bad. 21 mi. **Samuel Parker Diary** *[Camped at the fork of Long Hollow and Dry Creek.]*

Mon 6: Road still Broken Weather fine Come about 3 miles and struck a creek and come about 1 mile Down it and crossed plenty of grass and Wood about 3 miles farther crossed a creek plenty of grass and Wood here and about 5 miles further Arrived at the Methodist Mission on the Bank of the Columbia and camped. 12 **Eli Cooley Diary**

Oct Tue 7: Weather fine to day Laid here to day Flower is $8 per hundred Beef 6 cts per pound Potatoes 60 cts per Bushel. **Eli Cooley Diary**

7th: 8 ms braught us to the mission on the Columbia river where we got a fresh supply of provisions **Jesse Harritt Diary**

7: this morning nothing to eat got to the mission at dark got in a house with my family got something to eat This was the first day we had gone without something to eat. But some of the Company had been without bread for 15 days and had to live on pore beef without anything else I will gist say pen and tongue will both fall short when they gon to tell the suffering the Company went through. 17 mi. **Samuel Parker Diary**

On October 4th, the Savannah Oregon Emigrating Society made their way westerly up Tygh Valley somewhat paralleling Oregon State Highway 216. Eli Cooley describes traveling 3 miles to an Indian village.[1] He observed the Indians living here as being farmers, raising garden produce such as peas and corn. Here, Eli Cooley mentions turning northwesterly of the Indian village and following the trail about one mile farther to a spring, where they camped at the foot of a large hill that the road ascends. Cooley states that some of the wagons have gone on. Solomon Tetherow's Company of wagons could easily be seen making the long ascent to the summit of Tygh Ridge.

General Vicinity of Eli Cooley's Camp. *"...Come up the Creek about 3 miles to an Indian Village then Turned to the rite up a hollow and Went about 1 mile further and Camped at a Spring..."* Eli Cooley, October 4 1845. Location 1 viewed northerly on Tygh Valley (Modified) map, p. 156.

Tygh Ridge Road. *"...Some waggons has gon on wee are now at the foot of a Big hill which the road runs up..."* Eli Cooley. They were now on the main trail between the Indian village in Tygh Valley and The Dalles. Today four-wheel drive vehicles travel over Tygh Ridge. Location 2 viewed northeasterly on Tygh Valley (Modified) map, p. 156.

[1]This Indian village was located about a mile and a half easterly of present-day Tygh Valley, Oregon

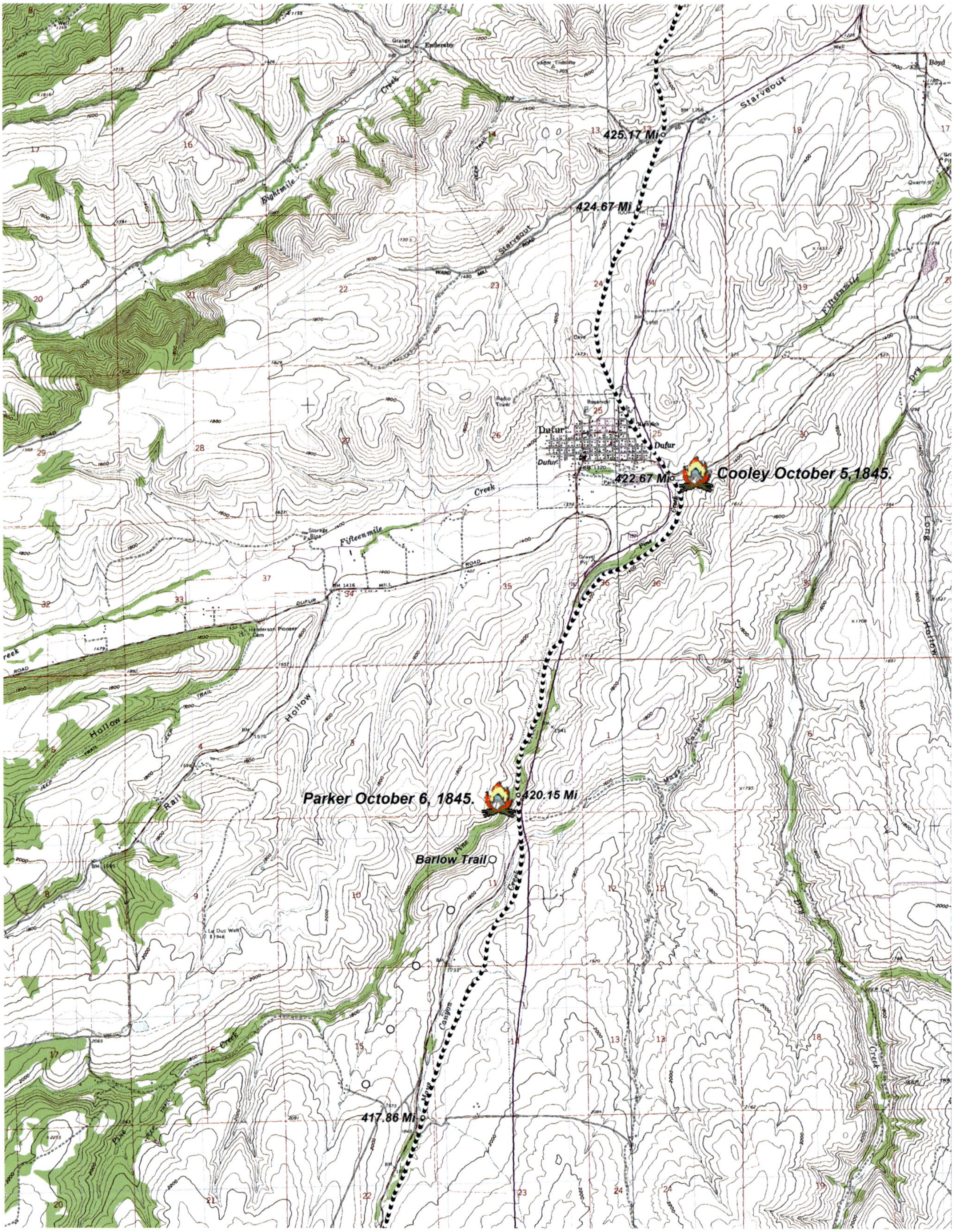

Dufur (Modified)

Circles: Picture Number and Its Location.
Solid Line: Traces of the Trail. Verified on the ground by these authors.
Dashed Line: Projected Trail Location. Verified on the ground by these authors.

Michael Davis, Owner of Tygh Ridge Ranch. He is standing on the edge of wagon swales going up Tygh Ridge. Location 3 viewed northeasterly on Tygh Valley (Modified) map, p. 156.

The road that Eli Cooley mentions is most likely the same road that Joel Palmer came down the day before. This was the main trail from Tygh Valley to The Dalles. In addition, it was the same trail Peter Skene Ogden followed in 1825. Upon reaching the summit of Tygh Ridge, Peter Skene Ogden wrote this comment *"...about 12 o'clock came to the end of the hills - a grand and noble sight- Mount Hood bearing due West, Mt. St. Helens and Mt. Nesqually (Mt. Adams) Northwest, covered with eternal snow, and in the southern direction other lofty mountains in form and shape of sugar loaves."*[1] Peter Skene Ogden went on to write that it took nearly two hours to descend the last hill putting them in Tygh Valley. This author, James Hambleton, had the privilege of being escorted up Tygh Ridge over this trail by Michael Davis, owner of the Tygh Ridge Ranch. Today, there is a road up Tygh Ridge used by vehicles to access the northern reaches of the Tygh Ridge Ranch. There are several locations along the present road where traces of the original trail can be identified. Mr. Davis explained that his great-grandfather, Lafayette Davis, had settled in this area about 1886. He proved up on his homestead of 160 acres and received his patent on October 21, 1891. Mr. Davis said that his great-grandfather traveled to Tygh Valley using horse and buggy along this road. The summit of Tygh Ridge, where the trail crosses, is at an elevation of 2900 feet above sea level. It is the most westerly point along the main Tygh Ridge and the most extreme westerly location that would fit Peter Skene Ogden's observations of the snow-capped peaks. We stood on this summit, seeing the same view as described in detail by Peter Skene Ogden. Mt. Hood looms up in the sky due west of this location, while Mt. St. Helens is still visible in the distant northwest, even after its eruption in 1980. Mt. Adams is in full view in a general north-northwesterly direction. It must be noted that Mt. Rainier falls in direct line with Mt. Adams and cannot be seen from any location along Tygh Ridge. Turning in a southwesterly direction, Mt. Jefferson is in clear view,

Looking Down the Hollow/Draw. The wagons came up this hollow/draw from Tygh Valley and there Eli Cooley says they camped at a spring. Location 4 viewed southwesterly on Tygh Valley map, p. 156.

[1]T. C. Elliott, "Journal of Peter Skene Ogden; Snake Expedition, 1825-1826," *The Quarterly of the Oregon Historical Society, Vol. X, No. 4, Dec. 1909,* http://user.xmission.com/~drudy/mtman/html/ogdn2526.html.

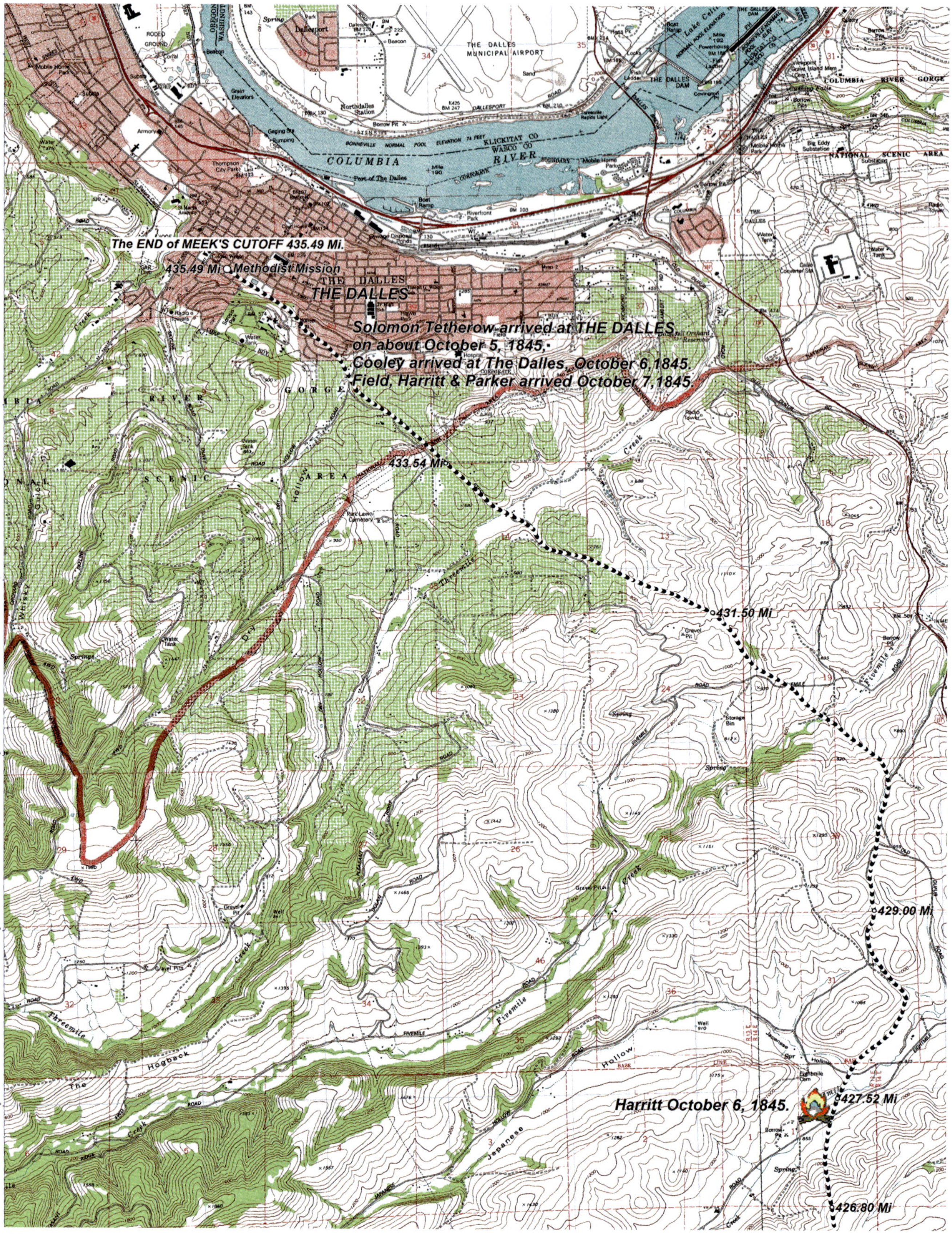

The Dalles (Modified)

Circles: Picture Number and Its Location.
Solid Line: Traces of the Trail. Verified on the ground by these authors.
Dashed Line: Projected Trail Location. Verified on the ground by these authors.

Oak Grove on Mays Canyon Creek. *"...encamped in a butiful white oak grove found no water."* Jesse Harritt. This Oak Grove is in the general vicinity of where Jesse Harritt wrote that they camped. Location 5 viewed northeasterly on Tygh Valley map, p. 156.

as are the Three Sisters and Mt. Bachelor to the far distant south.

From the top of the summit of Tygh Ridge to The Dalles, traces of the wagon trail are nonexistent. This area has been heavily homesteaded by early settlers. Extensive farming, as well as other types of developments, have destroyed traces of the original trail. The terrain dictates a general idea where the trail may have been. Therefore, the wagon road probably leaves the summit of Tygh Ridge, but staying on the top of the ridge, it continues over gently rolling hills, descending to where the Tygh Ridge Road and Mays Canyon Creek meet. This location is where Jesse Harritt wrote in his diary on October 5th, *"travleed 12 ms and encamped in a butiful white oak grove found no water."* Leaving the White River encampment, there are no oak trees to be found along the wagon road until reaching this location. The distance from White River to this location is 12.1 miles which fits very closely to the distance given in Jesse Harritt's diary.

The trail probably followed Old US Highway 197 down Mays Canyon Creek to Pine Creek which was the general location that Samuel Parker's Company camped on October 6th, their last night on the trail. Then from Pine Creek, the trail turns northerly to the present town site of Dufur, Oregon. Near this town site, located on Fifteenmile Creek, is the location described on October 5th by Eli Cooley as being their last campsite. The trail crosses Eightmile County Road on Eightmile Creek, the general location of the last encampment of the St. Joseph Company as described in Jesse Harritt's diary entry of October 6th. The trail continued northwesterly, crossing Fivemile County Road on Fivemile Creek. The trail continued on crossing Threemile County Road on Threemile Creek, before reaching the Methodist mission in The Dalles.[1]

With Stephen Meek and Tetherow's Company of the Savannah Oregon Emigrating Society in the lead, it is presumed that they arrived at The Dalles on October 5th. The remaining companies of the Savannah Oregon Emigrating Society, including Eli Cooley, arrived at the mission on October 6th. After a final 8 mile push, the St. Joseph Company arrived at the mission in the early afternoon of October 7th. Samuel Parker's Company made an early start on October 7 without anything to eat. Many members of his company were very sick. They completed the last 17 miles that day, arriving at the Methodist mission after dark. The entire Meek Wagon Train had arrived at The Dalles, Oregon, within a three day time frame. They had traveled 435 miles along the Meek Cutoff. They spent 45 days on the trail, averaging about 9½ miles each day.There have been many rumors and speculations that Stephen Meek disappeared, abandoning the wagon train because of fearing for his life. Solomon Tetherow wrote he had been over the ground with Stephen Meek, indicating Stephen Meek never abandoned the wagon train as many writers have stated.

Samuel Parker has one final statement that he writes in his diary, *"Thare my wife and child died and I staid till the 3rd November when I left for Oregon City."*

Jesse Harrit writes, *"the prices is as follows flower $8.00 per hundred beef 6 and 7 potatoes 62 1/2 cts per bushel wheat $1.50 coffee 33 1/3 cts tea $2.00 shugar the soil here is quite productive for almost every kind of produce the Indians here beecome verry much civilized [and]turned their attention to aggraculture."*

[1]The names given to these creeks are referenced to their approximate distance traveling southeasterly from The Dalles, i.e. the creek five miles southeasterly from The Dalles is named Fivemile Creek.

ALLEGED SPLIT

Over time, there have been various opinions about a supposed split in the Meek Wagon Train of 1845. These views have the Savannah Oregon Emigrating Society, under Solomon Tetherow's command (which included Eli Cooley), leaving the large springs at the present G I Ranch location, turning westward through the mountainous region of the Gerry Mountains. Supposedly, they would have then continued south of the Maury Mountains, crossing a large desert region, and traveling nearly 75 miles before reaching the Deschutes River near present-day Bend, Oregon. Various historical places have been used and connected by a hypothetical route in support of this theory. These authors will review what would have been involved if the emigrants had actually used such a route. The following are six historical points of interest that we will discuss and examine as we describe the route of this alleged trail:

1. Alonzo Gesner's Survey Map near Pringle Reservoir.
2. A 40 mile stretch of wagon road having various names.
3. Juniper tree scribed "Sacred to the Memory of Jessie."
4. Meeks Camp along Huntington Road.
5. Juniper limb with words carved "1845 Lost Meeks."
6. J. P. Huntington claiming to be on alleged Meek's Cutoff split.

First, let's pick up the Meek Cutoff Wagon Trail at the large springs where the G I Ranch is located today. These springs are the headwaters of the South Fork of the Crooked River. At the springs, Eli Cooley writes in his diary on the evening of September 17, 1845, *"Mr. Tetherow started this Morning and camped just Below us."* In the following two days, the wagon train advanced nearly 30 miles to the northwest of the springs. This advancement places the companies near the confluence of the North Fork of the Crooked River and the main stem of the Crooked River, near the present-day Les Schwab Ranch headquarters. Again Eli Cooley makes a very important entry in his diary dated September 19, 1845, *"Tetherow just below [us] on the creek."* Further documentation, written by Solomon Tetherow, shows he was at this location on the Crooked River.[1]

Upon arriving at the springs at the present G I Ranch location on September 17, 1845, Samuel Parker made an important entry in his diary, when he writes, *"198 wagons in company, 2299 lose cattle, oxen 811 head. All these cattle to get water and 1051 soles [people] also consume a heap of water."* Samuel Parker had just made an accounting of the large Meek Wagon Train. Then the Meek Wagon Train advanced forward, and nine days later they had traveled a total of 115 miles, averaging about 12.8 miles a day. They were now located at a good spring called Porter Springs, near the north edge of Gateway, Oregon. Here on September 26, 1845, Jesse Harritt makes a very important statement in his diary although it is very brief. He writes *"turned a north east direction traveled 3 ms and encamped at a good spring in company with about 200 waggons."* Both Samuel Parker and Jesse Harritt have now accounted for the entire Meek Wagon Train to within two wagons. This dramatically dispels any possibility of a split or division in the wagon train.

Further supporting information that there was no split of the Meek Wagon Train near the location of the G I Ranch are some diagram maps of public surveys of Oregon prepared periodically by the Surveyor General. In particular, some examples of these diagram maps are dated August 31, 1859, September 30, 1860, and August 24, 1863. The primary purpose of the maps was for organizational purpose only; they showed what cadastral surveys of public lands were completed, future proposed surveys, and the many surveys under contract but not yet completed. These diagram maps also show

[1]Solomon Tetherow, *Oregon Spectator,* Thursday, March 18, 1847, p. 3 column 2+. See pages 103-104 of this book.

physical features and road improvements. The data was sketched on the map at a very small scale of 18 miles to the inch, showing a very general location of physical features and improvements. These maps were not prepared with the intention of accurately depicting these features but gave insight as to the general location of many of the roads that had been previously developed, and in many cases, gave the names of the roads. One of the roads displayed on one map is called Meek Trail. Another map shows the same trail, but calls it Mix's Trail. As we have mentioned, the location of the sketched route of Meek's Trail on these maps is very general. However, the sketched lines follow the actual route of the Meek Cutoff Wagon Trail as it has been verified on the ground through this area. Taking particular note though, these maps do not show any split in the Meek Cutoff Wagon Trail as it has so adamantly been purported by several researchers and writers. Between the diaries, Solomon Tetherow's letter, and the diagram maps, there are sufficient facts and evidence to dispel any belief that there was a split in the Meek Wagon Train. Instead, the facts and evidence supports the one trail theory.

However, in case the diaries and the maps are not sufficient evidence to convince the skeptics, let's use logic as our guide. Let's begin to follow the alleged split of the trail from the large springs at the G I Ranch location. Solomon Tetherow has been clearly placed on the main stem of the Crooked River 30 miles to the northwest of the large springs at the G I Ranch location.[1] Therefore, the first logical step must have Solomon Tetherow and his company, as well as any other would-be followers, return to the springs. They had originally made that trip of 30 miles in a two-day journey. Having already descended two very steep hills, one located at Camp Creek and the other located at Crooked River, they must ascend now both of these steep hills to make their return trip to the big springs. One might say it could take 2½ days to make the return trip, instead of the two days when they descended down to the Crooked River. Therefore, once at the springs at the G I Ranch location, Solomon Tetherow and his company, having lost 2½ days, are now going to have to hurry for the next 6½ days through uncharted country on this alleged split trail, in order to arrive at Porter Springs on September 26, 1845, for the next accounting of the complete wagon train.

As these authors cover the following points of interest relied upon by the advocates of the alleged split of the Meek Cutoff Wagon Trail, please keep in mind that as we describe the trail in the following paragraphs, we are describing a hypothetical trail supported by these advocates of the alleged split in the Meek Cutoff Wagon Trail.

1. Alonzo Gesner's Survey Map near Pringle Reservoir.

Let us assume that Solomon Tetherow and his company did take the alleged trail west from the big springs at the G I Ranch location. They would have had to traverse the southern reaches of the Gerry Mountain range through a mountainous region before breaking out onto the vast desert plain. They would have traveled about 22 miles before reaching the first historical point of interest that the "split theory" researchers have them passing. This location is in Township 19 South, Range 19 East, W.M. It was surveyed in 1876 by Alonzo Gesner, Cadastral Surveyor. Alonzo Gesner traveled with his father, Ruben Alonzo Gesner and his mother, Mary (Bailey) Gesner, and one sister Mary Elizabeth, all of whom were reported to be a part of the Meek Wagon Train of 1845. Alonzo Gesner was three years old, while his sister Mary Elizabeth was one year old. Alonzo Gesner grew up in the Willamette Valley and learned the profession of surveying and became a Deputy Cadastral Surveyor working for the General Land Office, and took on contract No. 251, dated September 6, 1876. During the course of his survey of T 19 S, R 19 E. W. M., he was instructed to make note of any prominent physical features or man-made improvements such as wagon roads or any settlers' houses that might be found throughout this area. His field notes reveal a settler named Andrew Jackson Hampton. Hampton's house was located

[1]Tetherow, *Oregon Spectator.*

at a spring which today is recognized as the Barb Wire Ranch. Andrew Jackson Hampton was one year old when his family emigrated west to settle in the Willamette Valley. They were also reported to have been on the Meek Cutoff of 1845. By 1876, at the age of 32, Andrew Jackson Hampton took up squatters rights on the northwesterly reaches of Hampton Buttes, named in honor of his family. Andrew Jackson Hampton had two brothers, John Hampton and Jesse Green Hampton. The three brothers roamed this desert region far and wide, each obtaining land patents across this area. Also, about nine miles to the northwest of Andrew J. Hampton's house, there was another settler, Octavius Pringle, who had taken up squatters rights at the location presently called Pringle Flat Reservoir. Octavius Pringle emigrated to Oregon in 1846 by way of the Applegate Trail.

The main point of this background information is the fact that when Alonzo Gesner completed the survey of T 19 S, R 19 E W. M., he prepared a map of that survey. On this map, he shows a short stretch of wagon road and the location of Octavius Pringle's house being about 600 feet east of one of the section corners that he established. Gesner's field notes show he crossed this particular road eleven times. With seven of these times he specifically names the road "Meeks Old Emigrant Road." All of these specific names are within a three mile stretch around Octavius Pringle's house. The remaining four crossings, he only designates as "road." It is very clear to us that Octavius Pringle influenced Alonzo Gesner with respect to naming the road as it passed so close to his house. Pringle also had a great deal of ownership in the development of this road. However, since Octavius Pringle was not a part of the Meek Wagon Train, and the Hampton brothers were members of the Meek Wagon Train, speculation might be that Octavius Pringle was lending credit to the Hampton brothers, calling the road "Meeks Old Emigrant Road." Certainly Alonzo Gesner would have became well acquainted with these settlers as he worked in this area, passing very close to each settler's home site. During the course of Gesner's Cadastral Surveying career, which spanned somewhere between seven to ten years, he covered about 2700 miles of section line, establishing section corners and quarter section corners many times as he crisscrossed the actual location of the Meek Cutoff Wagon Trail and also the alleged split trail. Alonzo Gesner never mentions anything pertaining to the Meek Cutoff Wagon Trail again in any of his work other than these exclusive seven named locations, all within the three mile stretch of Octavius Pringle's house. Yet he mentions the names of many roads and trails throughout the area he surveyed. It appears he was very conscientious in his survey work. In any respect, these authors feel the designated "Meeks Old Emigrant Road" sheds no evidence to justify any alleged split of the Meek Wagon Train.

Further, exploring the possibilities of what this five mile stretch of wagon road surrounding Octavius Pringle's home might be, these authors look to the years 1853 and 1854. In 1853, the Elliott Wagon Train followed the Meek Cutoff Wagon Trail until they reached the Harney Valley, as evidenced by the detailed accounts Andrew McClure describes in his diary. Andrew McClure was a part of the Elliott Wagon Train. However, upon reaching the Silvies River in Harney Valley, this wagon train left the Meek Cutoff and turned toward the Steens Mountains, believing them to be the Cascade Mountains. This wagon train became hopelessly lost for several days. In the meantime, a party of young men, including Andrew McClure, left in advance of this wagon train for the purpose of obtaining much-needed supplies when they themselves also became lost. Andrew McClure and this small group of men on horses wandered westerly across this desert region rendering Andrew McClure's diary useless as far as the main Elliott Wagon Train was concerned. There does not appear to be any known documented evidence available to establish the actual route Elijah Elliott took crossing this area. His intended goal was the Willamette Valley by way of a poorly developed road that later became known as the Free Emigrant Wagon Road.

With no apparent documentation, it is speculation on these authors' part that it was the lack of water in the desert south of Harney Lake that forced the Elliott Wagon Train back in a northwesterly direction. They eventually returned to the Meek Cutoff somewhere west of Harney Lake and Silver Creek. If this actually happened, as we know was true of the Andrew McClure group, then the Elliott Wagon Train would have advanced westward to at least the Lost Hollow encampment. In 1854, the Macy Wagon Train also followed the Meek Cutoff but avoided the mistakes made by the Elliott Wagon Train. They continued following the Meek Cutoff until they reached the Lost Hollow encampment. The Macy Wagon Train experienced little difficulty in their journey.

It has been asserted by some researchers and writers that the Elliott Wagon Train and the Macy Wagon Train made their way to the large springs at the G I Ranch location and then turned westward following the alleged split of the Meek Wagon Train to the Deschutes River before turning south along what was later called the Free Emigrant Road. While there is no evidence or documentation supporting this theory, these authors have a different approach that might help more in understanding the Elliott/Macy wagon trail. We believe the Elliott Wagon Train and the Macy Wagon Train left the Meek Cutoff just north of the Sinks of Lost Creek, and turned in a northwesterly direction traversing along the base of the mountainous region of the Glass Buttes and the Hampton Buttes. This trail location would skirt the northerly reaches of the desert plains lying westerly between Lost Hollow and the Deschutes River. The terrain along this route is very flat with very few, if any, mountains to ascend or descend, making it a very good road. No doubt this route, being about 38 miles long before reaching the present-named Pringle Flat Reservoir, would require having at least one night's dry camp before passing a spring at the location where Andrew Jackson Hampton later settled, and where the present-day Barb Wire Ranch is located. This route would continue directly to the wagon road leading to the location of a spring that Octavius Pringle settled near. This road continues generally northwesterly about five miles beyond Octavius Pringle's house, reaching a spring near the headwaters of the present-day Ant Creek, where a set of corrals was shown on Alonzo Gesner's map of this area dated 1876. Once again, these authors feel the designated "Meeks Old Emigrant Road" sheds no valid bit of evidence to justify any alleged split of the Meek Wagon Train.

2. A 40 mile stretch of wagon road having various names.

From the corrals on Ant Creek, the terrain dictates that the location of the trail that the Elliott Wagon Train and the Macy Wagon Train probably followed appears to have continued down Ant Creek, crossing Bear Creek near the mouth of Cow Creek Canyon. It then followed up Cow Creek to an unnamed canyon, possibly referred to as the west fork of Cow Creek. Then it reached a house and spring in the southwest quarter of the southeast quarter of Section 22, T 18 S, R 18 E. WM. This is shown on Gesner's 1876 map of this area. It had been 22 years since the Macy Wagon Train was at this location, so Gesner's omission in his field notes of any trail or road for about 7 miles through the Ant Creek and Cow Creek drainages might be attributed to erosion of these creek bottoms. In any respect, whatever the reason for these omissions, a 40 mile continuous road can be retraced from this house using several different Cadastral Surveyor's field notes and maps. Several Cadastral Surveyors, including Alonzo Gesner, have given several names to this same 40 mile stretch of the road. The names include Macy Emigrant Road, Macy Wagon Road, Old Emigrant Road and Road [sic]. A point of interest is that the old Emigrant Wagon Road was used by the Macy Wagon Train in 1854, and most likely the Elliott Wagon Train of the previous year. There is no credible evidence of this road being used by the Meek Wagon Train of 1845.

Scribed Juniper Tree. Photo from *"Terrible Trail: the Meek Cutoff of 1845"* authored by Keith Clark and Lowell Tiller Plate XXV. Courtesy of the Families of Keith Clark and Lowell Tiller. Juniper tree showing scribing "Sacred To The Memory of Jessie" has been misinterpreted by others who believe part of the scribing is missing, when in fact the message is all intact.

HIGHLIGHTED SCRIBED JUNIPER TREE. Scribing is highlighted to enable the viewer to make out the letters of the original photo.

3. Juniper tree scribed "Sacred to the Memory of Jessie."

From the Ant Creek and Cow Creek drainages, the 40 mile stretch of road turns westerly passing near the well known Cofelt Ranch and continues westerly across Little Bear Creek. The trail then ascends out of Little Bear Creek, crossing through the headwaters of both Home Hollow Creek and Salt Creek, before reaching the southerly reaches of what is called Alkali Flat. Crossing the Alkali Flat area, the trail descends Crockery Rim, dropping into Bear Creek Canyon. It then leaves Bear Creek and continues in a westerly direction ascending to the head of a canyon just south of Taylor Butte. County Road No. 27 follows a portion of this canyon. Reaching the head of the canyon, the trail breaks out onto a high desert plain that stretches all the way to the Deschutes River.

Continuing in a westerly course, another historical point of interest is reached.This was a juniper tree with scribing on it. This tree was located about 1½ miles south of the community of Alfalfa, Oregon. A number of trail researchers and writers say that this juniper tree was a direct link to the Meek Cutoff Wagon Trail, as they continue attempting to perpetuate the alleged split in the Meek Wagon Train. This tree was found in the late 1800s with people assuming it to be a reference to a grave of the Meek Wagon Train. Later, it was in jeopardy of being destroyed during the construction of an irrigation canal. Eventually the tree was cut down. The portion of the stump where the scribed words "Sacred to the Memory of Jessie" appeared, was placed somewhere for safekeeping. However, the place is so safe that the location of the artifact remains unknown. Rumors said the Oregon Historical Society was the recipient, yet when asked about its whereabouts, they had no knowledge of its existence. The only evidence remaining of this artifact that these authors have been able to acquire is a copy of a picture appearing in the book *"Terrible Trail: the Meek Cutoff of 1845"* authored by Keith Clark and Lowell Tiller Plate XXV. (See page 166 for a copy of that photograph).

To the untrained eye, the scribing of the tree appears to be incomplete. The scribing has been interpreted to read “Sacred to the Memory of JE--IE”. However, to a more trained eye all the letters are present, clearly rendering the word “JESSIE”. On Page 167 is a copy of the photo with enhancement to help one see the words. There is a great deal of weathering of the wood on the face of this blaze and on the scribing, scribing not carving. The unique and distinct characteristics remaining, as well as the technique used to produce each letter, clearly indicates that these letters have been scribed using a timber scribe and not a knife. During this author’s Professional Land Surveying career of over 50 years, I have scribed many "witness trees" to corners in just such a manner. On page 169 are photos of a timber scribe and a sample of its use on a piece of wood. Very few people would have a timber scribe in their possession, as this tool is used predominantly in the surveying profession. With this in mind, there may be a logical explanation as to how the scribing might have been placed on this juniper tree and possibly even the date the scribing was made.

On May 10, 1879, Rufus S. Moore, Deputy Cadastral Surveyor, along with his survey crew consisting of J. W. Graves, George A. Burris, and S. H. Rock, were working under Survey Contract Number 344. On this particular day, they were surveying the section line between Sections 34 and 35, T 17 S, R 14 E W. M. Moore states in his field notes that he was running north between these two sections, and at a distance of 33.70 chains he crossed a road that he called the Old Emigrant Road, which is the same road that these authors have been describing. Surprisingly, just three chains (194 feet) easterly of this road crossing is the location of the juniper tree artifact. Today, a memorial has been erected at its location 44° 03’16.76”N 121° 01’34.34”W. Just 6.30 chains (415.8 feet) north of the road crossing mentioned, Moore set a one quarter corner stone measuring 12” x 8” x 8”, along with a juniper witness tree. The tree was scribed "1/4 S BT". Rufus S. Moore, being a surveyor, had in his possession a timber scribe. While it is possible the juniper tree artifact was established by some unknown source, these authors believe it was likely that the survey party of 1879 was involved with the scribing of this

Scribe and Sample Scribing Done on May 5, 2014.
Author's personal "Timber Scribe," similar in nature to the scribe Rufus Moore was using during the course of his 1880 survey.

Showing How Scribing Weathers. A juniper tree scribed in 1990. Photo taken March 2009. This is an example of a witness tree.

tree. In any case, there is no supportive evidence the Meek Wagon Train had anything to do with the tree at this location.

4. Meeks Camp along Huntington Road.

From the tree location, the Macy Road, better known as the Free Emigrant Road, continued in a generally westerly/southwesterly direction to Pilot Butte. Pilot Butte is located in the city of Bend, Oregon. Near the southerly side of Pilot Butte, a wagon road called the Huntington Wagon Road joined the Free Emigrant Road. Both roads became synonymous and turned in a southerly direction. Here at this location these authors leave this portion of the road.

From the intersection of these roads and turning northeasterly skirting the westerly side of Pilot Butte and following the Huntington Wagon Road about 5½ miles to a location that has been purportedly called Meeks Camp, is another historical point of interest which is shown on maps. Some trail researchers and writers have made the assumption that the group from the alleged split of the Meek Wagon Train could have possibly camped at this location. However, the Hudson Bay Expedition of 1836, under the command of Thomas McKay and of which Stephen Meek was a member, also could have camped at this location as they made their return trip from California to Vancouver going along the eastern flanks of the Cascade Mountains. The 1836 journey could have been the time Stephen Meek passed this location near the Deschutes River. Even though researchers have determined this to be an authentic historic campsite, there is no credible evidence or documentation that this site had anything to do with the Meek Wagon Train of 1845.

5. Juniper limb with words carved "1845 Lost Meeks."

Continuing northeasterly from this campsite, following along the Huntington Wagon Road for about three miles, another historical point of interest is located one and three-quarter miles easterly of this wagon road. This is a highly controversial artifact that was found in the early months of 1949. The words "1845 Lost Meeks" are carved with a knife, on the surface of weathered wood on a dead juniper limb. While this carving was intended to appear ancient in nature deceiving the average history buff, the trained eye can tell otherwise. Careful analysis of the carving of this limb reveals some very interesting facts. First, it is quite apparent the limb had been dead for many years prior to the time the carving was

1845 Lost Meeks Limb. This photo was taken with the limb still attached to the tree. Photo Courtesy of the Families of Keith Clark and Lowell Tiller.

1845 Lost Meeks Limb
Photo courtesy Oregon Historical Society Image #6214.

1845 Lost Meeks Limb This photo was taken through the glass case at the Des Chutes Historical Museum in Bend, Oregon.

made. Second, the carving was accomplished by someone with very little experience in carving, as his knife control is somewhat sloppy. Third, either a large pocket knife or more likely a fixed blade knife such as a hunting knife was used to make the carving. Fourth, and most importantly, the knife marks are clearly sharp and distinct on many of the figures and letters showing virtually no weathering action on the carving itself, while clearly there is a great deal of weathering of the limb. However, the words on this juniper limb are crisp and clear as well as the visible knife marks which all show very little weathering. Reflect back to the scribing of the words "Sacred to the Memory of Jessie" on the juniper stump near Alfalfa, Oregon. The scribing on this tree stump clearly demonstrates a considerable amount of weathering synonymous with the weathering of the wood on the face of the blaze. The "Lost Meek Limb" in question shows very little if any such weathering. Since this limb was found in 1949, making it 104 years from the date of 1845 when the Meek Wagon Train allegedly passed somewhere near this location, there should have been a great deal of weathering evident on the limb. Examples of weathering can clearly be seen in the photos on pages 166, 169, and page 170. The photo of the juniper on page 169 was scribed in 1990. The photo was taken in March 2009. Comparing these exhibits demonstrate the amount and type of weathering that should be evident on the "Lost Meeks" limb. The photo of the limb that is still intact with the tree shows where the knife carvings have just recently exposed wood. This wood has no discolaration associated with the wood being exposed to the weather elements.

This evidence indicates this limb is fraudulent in nature. Perhaps the carving displayed on the limb was deviously placed there to confuse people interested in the Meek Cutoff and to lend supportive evidence that the Meek Wagon Train was woefully lost. These authors speculate that the carving on the limb was made within a years time frame prior to its discovery in 1949. This would-be artifact has nothing to do with the alleged split of the Meek Wagon Train of 1845.

6. J. P. Huntington claiming to be on alleged Meek's Cutoff split.

Returning to the Huntington Wagon Road and following it in a northeasterly direction for about 15½ miles brings one to a prominent crossroads of the Crooked River Canyon near the location called O'Neil. Historically, this has been the main crossing of the Crooked River used by Indians for many centuries, as well as trappers, explorers and the many emigrants arriving in this vicinity after 1853. It is the first feasible crossing of the Crooked River from the mouth where it empties into the Deschutes River. Here, John Webster Perit Huntington, without a doubt, identifies this crossing as the location where the Meek Wagon Train crossed the river. While all modes of travel used this crossing long before J. P. Huntington ever set foot in the general area, a question comes to mind: If the Meek Wagon Train had traveled this route, how was it possible that J. P. Huntington was able to so positively identify the tracks of the Meek Wagon Train that would have been 19 years old? Clearly J. P. Huntington likely followed much of the Meek Cutoff Wagon Trail from Sherars Bridge to Rimrock Springs and on to the headwaters of Lone Pine Creek. At the head of Lone Pine Creek, he turned to the right, leaving the Meek Cutoff Wagon Trail, followed a prominent Indian trail southwesterly down Lone Pine Creek, passing by Lone Pine Springs and on to the crossing of Crooked River. Possibly he was making an assumption he was still following the Meek Cutoff Wagon Trail as he continued to follow this prominent Indian trail on to the Bend, Oregon, area where he then joined the already existing Free Emigrant Road. The question is why would he not have mentioned the Meek Cutoff Wagon Trail any further south of the Crooked River if he was so sure he was on the trail at the river crossing? These authors continue to believe there is no supportive evidence of any split in the Meek Wagon Train.

The split trail idea has covered the given historical points of interest but would have caused the Savannah Oregon Emigrating Society, under the command of Solomon Tetherow and including diarist, Eli Cooley, to travel 145 miles out of their way minus the last 30 miles from the headwaters of Pine Creek. They would have averaged about 23 miles of travel each day. This rate of travel would have been over twice their average rate of travel for the past 1500 miles of their entire journey up to this point and would be necessary in order to arrive at Porter Springs, near Gateway, Oregon, on the same day that Jesse Harritt made an accounting of a total of 200 wagons in his diary entry, September 26, 1845. Such an effort would be nothing short of impossible given their mode of transportation and amout of accompanying livestock.

Now if this data does not provide enough proof that there was not a split between the Savannah Oregon Emigrating Society and the St. Joseph Company at the large springs in the G I Ranch location, then let's carefully examine the diary entries of each of these companies regarding the nine days after leaving Lost Hollow and traveling to Porter Springs. The diarists were actually present on the Meek Cutoff Wagon Trail in 1845 describing the daily travel in their own words. Let us scrutinize the diary of Eli Cooley, a member of the Savannah Oregon Emigrating Society under the command of Solomon Tetherow, and the diary of Jesse Harritt, a member of the St. Joseph Company under the command of James McNary. We will examine their entries on a day-by-day location basis, demonstrating how they were following in one another footsteps, although they were in separate companies.

> **Sept Tue 16:** Weather fine to day all of our Waggons that had started out the other day got in to day, news come that thare was water and this Evening we started and got to Branch next Morning at Sun rise Traveled down the hollow out at the Mouth which is about 2 miles and along the way wee first started for about 3 miles further the corse this far is about South west then wee Turned to the rite and Traveled about a north corse for about 19 miles and camped on a Branch plenty of Grass and Some Willow and plenty of sage here for 5 miles the road is good then rocky and some what Broken for about 15 miles then good and level to the Branch. 24 miles. **Eli Cooley Diary**

> **16th:** the hunters returned this morning at 9 oclock found water in 25 ms in a fiew minits the company were in parade for their oxen made a general collection of stock betwin 4 olock and sundown about 80 waggons left the branch for the next encampment travleed all night at day brake we reached the place of encampment at a small mountain stream winding its way through a level vally found no wood except sage which grew in abundance near its margin haveing come 25 ms we stoped to take some refreshment and rest our teams. **Jesse Harritt Diary**

Eli Cooley makes a mistake when he says "South west." He meant northwest. This was a transitional change. The terrain dictates this direction. There is not any way to travel down out of the hollow without going northwest. Notice Cooley says they traveled 24 miles while Harritt says 25 miles.

> **Sept Wen 17:** This Morning wee camped about sun rise and about 12 o clock started again and in about 6 miles struck a spring creek and camped near the head plenty of grass some Sage no Willow Mr Tetherow started this Morning and camped just Below us Weather fine. 6 miles. **Eli Cooley Diary**

> **17th:** after takeing some refreshment we yoaked our teams at 2 oclock PM travleed 6 mi and encamped on sandy delightful stream running to the north west affording an abundence of fine grass no wood. **Jesse Harritt Diary**

Notice both companies traveled six miles farther and camped on a spring creek: a "sandy delightful stream." This is the main headwaters of the South Fork of Crooked River running to the northwest.

> **Sept Thu 18:** Weather fine to day road Tollerable good come down the creek north west about 3 miles and crossed it and in about 11 miles further struck a hollow and come Down about 1 mile further and camped at a Spring Plenty of grass and Some Wood on the Bluff here. 15 miles. **Eli Cooley Diary**

> **18th:** 3 ms down we crassed over to the west side and after a travle of 12 ms we encamped at a good spring found good grass and some ceder timber. **Jesse Harritt Diary**

Notice both companies went 3 miles and crossed the South Fork of Crooked River and went 12 miles and camped. This is Jaggi Spring on Camp Creek.

Sept Fri 19: road Tallorable good today Weather fine Come down the Branch about 2 mile and Turned to the left up the hill and in about 5 mile struck the same creek wee crossed yesterday and Traveled Down it at about 3 mile and Camped plenty of grass and some Willow Tetherow just below on the creek the corse to the creek is about North west then down the creek this far about west Some Ind to see us to nite. 10 miles. **Eli Cooley Diary**

19th: made an advance of 12 ms and encamped again on sandy found grass and a fiew small willows. **Jesse Harritt Diary**

The companies traveled in a northwest direction and arrived on the main stem of the Crooked River near the confluence of the North Fork of the Crooked River. Cooley goes into a little more description of the day's travels than Harritt. Cooley's extra description fits the actual terrain of the ground that the companies traveled over. Harritt says they were "again on sandy." "Sandy" is the term he used in describing the delightful stream on the 17th. The mileage again is very close.

Sept Sat 20: Bad road to day Weather fine Traveled down the creek to day and Generally in the Bottoms of it some scattering seder and pine Timber on the hills they is plenty of grass and Willow to camp any whare on the creek Camped on the creek plenty of grass and wood here. 12 miles. **Eli Cooley Diary**

20th: continued down the creek passed through several narrow evenus where the mountains closed in on both sides where we ware compelled to follow down the channel of the for several hundred yards in water up to our waggon beds continued to follow its meanders crassing its channel a number of times after an advance of 13 ms we encamped found grass and willows. **Jesse Harritt Diary**

Please note that both companies traveled down the creek where they were constantly in and out of the river. It is very apparent that both companies are following the same route. Most assuredly, the Savannah Oregon Emigrating Society did not take another route away from the St. Joseph Company.

Sept Sun 21: Still Bad road Weather fine Traveled down the creek to day and have crossed it several times to day and have Camped on it plenty of grass and Willow here and all along the creek still Seder and pine on the hills West 12 miles. **Eli Cooley Diary**

21st: down the creek 10 ms had bad road we encamped found grass willow and ceder timber in abundence. **Jesse Harritt Diary**

Both companies are still traveling down the river and seeing the identical vegetation along the river with plenty of grass and willow.

Sept. 22. Mon: Bad road today Weather fine come down the creek about 2 miles and then Turned to the rite and left it after crossing it 3 times Here wee had a very steep hill to pull up and about 8 miles further struck a creek and camped in the forks the creek wee camped on is to our rite some cedar on the hills the corse to whare wee left the creek is about west then about North to here. 10 miles. **Eli Cooley Diary**

22nd: 3 ms braught us to the foot of a huge mountain where we commenced ascending through thick ceder timber at 2 oclock P.M. we gained the top the seen of the country became butiful and levle passed through several groves of pine and ceder timber at 11 oclock we came to a stream affording an abundence of water grass and timber where we encamped haveing come 14 ms. **Jesse Harritt Diary**

Both companies had a very steep mountain to ascend in order to leave the river. Here Harritt writes that after the steep climb, the country was beautiful and level and Cooley writes that his company camped at "the forks." The forks he is talking about is Crooked River and Ochoco Creek at Prineville.

Sept Tue 23: The road to day has been Tollerable good Weather fine Crossed the Creek this Morning near its Mouth whare it runs into the same creek wee have been traveling Down and come about 3 miles down the creek here leaving it to our left and have Traveled about a South West corse about 3 miles from whare wee left the creek is a Spring plenty of grass and Some few Willow Camped about 8 miles further at a Branch or spring plenty of grass and some seder Wood on the hills to the left about ¼ mile. 12 miles. **Eli Cooley Diary**

23rd: started late had good road travleed 12 ms stoped at 9 oclock at a spring found good grass no wood except a little sage. **Jesse Harritt Diary**

Cooley again makes a transitional error in his direction, meaning northwest instead of southwest.

Once again, the terrain dictates the direction they had to take. Southwest would have them crossing Crooked River and then climbing the steep rimrock bluffs of the Crooked River canyon. Here both companies traveled 12 miles for the day. Cooley describes where the companies camped at Rimrock Springs very accurately.

> **Sept Wen 24:** The road to day has been Tallerable good Weather fine Traveled about a North west corse for about 10 mile then Turned about west with the Expectation of Striking the river But did not Strike it and stopped without any water. 12 miles. **Eli Cooley Diary**
>
> **24th:** the roade good travleed 14 mi through the levle plain and stoped for the night without wood or water. **Jesse Harritt Diary**

Upon leaving the encampment located at the present-day Rimrock Springs, both the Savannah Oregon Emigrating Society and the St. Joseph Company passed through the headwaters of the Willow Creek drainage. This location is the present-day town of Madras, Oregon, just before Willow Creek enters a deep gorge and flows down toward the Deschutes River. Crossing these headwaters, they reached a nearly level plain where they traveled about two miles farther. Both companies have now traveled nearly the same mileage to a location near the northerly rim of the deep chasm of Willow Creek. This location is northwesterly of the present-day Madras, Oregon. Here they made a dry camp and did without water.

> **Sept Thu 25:** The road to day has been Tollerable good Except Some few rockey places Weather fine this Morning wee Started Early and Traveled nearly North for about 8 mile and Camped on the hill about 1½ mile from Shoots or Falls River and drove our cattle down a hollow to water Some seder wood here and some grass the rite hand road is some nearest as the Company biching made a cutoff on us. 8 miles. **Eli Cooley Diary**
>
> **25th:** made an erly start travleed 6 ms and encamped on Shouts or fall river this river is the most singula in its carrecter of any we have seen it washes the eastern margin of the Cascade mountains and flows with a rapid current through a deep cavern of rock haveing a channel from 20 to 30 yards wide and is from 3 to 4 hundred feet below the levle plain. **Jesse Harritt Diary**

The companies arrived on the northerly reaches of the Agency Plains where water again was not available. Here a decision was made that both companies would drive their cattle about a mile and a half down a hollow to the Deschutes River.We must remember that Harritt is a drover and did not go into detail about where the wagons camped but went into great detail about what the river was like when he and the cattle reached it and camped. In turn, Cooley clarified that the wagons camped on a hill, while he drove the cattle down the hollow to the river. The drovers returned to the wagon train with the cattle the following morning. In addition, Cooley mentions that one of the straggling companies made a shortcut across Agency Plains grumbling and complaining.

> **Sept Fri 26:** The road to day has been Tollerable good Except one Big hill to come Down which is Rockey. Weather fine. Traveled about a North East corse and camped at a spring plenty of grass here some seder Wood Some Distance off. 3 miles. **Eli Cooley Diary**
>
> **26th:** turned a north east direction travleed 3 ms and encamped at a good spring in company with about 200 waggons. **Jesse Harritt Diary**

Both companies traveled northeast three miles to a good spring. Cooley says the road was good except one big hill to go down which was rocky while Harritt made the point that they were in the company of about 200 wagons. All companies were camping together again at this point.

With the diaries properly correlated, there is no doubt that the Savannah Oregon Emigrating Society and the St. Joseph Company did in fact follow the same route along the Crooked River. There was NO SPLIT in Meek Wagon Train.

WHERE WAS THE GOLD?

Gold was discovered in the United States in California in 1848. Word quickly spread, and the emigrants of 1845 recalled an important incident! Someone on the journey across central Oregon with Stephen Meek had found something that now they realized must have been "gold!" Stories flew rampant with this emigrant and that emigrant having been the one that found it somewhere along the Meek Cutoff. Each time a descendant would utter this exciting gold story, they would embellish the story a little bit more and some different ancestor would be placed in the forefront in an attempt to assure that they might receive the credit for the initial discovery. It was soon called the "Blue Bucket Diggins," and later dubbed the "Lost Blue Bucket Mine." The legend of the Blue Bucket Gold discovery has swirled around the country ever since. However, the diaries do not mention anything that could have been attributed to gold.

People have been searching for years for the location where the gold on the Meek Cutoff may have been found. In 1861, David Littlefield, Henry Griffin, William Stafford, and G. W. Scriver met a man by the name of Adams in Portland, Oregon, who said he could lead them to the famous Blue Bucket Diggins. A large group of men and equipment congregated and left The Dalles. Eventually Adams began to show evidence that he was lost. By the time they had wandered all over the area, somewhere near the North Fork of the Malheur River, the group expelled Adams from the camp. The large group of men split and many of them returned to Portland. Littlefield, Griffin, Stafford, and Scriver continued on their own prospecting expedition but abandoned the search for the Blue Bucket Diggins. They crossed the divide between Burnt River and Powder River and camped on a creek the night of October 23, 1861. Here Griffin prospected and found the first gold in Eastern Oregon. From this discovery, Auburn, Oregon, sprang up, and all over Eastern Oregon gold was discovered and towns were formed.

In 1868, Stephen Meek guided a group of thirty men to the Malheur River where rumor had it that the famous Blue Bucket Diggings had been found. Stephen called it a "wild goose chase". Trail retracers have been continuing to search for this prize since 1849, all in the hopes of becoming rich. As far as we know, the "Lost Blue Bucket Mine" has not been located.

William Armstead Goulder, a wise young man, was a member of the Meek Wagon Train. He was a cattle drover traveling with the Savannah Oregon Emigrating Society. Daily, he had observed the precious gold and later told the whole world where it could be found. William Goulder wrote the following:[1]

> Not a word was ever heard of the marvelous find until after the discovery of gold in California in 1848, and though many attempts have been made by prospecting parties to rediscover the place where the nuggets were found, no one has yet been able to find the hidden locality or discover any evidence of the presence of gold anywhere in that region. But all that detracts nothing from the interest of the story. Were all myths sifted from history, the residue would form a dreary and uninteresting mass of commonplace rubbish.
>
> There was however a great deal of real gold found that year, not only on the "Cut- off," but also along every mile of that long, dreary transit across the wilderness, and it was gold of the truest and purest type, without any alloy or admixture of baser metal. It was the gold that was found in the courage and fortitude, the patience and cheerfulness of the brave and persevering immigrants. But in none did these qualities shine out in such resplendent lustre as among the women of the immigration.

Yes, William Goulder was a wise young man. The real gold found on the Meek Cutoff was the courageous women of the emigration.

[1]W. A. Goulder, *Reminiscences: Incidents in the Life of a Pioneer in Oregon and Idaho,* ed. Timothy Reagan (University of Idaho, 1989), 131-132.

CONCLUSION

Arriving at Fort Boise having just traveled 1300 miles in 97 days, the emigrants were exhausted. Just when they thought their journey couldn't get any worse, panic swept through the people as tales of Indians on the warpath spread throughout. In an effort to calm the chaos, Stephen Meek, knowing that renegade Indians could be extremely dangerous, explained to the emigrants their options. They could continue along the Oregon Trail and take their chances with the Indians, or he knew of a route that would lead them to The Dalles that would avoid the Indians altogether. However, it had never been traveled by wagon. The emigrants, weighing their options and fearing for their lives, were willing to risk a new trail if it meant avoiding the hostile renegades. Putting their faith in Meek, the emigrants hired him to guide them on this new route. They let their fear override their common sense. The new trail they took required so much more work than if they had stayed on the Oregon Trail. Nevertheless, these emigrants were very determined, resourceful, creative, strong-willed and hardworking people. Just like the oxen that bowed their necks and pulled those heavy wagons, the emigrants bowed their necks, doing what had to be done each day. Credit should be given to them, as they were the ones that opened up the central part of Oregon.

Correlating the diaries on a day-by-day location basis enabled these authors to see the bigger picture with more detail. Several key points came to light:

The first, being a common misconception by the public, is the belief that the emigrants traveled during daylight hours. Therefore, one would expect that soon after daylight they would rise, fix breakfast, and leave the encampment to continue down the trail. However, the time of departure was contingent upon a lot of factors such as the readiness of the other wagons in the company, the animals, especially the cattle and cattle drovers, the weather, and the wagon master, as well as the guide. Reading the diary entries gave a better insight as to how the companies traveled and often they referred to beginning later in the day, and sometimes they traveled at night. Usually when traveling at night, it was under bright moonlight, and was necessary in order to make the 25 to 30 mile jaunts to reach the next encampment and water source.

The second key point is that although there were four occasions when the emigrants did not have adequate water for their livestock, this was not much different than when they traveled over the Oregon Trail. They did, however, have a reserve supply of water that they carried in water kegs for their personal use. Visiting this desert region has revealed that even today water is still present at the locations of nearly every historical encampment. Hibbard Spring, near the Double O Ranch headquarters, and the large springs at the headwaters of the South Fork of the Crooked River where the G I Ranch is located, are very large springs running impressive volumes of water. Certainly, the size of these springs astonished the emigrants of 1845, just as they do travelers in that area today. The local people throughout this region and the present-day owners of these properties indicate there was a larger supply of water available historically than what is present today.

The third key point and possibly one of the most important, is the fact when the emigrants saw the snow-capped Steens Mountains, they mistook them for the Cascade Mountains. At that time, they began losing confidence in their guide, Stephen Meek.

The fourth key point is that although the diarists, tired from the day's journey, were not very long-winded in their entries, it was the quality of the wording, not the quantity, that has led these authors to the conclusion that there was no split in the Meek Wagon Train at, or near the G I Ranch, or anywhere else along the trail. Without their guide, they were at a complete loss of where to go.

Fifth, death claimed the lives of twenty-four people along the Meek Cutoff Wagon Trail. Apparently, the first death was Sarah Chambers; although her death is not mentioned in the diaries, a grave marker bearing her name and date has been found and monumented along the trail. The first death that was mentioned by three of the diarists was baby Elkanah Packwood. While there is very little known pertaining to the deaths of the remaining twenty-two people who later died along the trail, these people all appear to have been from Samuel Parker's Company. Samuel Parker made an accounting each time the company laid a member to rest at the several encampments along the trail. If there were deaths of members of the other companies, the diarists would have reported them in their diary entries. What caused these twenty-two deaths? These authors conclude that they were caused from the consumption of alkali. Even though that is our conclusion, it would be prudent for the reader to research this subject further, obtaining more professional opinions for one's own satisfaction.

The sixth key point is that the crossing of the Deschutes River was taken in stride, as the diarists made little mention of it. They knew what needed to be done and they did it with speed and no grumbling. Ironically, they did have assistance from some of the Indians.

Seventh, the diarist do not mention a rescue party at the Deschutes River. Therefore, it is these authors opinion that there was not a rescue party at the river, as we are certain the diarist would have mentioned such an event taking place.

The final and eighth key point is that Stephen Meek was NOT lost when guiding this wagon train. Stephen Meek was a real mountain man. His abilities to survive in such a vast uncharted wilderness were such that he was never lost. Stephen Meek spent twenty years of his life crisscrossing the better part of this great continent, especially the Oregon territory. Prominent landmarks throughout this country were crucial to his daily life. It became second nature for him to observe these landmarks far off on the horizon, using them to guide his course across many hundreds, if not thousands, of miles as he journeyed far and wide. This, in itself, gave him the experience and qualifications to be a guide for the large group of emigrants in the year 1845. Stephen Meek was a man of few words. If he had communicated better with the emigrants, perhaps the misunderstandings would not have taken place. However, he was a man of good and honorable intentions. He was not a contriving, devious scoundrel. He led the wagon train over the very best possible route conducive for a wagon to travel through this area. It is these authors' opinion, that while it is nearly impossible to lead a stubborn mule along an intended path, in due time he can be encouraged to follow reluctantly. Lost Hollow was one of these instances. Stephen Meek knew where he must go and the arrival of Solomon Tetherow made the time right. It was at this location that we believe Stephen Meek led the wagon train back to his original intended course.

It is these authors' goal to eventually have the Meek Cutoff Wagon Trail mapped, marked and permanently monumented. When this takes place, if ever, it will be our tribute to the memory of Stephen Hall Meek.

IN MEMORY

Stephen Hall Meek
Photos Courtesy of Oregon Historical Society Research Library Images # 19905 and 25856.

Last Homesite of Stephen Meek. Located on the Josiah Doll Homestead near Etna, California. Photo Courtsey of Richard Silva.

Remains of Stepen Meek's Last Home. The remains of the house in 2009.

Stephen H. Meek Gravemarker. Etna Cemetery, Etna, California. Memorial plaque placed by Native Daughters of the Golden West, Eschscholtzia Parlor #112.

HUDSON BAY CO. TRAPPERS CAMPSITE OF 1836.
Located near Scotts River in Scotts Valley, California.
Photos Courtesy of Joe Molter.

In the 1880s, Stephen Meek showed this Hudson Bay Trappers campsite to the local residents of the area, including his friend, Jacob Lewis, grandfather of Oral Lewis. Oral Lewis was a prominent historian of the area. Camp was located on the top of the small knoll in the grove of oak trees. A spring is on the left.

Sign erected at the Hudson Bay Trappers Campsite by the Native Daughters of the Golden West, Eschscholtzia Parlor #112.

Musket Ball found on the campsite by Joe Molter and Richard Silva in about 2012.

OREGON PIONEER ASSOCIATION
ORGANIZED OCTOBER 18, 1873

GEO. H. HIMES
SECRETARY

ROOM C, SECOND FLOOR
PUBLIC AUDITORIUM
ENTRANCE, 253 MARKET STREET, CORNER OF THIRD
PORTLAND

October 4, 1925.

Mrs. D.C. Remington,

R.F.D. No.3,
Box 817a,

Portland, Oregon,

Dear Madam:

In response to your letter of 30th September, in which you allude to a diary kept by the grandfather of your husband, when he crossed the plains to Oregon in 1845, permit me to say that it has no particular value aside from its being a "keepsake." Its contents, of course, are interesting, but I have diaries as far back as 1832, , 1834, 1836, 1838, 1834, 1838, 1844, 1845, 1846. 1850, 1851, 1853, 1854, etc.; and most of them are in print.

Now, I should like to get yours as a gift to this Society, or as a loan, with the understanding that I can have it copied, and then, in due time, print it so that every member of your family might have a printed copy, and if desired, will return the original to you.

I presume I have something here that you may not remember, or it may be that you never knew. What I allude is the portraits of Mr. and Mrs. Ely Cooley, loaned by L. E. Remington in December, 1916, to the Pioneer Association.

Very truly yours.

Geo. H. Himes

Secretary.

OREGON PIONEER ASSOCIATION
GEO. H. HIMES, SECRETARY
AUDITORIUM
ROOM C, SECOND FLOOR
ENTRANCE, 253 MARKET ST., COR. OF THIRD
PORTLAND, OREGON

PORTLAND JAN 26 1 7 PM 1926 OREGON

Letter courtesy of Grace Armstrong, Great-Granddaughter of Eli Cooley.

LETTER WRITTEN BY JAMES FIELD'S TO A NEWSPAPER EDITOR

Port Chester, N.Y.
June 3, 1879

Friend Clarke:

Through the kindness of my old friend, R. Weeks of Portland, I am in receipt of three numbers of your paper, containing installments of my diary kept while crossing the plains in '45, with a request that I may complete it from memory. This it is impossible for me to do, as it was cut short by my illness with camp fever, which destroyed all memory of what transpired during the remainder of the journey. I have an indistinct recollection of crossing the Deschutes river in a wagon body, caulked tight and drawn back and forth by ropes, of being carried and laid upon a bed among the rocks that lined the river banks where we crossed, and of arriving at the Dalles so helpless that it was necessary to lift me out of and into the wagon like a baby. Then I remember going down to the Cascades in a boat such as the Hudson Bay Company then used on the river, of walking and crawling past the first steep rapid, then getting into a canoe with some Indians and running the remainder of the rapids to the landing place of the old Callapooia, Capt. Cook, owner and master; then of sailing down the Columbia and up the Willamette to Linton, a place on the west bank of the river below Portland, and then having the only wagon road to Tualatin plains below Oregon City from the river. From Linton to Oregon City I was a fellow passenger with old Mr. Fleming, the pioneer printer, so long connected with the press at that place, and I think it was late in November when we arrived there.

When I returned here overland in the spring of 1848, I deposited the diary with Capt. J. B. Riggs of Polk County and when I returned to Oregon in 1850, finding that he had used the blank leaves in the book to keep his business accounts I left it with him. If it is still my property and I know of no reason why it should not be, please hand it to the Society of Pioneers of Oregon with my compliments. I herewith present it to them. It was written up daily, after all my other duties as teamster and general assistant about the camp were performed. It has never been revised by me and I hope my old companions will overlook any errors I have made.

Your friend,
James Field

BIBLIOGRAPHY

Bancroft, Hubert Howe. *History of Oregon: In Two Volumes.* San Francisco: The History Company, Publishers, 1890.

Bassett, Karen, Jim Renner, and Joyce White. *Meek Cutoff 1845.* http://www.endoftheoregontrail.org/oregontrails/meek.html (accessed November 5, 2007).

Bennett, Lucy Hall. "In Earlier Days" by Fred Lockley. *Oregon Journal,* March 8, 1914, Section 2, p. 4 column 8.

Berry, Mike. *1908 Oregon Sticks & Stones.* http://www.i-boards.com (accessed April 5, 2009).

Bowers, Fidelia March. *An Account of the Wagon Train Mastered by Solomon Tetherow.* Lane County Pioneer-Historical Society. Eugene, Oregon, 1960.

Brier, Warren J. "Political Censorship" *Oregon Spectator.* February 5, 1846.

Brown, Jennie Broughton. *Fort Hall: On The Oregon Trail.* Caldwell, Idaho: The Caxton Printers, Ltd. 1932.

Bryant, Edwin. *What I Saw in California.* New York: 1848. Accessed June 2, 2014, http://user.xmission.com~octa/DonnerParty/Bryant.htm.

Bureau of Land Management Online, "Millican Valley Off-Highway Vehicle (OHV) Trail System" http:www.blm.gov/or/district/prineville/recreation/millican/

Burnt River History Group. *Lest We Forget: Remembrances of Upper Burnt River in Baker County Oregon.* Caldwell, Idaho: The Caxton Printers, Ltd., 2007.

Campbell, Loreita M., ed. *Etna: From Mule Train to 'Copter.* Eschscholtzia Parlor No. 112 Native Daughters Of The Golden West, 1965.

Clarke, S. A. *Pioneer Days of Oregon History.* Portland: J.K. Gill Co., 1905.

Clark, Keith and Lowell Tiller. *Terrible Trail: the Meek Cutoff, 1845.* The Caxton Printers, 1967. Reprint Maverick Press, 1992.

Cooley, Eli Casey. Diary, 1845. Original in possession of Mrs. Grace Armstrong, descendant. Hillsboro, Oregon.

Cornelius, Rachel McKinney. "In Earlier Days" by Fred Lockley. *Oregon Journal,* July 23, 1914, p. 8 column 8 pt 1 and pt 2.

Cornelius, Rachel McKinnery. "In Earlier Days" by Fred Lockley. *Oregon Journal,* July 24, 1914, p. 6 column 8.

Cornelius, Rachel McKinnery. "In Earlier Days" by Fred Lockley. *Oregon Journal,* July 27, 1914, p. 4 column 8 pt 1 and pt 2.

Durbin, Sol. "In Earlier Days" by Fred Lockley. *Oregon Journal,* June 20, 1914, p. 4 column 8, pt 2.

Eddins, Orland Ned. *The Winds of Change.* Price, Utah: Peczuh Printing, 2009.

Eddins, Orland Ned. *Mountain Man Plains Indian Canadian Fur Trade.* http://thefurtrapper.com (accessed January 5, 2010).

Elliott, T. C. *Journal of Peter Skene Ogden; Snake Expedition, 1825-1826.* The Quarterly of the Oregon Historical Society, Vol. X, No. 4. (December 1909). http://user.xmission.com/~drudy/mtman/html/ogdn2526.html (accessed March 17, 2014).

Field, James. Journal, 1845, "*Crossing the Plains.*" Willamette Farmer. Portland, Oregon. Mss 520 Oregon Historical Society Research Library.

Gilbert, Frank T. and Harry L. Wells. *History of Butte County. Volume I, History of California from 1513 to 1850, Volume II, History of Butte County.* 1882.

Goulder, W. A. *Reminiscences: Incidents in the Life of a Pioneer in Oregon and Idaho.* Published in 1909 by Timothy Reagan, Boise, Idaho. Moscow, Idaho: University of Idaho, 1989.

Haffen, LeRoy R. *The Mountain Men and the Fur Trade of the Far West, Vol. II.* Spokane, WA: The Arthur H. Clark Co. 2001.

Harritt, Jesse. *Overland Diary 1845.* Mss 947 Oregon Historical Society Research Library.

Herron, John. Diary, 1845, excerpt from Albany newspaper, Mss 224 Oregon Historical Society Research Library.

Hines, Rev. H. K.. *An Illustrated History of The State of Oregon.* Chicago: The Lewis Publishing Company, 1893.

Hoffman, Charles S. *The Search For Oregon's Lost Blue Bucket Mine: The Stephen Meek Wagon Train of 1845: An Oregon Documentary.* Medford, Oregon: Webb Research Group, 2003.

Howden, Arthur D., ed. *The Narrative of Samuel Hancock.* New York: Robert M. McBride & Company, 1927.

Holmes, Kenneth L. *Covered Wagon Women, Volume 1: Diaries and Letters from the Western Trails, 1840-1849.* Glendale, California: Arthur H. Clark Company, 1983.

jdb. Pengra, *Willamette (2), Odell, Pengra's, Military Passes.* http://www.trainorders.com/ (accessed April 5, 2009).

Jenott, John D. *Scott Valley Sketchbook.* Fort Jones, California: John D. Jenott, 1995.

King, Anna Maria. *Letter From Luckiamute.* http://www.all-oregon.com/king/annaletter.htm (accessed October 17, 2007).

Klausmeyer, David. *Oregon Trail Stories: True Accounts Of Life In A Covered Wagon.* Morris Book Publishing, 2004.

Land Status and Cadastral Survey Records. http://www.blm.gov/or/landrecords/survey/yNoteView2_2.php

Lockley, Fred. *History of the Columbia River Valley From The Dalles to the Sea, Vol. I.* Chicago: The S. J. Clarke Publishing Company, 1928.

Lockley, Fred. Mike Helm, ed. *The Lockley Files: Conversation with Pioneer Women.* Eugene, Oregon: Rainy Day Press, 1981.

Map of Oregon, 2009. http://topocreator/download (accessed February 20, 2014).

McClure, Andrew S. Diary, 1853, SLibrary cop 14053021520 Oregon Historical Society Research Library.

McClure, James F. Diary, 1853, Eugene, Oregon: Lane County Pioneer-Historical Society, 1959.

McClure, James F. *How We Came To Oregon: A Narrative Poem and Bruce Genealogy Diary* Eugene, Oregon: Lane County Pioneer-Historical Society, 1967.

McLynn, Frank. *Wagons West: The Epic Story of America's Overland Trails.* New York: Grove Press, 2002.

McNeal, Wm. H. *History of Wasco County, Oregon.* W. H. McNeal, unknown year.

Meek, Stephen Hall. *Autobiography of a Mountain Man, 1805-1889.* 92M4946a Oregon Historical Society Research Library.

Menefee, Leah Collins, and Donald F. Menefee, Kenneth Munford. *The Free Emigrant Road Over Willamette Pass.* Benton County Historical Society & Museum. http://www.bentoncountymuseum.org/research/freeemigrant.cfm (accessed April 5, 2009).

The Military Road: Why The Military Road Went Through. 1972-1973 Journalism Class of Dayville High School, Dayville, Oregon. http://gesswhoto.com/bluebucket.html (accessed January 21, 2009).

Munford, Kenneth. *Back When in Benton County, Part 3, Preparing for the Oregon Trail.* http://www.all-oregon.com/king/part%203.htm (accessed March 11, 2008).

Ontko, Gale. *Thunder Over The Ochoco: The Gathering Storm Volume I.* Bend, Oregon:Maverick Publications, 1993.

Oregon Blue Book: *Notable Oregonians: Joel Palmer - Pioneer, Writer.* http://bluebook.state.or.us/notable/notpalmer.htm (accessed January 23, 2009).

Oregon Historic Trails. *Free Emigrant Road, 1853.* http://www.oregonhistorictrailsfund (accessed February 12, 2010).

Oregon Historic Trails. *Meeks Cutoff, 1845.* http://www.oregonhistorictrailsfund (accessed February 19, 2010).

Palmer, Harriet. Diary. *Crossing the Great Plains by Ox-Wagons.* http://www.isu.edu/~trinmich/00.ar.palmer.html (accessed November 5, 2007).

Palmer, Joel. *Journal of Travels Over the Rocky Mountains.* Cincinnati: J. A. & U. P. James, 1847. Fairfield, Washington: Ye Galleon Press. Digitized by Google.

Parker, Samuel. Diary, 1845, Mss 1508 Oregon Historical Society Research Library.

Parker, Samuel. *Samuel Parker (Oregon politician).* http://en.wikipedia.org/wiki/Samuel_Parker (accessed November 5, 2007).

Pepper, Choral. "The Case of the Blue Bucket Gold." *Desert Magazine*, September 1967.

Peterson, Pete. "Steep price for free wagon road." *The Register-Guard,* October 5, 2003.

Peterson, Susanah Johnson. “In Earlier Days” by Fred Lockley. *Oregon Journal,* June 1, 1915, p. 6 column 8.

Pierce, Lois A. *Lost Immigrants of 1845 And The Blue Bucket Gold.* Shelton, Washington: Shelton-Mason County Journal, 1962.

Pillow, C. B., Adjutant. “The Battle on Burnt River” *Pioneer and Democrat.* August 22, 1856.

Ragen, Brooks Geer. *The Meek Cutoff: Tracing the Oregon Trail's Lost Wagon Train of 1845.* Seattle and London: University of Washington Press,2013.

Ruse, Dr. M. *Alkalis.* http://www.inchem.org/documents/pims/chemical/pimg012.htm#PartTitle:1. Alkalis (accessed March 10, 2014).

"Saleratus." *The Adams Sentinel and General Advertiser,* Gettysburg, Pennsylvania. August 15, 1853. p. 5.

Selenium. http://en.wikipedia.org/wiki/selenium (accessed January 21, 2010).

Shadden, Thomas. http://freepages.genealogy.rootsweb.ancestry.com (accessed January 26, 2010).

Shannon, Donald H. *The Boise Massacre on the Oregon Trail: Attack on the Ward Party in 1854 and Massacres of 1859.* Caldwell, Idaho: Snake Country Publishing, 2004.

Smith, Ross A., *Oregon Overland: Three Roads of Adversity.* Ross A. Smith, 2002. http://oregonoverland.com

Smith, R. Gess. *In Quest of the Blue Bucket Mine: May 02, 1919.* http://gesswhoto.com/bluebucket.html (accessed October 21, 2007).

Smith, R. Goss. *A Place Called Oregon.* Oregon Historical Quarterly Nos. 2 and 3 June, 1919 and Sept. 1919.

Stewart, John L. *Fremont's Greatest Western Exploration: Volume 1: The Dalles to Pyramid Lake.* Vancouver, Washington: SET, Inc., Publisher, 1999.

Tetherow, Solomon. *Oregon Spectator* (Oregon City) Thursday March 18, 1847, Vol. II, No.4 p. 3 column 2+.

Tetherow, Solomon. *Organizational Journal of an Emigrant Train of 1845* Lane County Pioneer-Historical Society, Eugene, Oregon, 1959.

Trails End. http://www.muskingum.edu/~rmunkra es/life/Daily/End.html (accessed January 4, 2008).

"Tulare Lake" http://wiki.ask.com/Tulare_Lake (accessed March 5, 2012).

"Tulare Lake" http://en.wikipedia.org/wiki/File:Tulare_Lake_1874.jpg. (accessed March 5, 2012).

Unruh, John D. Jr. *The Plains Across; The Overland Emigrants and the Trans-Mississippi West, 1840-1860.* Urbana and Chicago: University of Illinois Press, 1993.

Walling, A. G.. *Illustrated History of Lane County Oregon.* Portland, Oregon: A. G. Walling, 1884.

Walter, W. W., *Recollections.* Mss 739 Oregon Historical Society Research Library.

Wirfs, Charlotte. *We Called Her Sally Memories of Sarah King Chambers.* http://www.all-oregon.com/king/calledhersally.htm

Wojcik, Donna M. *The Brazen Overlanders of 1845.* Donna M. Wojcik, 1976.

Index

Symbols

A

B

C

D

E

F

G

H

I

J

K

L

M

N

O

P

Q

R

S

T

U

V

W

Y